QUICK CUISINE

Easy and Elegant Recipes
for Every Occasion

ANN CLARK

A PLUME BOOK

PLUME
Published by the Penguin Group
Penguin Books USA Inc., 375 Hudson Street, New York, New York 10014, U.S.A.
Penguin Books Ltd, 27 Wrights Lane, London W8 5TZ, England
Penguin Books Australia Ltd, Ringwood, Victoria, Australia
Penguin Books Canada Ltd, 10 Alcorn Avenue, Toronto, Ontario, Canada M4V 3B2
Penguin Books (N.Z.) Ltd, 182–190 Wairau Road, Auckland 10, New Zealand

Penguin Books Ltd, Registered Offices: Harmondsworth, Middlesex, England

Published by Plume, an imprint of Dutton Signet,
a division of Penguin Books USA Inc.
Previously published in a Dutton edition.

First Plume Printing, October, 1995
10 9 8 7 6 5 4 3 2 1

Copyright © Ann Clark, 1993
All rights reserved

 REGISTERED TRADEMARK—MARCA REGISTRADA

The Library of Congress has catalogued the Dutton edition as follows:

Clark, Ann.
    Quick cuisine : easy and elegant recipes for every occasion / Ann Clark.
        p.   cm.
    Includes index.
    ISBN 0-525-93571-1 (hc.)
    ISBN 0-452-27469-9 (pbk.)
    1. Quick and easy cookery.   I. Title.
TX833.5.C53   1993
641.5'12—dc20   92–18252
                                                         CIP

Printed in the United States of America

Without limiting the rights under copyright reserved above, no part of this publication
may be reproduced, stored in or introduced into a retrieval system, or transmitted, in any
form, or by any means (electronic, mechanical, photocopying, recording, or otherwise),
without the prior written permission of both the copyright owner and the above publisher
of this book.

BOOKS ARE AVAILABLE AT QUANTITY DISCOUNTS WHEN USED TO PROMOTE PRODUCTS OR SERVICES.
FOR INFORMATION PLEASE WRITE TO PREMIUM MARKETING DIVISION, PENGUIN BOOKS USA INC.,
375 HUDSON STREET, NEW YORK, NEW YORK 10014.

CONTENTS

INTRODUCTION

◆

It is interesting to watch one's own style of cooking change and evolve over the years. In some ways it seems I have done things backward, progressing from the most complex to the simplest. For instance, years ago, I cut my teeth in the kitchen on the most complicated classic and ethnic dishes I could find in cookbooks—dishes that took hours and sometimes days to prepare. They were works of art, and I admit that I loved every minute of this passionate pursuit of authenticity and extraordinary flavor. I also made wonderful discoveries of technique and style along the way. It was, for me, an excellent way to learn a great deal.

But when I call to mind favorite dishes I've either cooked or tasted in restaurants, invariably they are always the *simplest* and often the most *effortless* ones. I'll always remember every detail of the perfect tastes of a very simple meal cooked by an elderly French hotel keeper in a small spa town in southwestern France twenty years ago. The hotel had four modest rooms, and after a long drive, my companion and I were grateful to occupy the last one available. The decor of the place gave little hint of what was to come. We took our places in the tiny dining room, the last guests to be served that evening.

Nonetheless, Madame (arthritic and stern) prepared for these tired foreign latecomers a plump whole chicken with tarragon, seasoned and roasted to perfection, accompanied by the most sensual, melt-in-your-mouth potato-fritter delicacy called *pommes dauphine* (mashed potatoes combined with an unsweetened cream puff pastry and deep-fried). At an appropriate interval, this was followed by perfectly ripe tomatoes, still warm from the sun, thickly sliced and scattered with just-plucked basil leaves and small fresh goat cheeses, dusted with herbs and drizzled with just a little green olive oil—and, of course, crusty country bread. A bowl of fragrantly ripe, perfect peaches and figs was presented for dessert. No three-star meal I have ever eaten can compare to, replace, or diminish the memory of the simple perfection, the sensuality and enjoyment of that meal.

Simple, earthy, French country or regional cooking has been an important part of my culinary experience, and no region has been as important to me as Provence, my beloved second home, where I have returned year after year since 1968. Provençal food is the epitome of honest, simple, natural food, distinctly flavored with herbs, garlic, olive oil, olives, onions, anchovies. These Provençal seasonings have dense, full, rich flavors, as rich and colorful as the landscape of this magical region, where lavender and thyme perfume the air.

Even before I lived in Provence I always experimented in the kitchen with a wide range of herbs, spices, and condiments, cooking wonderful dishes from the world's great ethnic cuisines—Mexican, Thai, Moroccan, Indian, Middle Eastern—learning which seasonings worked well together and with which foods. I have always liked aromatic food, dishes that are redolent of a particular herb or spice. (One of the reasons I don't use the microwave oven much for cooking is that I can't smell anything cooking! And since I season by aroma as well as by taste, that frustrates me and diminishes my pleasure in cooking.) To me, seasoning is the soul of cooking. Being able to season well is both a skill and a sensibility that evolves over the years, depending on memory, on learning, and on active use of your senses. Developing your palate means becoming more keenly aware of a wider range of seasonings and being able to distinguish and separate out all the different flavors in a particular dish. Once you have had a certain sensory experience (tasting fresh tarragon in a dish, for example), it goes into a memory bank so that the next time that taste comes around, you'll say, "Ah, tarragon!" And so on with countless flavors, aromas, and combinations. It's really what makes cooking so exciting. Eating out can be a good way to develop your palate. When a dish is distinctive, ask what makes it so. Then experiment with that seasoning in your own kitchen.

I hope that the recipes in this book, which reflect my favorite seasonings and flavor combinations, will also inspire you. I have taught cooking for twenty

years, and one of the continuing pleasures I have is that of introducing seasonings that are less well known and underutilized, such as Hungarian paprika. It's
milder than cayenne, more complex and subtle in flavor, and should be used as
it is in its native Hungary—not as a timid and insipid garnish sprinkled over
cooked food, but as a distinctive full-blown seasoning in its own right. My recipes for Hungarian Paprika Chicken and Hungarian Paprika Mushrooms will, I
hope, give you a new appreciation of this delightful seasoning and show you how
to use it in your own creations.

To help you get a feel for how seasonings work together, I have included
menus with all the main-course recipes in the book. The menus are intended as
suggestions of interesting flavor, color, and texture matches, not as hard-and-
fast rules. You may have a favorite dish using similar ingredients that suits the
menu perfectly, or one you'd like to experiment with. These menus reflect the
flavor combinations I particularly like, but of course, there are many more possibilities. My intent is to encourage you to cook with an adventurous spirit and
develop your own personal taste.

But what about *quick* cooking? This is a dilemma we all face: How can we
nourish ourselves well *and* relax while so doing, but somehow do it all quickly?

Even though I am in the kitchen a great deal and food is my profession, as
a working person, I face the same problem everyone faces who leads a very full
life: *what to fix for dinner* four to six nights a week and how to squeeze in the
pleasures of good food and of having guests without being totally exhausted the
next day. Cooking and entertaining are to me a great joy—but as a caterer, restaurant consultant, and cooking teacher, I am fully aware of all the time and
work involved in preparing and presenting tasty, healthy, beautiful food. For the
last several years I have been teaching to a responsive audience at my school,
La Bonne Cuisine, series after series on "quick cuisine." Those classes are the
basis of this book, which I hope will show you how it *is* possible to have fabulous
meals of great simplicity, cooked quickly and easily.

"Quick" means different things to different people. For some, it is throwing
something in the microwave oven for a few minutes. For others, it is the simple
preparation of just one or two fresh items, such as sautéed fish and a salad, or
the preparation of one delicious dish at home, with purchased items added—an
appetizer or soup or a dessert tart, to complete the meal.

It should be clear by now that for me, "quick" does not mean putting meals
in the microwave; it means real cooking on a conventional stove with good, fresh
ingredients combined in interesting ways—but in a short amount of time. This
does not mean that I never use a microwave—on the contrary, I find it an extremely useful, time-saving tool for many chores—but because it alters the texture of many foods, it does not replace traditional cooking.

Having a well-stocked pantry *and* refrigerator is essential for preparing speedy meals and helps eliminate those unnecessary and time-consuming trips to the store to search for that one missing ingredient. To make my book easier to use, I have listed in chapter 1 the basic ingredients that recur in the recipes so that you can stock your pantry accordingly. I can't emphasize enough how much time you'll save if you keep these ingredients on hand. Shopping can then be simplified to one or two fresh, perishable items like fish, salad, and fruit every other day. And having so many good things on hand will inspire you to create delicious, simple dishes of your own.

It is important to learn to work efficiently and quickly in the kitchen. This is something that comes with practice and good habits, such as reading a recipe through from beginning to end, getting out all ingredients and utensils needed and organizing your work space beforehand, and proceeding in a clear and focused way. This alone will make any recipe you prepare go that much more quickly. Cooking is, to me, not a chore, but a skill, and one that can be practiced quickly and with pleasure in the preparation of your daily meals.

Since I opened my school in 1973, I have never really tired of teaching what I call the "basic skills of cooking," as illustrated in many dishes from simple French home cuisine. I have always preferred to teach the techniques of good *daily* cooking using fresh ingredients rather than focus on elaborate dishes I know my students will prepare only once or twice a year! The tips and hints in boxes and recipe notes throughout the book reflect the teacher in me. These bits of information are designed to help you save time in the kitchen, shed light on ingredients, seasonings, and cooking techniques, and, in general, help you simplify your approach to cooking. For example, the tips on vegetables (washing spinach, trimming greens, seeding cucumbers) can be applied to any dishes made with those ingredients.

My cooking style has evolved and changed from those early days when I was an ardent apostle of French country cooking. My travels and reading have taken me farther abroad and have introduced me to many wonderful new cuisines. My experience working as a private chef at Iron Horse Vineyards in Sonoma County, California, in the early eighties gave me an exceptional opportunity to explore all the different cuisines represented in California (especially every variety of Asian) as well as the joy of using the incredible produce, foodstuffs, and wines of Sonoma.

More recently, the professional catering seminars and health-spa classes I teach have oriented me squarely in the direction of efficient and *healthy* meals. I have modified many dishes using cream and butter, cutting the quantities way down. Seasonings offer a great way to cut down on fat and calories; use them to flavor dishes instead of butter and cream. At the health spa the premise of the classes is "no fat, no salt, no sugar"—restrictions that have really exercised my culinary imagination. Spinach Fettuccine with Tomato-Mint Sauce is one of the delicious recipes developed within those guidelines, and many other recipes in the book were inspired by this challenge. I still do use cream and butter, though in smaller amounts, because they taste so good, but in a number of recipes I suggest substituting buttermilk, light cream, or yogurt for cream where it will not vastly alter the result. In other cases, such as the Fettuccine with Lemon and Vodka Sauce, cream is the only thing that really gives the right taste. But where cream is used in a few of the richer dishes, it is divided among four to six people, so that the amount consumed per person is quite modest.

The traditional evening meal of soup or appetizer, meat or other protein, vegetable, starch, salad, and dessert seems to me like just too much food to eat and definitely too time-consuming to prepare. My smaller, lighter meals are quicker, easier, and more fun to assemble. They have fewer courses, livelier combinations, and a healthy ethnic flair, with a focus on imaginative use of seasonings.

While we are all concerned with time and are always striving to do more in what seems like less time, let us not forget that cooking is not an unpleasant chore to be gotten out of the way, but a joy and a delight, and that food is what sustains our life and nourishes our spirit. Time spent enjoying the simple pleasures of the table, sitting with others over good, honest food and wine, is truly one of the main sources of well-being. It seems to me more and more that cooking is, ultimately, an act of love, of grace, of giving and sharing, of real communion, of living fully in the moment.

THE QUICK-CUISINE KITCHEN

♦

Cooking is a lot easier if your kitchen is well organized. You need good-quality basic pots and pans, a few time-saving gadgets, and a well-stocked pantry, refrigerator, and freezer. The following suggestions should really help simplify the preparation of your evening meals.

KITCHENWARE

♦

Everyone has his or her own favorite pots, pans, and kitchen utensils. My favorite tool is a large wooden mortar and pestle, brought back from a Provençal market years ago. I can't imagine skinning and mashing garlic with anything else! I use it every day to pound nuts, mash garlic, incorporate herbs into butter, blend herb and spice mixtures, crush peppercorns, etc. My time-saving olive pitter is another tool I find indispensable.

I use oval gratin dishes of various types—a small white cast-iron enameled gratin dish is perfect for baking fish or broiling vegetables, and it is attractive enough to go right from the stovetop or oven to the table. My large, glazed earthenware gratin dish is useful for dessert gratins and for roasting meats and vegetables in larger quantities.

I recommend that you have the following basic kitchenware on hand for cooking the recipes in this book: a 2-quart cast-iron enameled saucepan and 4- and 6-quart cast-iron enameled casseroles (I prefer Le Creuset; these heavy-bottomed pans will help prevent burning when you are cooking a little *too* quickly!); two cast-iron enameled gratin dishes, one large and one small; two skillets: one fairly heavy 9- or 10-inch one with a nonstick coating and a heavier 12-inch one made of enameled or specially coated cast iron. I don't cook in stainless steel because it's not an even conductor of heat, but I do use a 5- to 6-quart straight-sided stainless-steel mixing bowl to boil large amounts of water for cooking pasta or blanching vegetables. An 8- to 10-quart pot made of enameled cast iron or hard anodized aluminum is also useful for soups and stews.

As for machines, these six save me a lot of time in the kitchen: a food processor, a blender, a large mixer (I prefer Kitchen-Aid), a small hand mixer, a microwave oven, and a hand blender. I find the microwave to be a very useful tool for cooking certain vegetables simply, for heating water, broth, and sauces rapidly, for toasting nuts and plumping sun-dried tomatoes, for melting chocolate, for thawing frozen foods in minutes, and, of course, for quickly reheating leftovers. I don't like the way it cooks meats or poultry. The French *mini-pimer,* known on the American market as a hand blender, is a wonderful gadget, a sort of "blender on a stick" that is primarily used to puree soups and sauces directly in the pots in which they are cooked. It's a great convenience since it eliminates the laborious transfer to a food processor or blender. I highly recommend it.

And let's not forget the importance of good sharp knives for any kind of cooking: a 10- to 12-inch chef's knife for chopping vegetables; a 10- to 12-inch slicer for meats and fish; a 10-inch serrated bread knife; and small paring knives for many other tasks. To prevent nicks and dulling, store them separately in a wooden knife block, or if storing in a drawer with other utensils, cover each knife with a cardboard sleeve.

Finally, several strainers of varying sizes and a few colanders (I have and use at least eight) will always make work in your kitchen easier.

I recommend putting your most frequently used utensils—spatulas, wooden and slotted spoons, tongs—in a big container on your counter so you don't have to waste time hunting for them in drawers and cupboards.

STAPLE INGREDIENTS

◆

*T*he state of your larder plays a big role in how efficiently you can prepare meals, especially on those nights when you haven't had time to shop. Keeping your pantry stocked with such basics as good-quality canned tomatoes, dried mushrooms, pastas of all sorts, rices and beans, canned chicken broth, onions, garlic, and shallots, and lots of herbs, spices, and condiments will enable you to prepare an interesting meal from scratch without investing a lot of time.

Having available a number of condiments and flavoring ingredients that keep well in the refrigerator expands the variety of dishes you can put together quickly. Ingredients such as ginger, soy sauce, mustard, horseradish, Parmesan cheese, capers, paprika, chilies, nuts, and oils, as well as lemons, parsley, scallions, yogurt, eggs, and cheese, can make a critical difference in seasoning a simple quick dish. And many ingredients, such as stocks and sauces, can be kept on hand in the freezer and thawed for a few minutes in the microwave oven or overnight in the refrigerator to give you "culinary insurance" for your quick meals.

To help you stock your larder, I have provided lists of basic ingredients that keep well and recur in the recipes; add to them *your* favorite foods.

PANTRY (DRY) STORAGE

ANCHOVIES: The best are rolled in jars with olive oil; try different brands of canned anchovies to find the ones that are firmest (see box, page 22).

ARTICHOKE HEARTS, CANNED

BAKING INGREDIENTS: Dry yeast, baking powder, baking soda, cornstarch.

BEANS, CANNED: Cannellini, chickpeas, black beans.

CORNMEAL: Yellow (medium to finely ground).

DRIED APRICOTS, RAISINS, AND CURRANTS

FLOUR: All-purpose, unbleached, whole-wheat, rice flour.

GELATIN, PLAIN

GRAINS: Instant grits, couscous, kasha.

HERBS, DRIED: Imported bay leaves (not California—see box, page 228), thyme, rosemary, oregano, marjoram, sage, basil, summer savory.

KOSHER SALT: See box, page 14.

MUSHROOMS, DRIED: Porcini, morels, chanterelles, shiitakes.

OLIVE OILS: Italian and Provençal virgin and extra-virgin (see box); Spanish and Greek olive oils are also good but tend to be more gutsy and full flavored.

PASTAS: Dry angel hair, fettuccine, capellini, spaghetti, spaghettini, bow-tie pasta, linguine, farfalle, orzo, penne.

PEPPER: Never use packaged ground black pepper, as it is much less flavorful than freshly ground pepper; always grind your own. Use black, white, green, and pink peppercorns (see box, page 77). Ground red pepper (cayenne) is fine, but it must be fresh (see box, page 55).

PIMENTOS: In a jar.

RICES: Long-grain, basmati, Texmati, arborio, wild, pecan.

ROASTED RED PEPPERS: In a jar; Pelopenesse brand are excellent.

SOY SAUCE: The best soy sauces need refrigeration.

SPICES: Saffron threads (see box, page 98); cumin and cumin seeds; cardamom, coriander, and fennel seeds; ground cinnamon and cinnamon sticks; allspice; ground ginger, ground nutmeg; juniper berries; dried red-pepper flakes; curry powder; turmeric; mustard powder and seeds.

STOCK AND BROTH: If homemade is

OLIVE OILS
◆

Olive oils impart a rich and subtle flavor to foods. I generally like to cook vegetables in extra-virgin olive oil, and I use both virgin olive oil and extra-virgin olive oil (which is more distinctly olive-flavored) for salads. For lighter flavor use virgin or pure olive oil. For heartier flavor use extra-virgin olive oil. Store olive oil in a cool dark place. It is not necessary to refrigerate it unless you buy it in very large quantities and use it sparingly. In that case keep a small jar of olive oil in your pantry for daily use and refrigerate the rest.

---

unavailable, use canned regular or low-salt Swanson's, Hain's, or College Inn chicken broth or Knorr's chicken or beef bouillon cubes (most other brands are too salty and taste bad); bottled clam juice.

SUGAR: Granulated and confectioners'.

TOMATO PASTE: Progresso brand; or imported double-concentrated tomato paste in a tube.

TOMATOES, CANNED AND BOXED: Progresso canned Italian plum tomatoes with basil and Pomi boxed Italian tomato chunks are the best, but use domestic brands if these are not available.

TOMATOES, SUN-DRIED: Use the

dry-packed type (see box, page 95).

VEGETABLE OILS: Safflower, sunflower, canola, grapeseed and corn oils; they keep longer if refrigerated.

VEGETABLES: Onions, shallots, garlic, potatoes.

VINEGARS: La Marne champagne vinegar, Fini or Mondari balsamic vinegar, raspberry wine vinegar, Spanish sherry wine vinegar, red-wine vinegar, rice-wine vinegar.

WHITE OR GOLDEN HOMINY, CANNED

WORCESTERSHIRE SAUCE

REFRIGERATOR STORAGE

SHORT SHELF LIFE
(about 1 week)

BACON: Slab bacon in slices.

DAIRY: Yogurt; milk (2 percent is usually fine for cooking, skim is terrible); unsalted butter; cream; buttermilk; *crème fraîche* (see page 210).

EGGS: Large; farm-raised or brown organic if available (see box, page 90).

FRUITS: Lemons, limes, and oranges.

GOAT CHEESE: Texas or California brands or French Montrachet.

HERBS, FRESH: Parsley, basil, coriander, dill, tarragon (see box).

SALAD GREENS

VEGETABLES: Chili peppers (jalapeños, serranos, poblanos—see box, page 36); bell peppers; scallions.

LONGER SHELF LIFE
(1 week to 6 months)

CAPERS: Nonpareil or smallest type you can find.

GINGER, FRESH: Store in a jar, covered with dry sherry.

GOAT CHEESE: Cover in oil and

HOW TO STORE FRESH HERBS

◆

Fresh herbs keep best when they are rinsed, shaken of excess moisture, gently wrapped in a paper towel or two, and stored in the refrigerator in small sealable plastic bags. They will stay fresh for a day or two, or at the very most three. Parsley is an exception—it will keep up to a week if stored this way.

> ### PARMESAN CHEESE
> ◆
>
> *The best Parmesan cheese, now widely available, is the true Parmesan cheese from Parma, Italy, called Parmagiano-Reggiano. Buy it whole, in chunks, keep it refrigerated in a tightly sealed plastic bag, and grate it fresh for each use—it keeps for weeks this way. Or, buy a small amount already grated and use it up within ten days (after that it tends to go moldy). Domestic and Argentinean Parmesan can be acceptable substitutes in a pinch, but they are not nearly as fine-flavored as the real thing.*

herbs (see page 228); keeps about one month.

HORSERADISH: Creamy.

MUSTARDS: A Dijon or smooth French mustard, such as Maille, and a country mustard with seeds, such as Zatrains Creole.

NUTS AND SEEDS: Pine nuts, walnuts, almonds, hazelnuts, pecans, peanuts, sesame seeds; store in covered jars; keep best for 2 to 3 months

OILS: Oriental (dark) sesame, walnut, hazelnut, peanut, any cold-pressed oils; smell these perishable oils for rancidity before using.

OLIVES: Niçoise, Kalamata; (see box, page 12); keep about 6 months if covered in brine or oil.

PAPRIKA: Hungarian, sweet and hot (see box, page 43).

PARMESAN CHEESE: Italian Parmigiano-Reggiano in large chunks (see box).

SOY SAUCE: Pearl River Bridge Mushroom Soy and Superior Soy Sauce (which is a little lighter in flavor) are the best Chinese brands and are inexpensive and readily available.

TABASCO: Buy smallest bottle and replace every year because it sours with age.

THAI OR VIETNAMESE FISH SAUCE: Squid brand is one of the best.

VEGETABLE SHORTENING: Crisco, smallest size, for making tart pastry.

VEGETABLES: Carrots, cabbage, winter squash, fennel, endive; keep 1 week to 10 days.

FREEZER STORAGE

BREAD: French, whole-wheat, white for bread crumbs, pita.

BREAD CRUMBS: Grind in food pro-

cessor and store in tightly sealed jars.

CHEESES: 4- or 8-ounce packets of Roquefort, fontina, mozzarella, feta, cream cheese, Monterey Jack.

COFFEE BEANS: French Roast, Viennese, Colombian.

FLAVORED BUTTERS: Roquefort-Walnut (page 214), Green Chili–Cumin (page 214).

FRUITS: 10-ounce to 1-pound bags of commercially frozen cherries, blackberries, peaches, blueberries, raspberries, strawberries, and rhubarb.

HERBS, DRIED: Freeze in small jars (helps retain flavor of these more quickly perishable dried herbs): tarragon, dill, mint, and chervil.

MEATS: Lamb chops, pork chops, chicken breasts and thighs, ground beef, ground lamb, ring sausage, Italian fennel and plain sausage, bratwurst, bacon (wrap slices separately), thin slices prosciutto (wrap slices separately).

STOCK, HOMEMADE: Freeze chicken, beef, or veal stock in ice cube trays, then bag the cubes in sealable plastic bags.

VEGETABLES: Peas, corn, artichokes, spinach, lima beans.

WINES AND SPIRITS

LIGHT AND DELICATE WHITE WINES: Mâcon, Muscadet, champagne, Soave, Verdicchio.

FULLER-BODIED WHITE WINES: Graves, champagne, Orvieto, Vouvray, Chenin Blanc, Chardonnay, Sauvignon Blanc, Chablis, Meursault, Sauternes, Gewürztraminer, Riesling.

LIGHTER-BODIED RED WINES: Valpolicella, Haut-Médoc, Merlot, Pinot Noir, Beaujolais, Rioja.

FULLER-BODIED RED WINES: Cabernet Sauvignon, Syrah, Chianti, Barolo, Zinfandel.

SPIRITS: Cognac, Cointreau, Grand Marnier, *crème de cassis,* vodka, gin, Madeira (Sercial), port, dry sherry (Amontillado).

FRENCH OR SPANISH ALCOHOLIC CIDER

BEERS: lagers, pilsners, dark beers, Asian beers.

♦

HORS D'OEUVRES, APPETIZERS, AND SANDWICHES

♦

Small meals often bring the greatest delights. A delectable hors d'oeuvre like the cheese puffs in this chapter; a simple lunch of delicious country bread toasted, spread with goat cheese and sprinkled with shallots; marinated olives, served with a ripe tomato salad; an unusual sandwich—all provide much pleasure in small ways.

It has been my experience in my classes, in my catering work, and in my own entertaining in the last several years that smaller *lighter* meals are here to stay. Buffets of heavy foods at parties are being replaced with an array of lighter but substantial hors d'oeuvres, like the Spanish *tapas*. Guests want to have their fill, of course, but *lighter* is definitely more and more appreciated by a wider public. Mini-meals during the day, light evening meals, and late-night suppers after work, meetings, or the theater, are all replacing heavier fare.

    The recipes in this chapter are all appropriate for delicious small meals. A number of these dishes can be served as elegant and unusual light main courses for entertaining at lunch or at a light supper—the Carpaccio with Lemon-Shallot Mayonnaise, the Smoked Trout Mousse with Horseradish and Dill, and the Quick Shrimp Pâté, for example. Add a salad or soup and fruit or other dessert to complete the menu.

    I've often made an impromptu light supper for friends from a collection of the quickest and easiest hors d'oeuvres—the Easy Tomato and Prosciutto Bruschetta, the Marinated Olives with Garlic, Lemon, and Herbs, the Amandes Grillés, and the Mushrooms Stuffed with Ricotta, Prosciutto, and Herbs.

HORS D'OEUVRES AND APPETIZERS

SANDWICHES

HORS D'OEUVRES AND APPETIZERS

◆

MUSHROOMS STUFFED WITH RICOTTA, PROSCIUTTO, AND HERBS

SERVES 8

◆

A wonderful and filling appetizer, these stuffed mushrooms could precede a simple fish dish, a veal or chicken *piccata* with lemon, or any entrée with an Italian flair.

1 cup part-skim ricotta
3 tablespoons light cream
¼ cup freshly grated Italian Parmesan
½ teaspoon freshly ground black
 pepper
8 thin slices prosciutto, fat removed,
 finely chopped
3 tablespoons finely chopped fresh
 Italian or curly-leaf parsley
1 tablespoon finely chopped fresh basil
 (see box, page 88)
1 teaspoon finely chopped fresh thyme
Kosher salt (optional)
16 large fresh white button mushrooms
 or shiitakes (2 to 3½ inches wide),
 cleaned, stems removed, and
 blanched 1 minute (see box)

Preheat the oven to 375°. Beat the ricotta with the cream, stir in the Parmesan and pepper, then add all the remaining ingredients except the mushrooms. Combine well. Taste and add salt if needed (some prosciutto is saltier than others).

Stuff the mushrooms with the mixture, place in a lightly buttered or oiled baking dish, and bake for 10 minutes, or until well heated through. Place on a serving dish and serve warm.

MAKE AHEAD: up to 24 hours; stuff the mushrooms and refrigerate in wrapped baking dish until ready to bake

---

BLANCHING MUSHROOMS

◆

It's best to blanch large fresh mushrooms such as shiitakes if they are going to be stuffed or cooked in a dish with other ingredients. Drop them in boiling salted water for 1 minute, drain, pat dry, and add to the dish. This removes the moisture that would otherwise make the dish watery.

MARINATED OLIVES WITH GARLIC, LEMON, AND HERBS

MAKES 1 POUND

◆

*T*wo foods I really can't live without are olives and goat cheese. Olives by themselves are a ready-made hors d'oeuvre; these marinated olives, which can be made weeks ahead, are spectacular. Serve them with Amandes Grillés (page 17) and crusty French or Italian bread.

8 ounces Spanish green olives
8 ounces imported black Kalamata or
    Niçoise olives
3 whole cloves garlic, mashed to a
    paste (see box, page 62)
2 tablespoons of one or more of the
    following chopped fresh herbs:
    thyme, oregano, rosemary
2 imported bay leaves
4 thin lemon slices
1 teaspoon crushed black peppercorns
1 to 1½ cups extra-virgin olive oil

> ### OLIVES
>
> ◆
>
> *M*any markets now offer a wide selection of imported olives in bulk. I prefer imported black and green olives. American-produced green olives in jars (especially from Santa Barbara) are also good, but American canned black olives will not work in my recipes because they are so much less flavorful than imported types.

Drain the brine off the olives and rinse them in cold water. Place them in a clean 16-ounce glass jar. Add all of the seasonings and the oil, cover tightly, and shake well to mix. Let stand for at least 20 minutes before serving. Remove the garlic and lemon after a week for long-term storage in the refrigerator.

VARIATION: If you can find a store that specializes in olives, make this recipe with 8 ounces each of three or four different types of olives of different colors and sizes, and increase the other ingredients accordingly.

MAKE AHEAD: Prepare up to 2 months ahead; refrigerate

YUGOSLAVIAN CHEESE SPREAD
SERVES 12; MAKES 1 POUND

◆

I learned how to make this super-easy cheese spread, a great favorite in my cooking school, from a fine cook of Yugoslavian specialties, Rosa Rajkovich. Serve it with country bread or a variety of imported crackers.

4 ounces feta cheese
8 ounces cream cheese
½ cup (1 stick) unsalted butter
½ teaspoon freshly ground black
    pepper
3 to 4 sprigs fresh rosemary, for
    garnish

Rinse and drain the feta, and beat it in a mixer or food processor until smooth. Add the cream cheese, mix well, then add the butter and pepper. Place in a small bowl, cover tightly, and refrigerate until ready to serve. Serve garnished with rosemary.

VARIATIONS: Add ½ tablespoon chopped fresh oregano, ¼ cup chopped fresh parsley, or ⅓ cup finely chopped walnuts to the spread just before serving.

MAKE AHEAD: prepare up to 1 month ahead; refrigerate

GOAT CHEESE, SHALLOT,
AND FRESH HERB TOASTS
SERVES 2

◆

*I*n my home, this simple hors d'oeuvre doubles as lunch quite often. Make the toasts any time you have a variety of fresh herbs in the refrigerator or garden, and enjoy them with a glass of light red wine.

3 ounces goat cheese
2 large slices French country or
    Tuscan bread, in big round loaves,
    if available, lightly toasted (if not
    available, use French baguettes or
    whole-wheat bread)
2 large shallots, finely chopped

1 heaping tablespoon of one or more of
    the following chopped fresh herbs:
    basil, thyme, chives or garlic
    chives, oregano, marjoram
Kosher salt
Freshly ground black pepper
Extra-virgin olive oil

Spread the goat cheese evenly on the two large slices of bread. Sprinkle each with the shallot, chopped herbs, and a little salt and pepper, then drizzle generously with olive oil. Cut the prepared toasts into smaller pieces, and serve immediately.

NOTE: If increasing the recipe, mix together the goat cheese, herbs, and seasonings for easy spreading. The mixture can be prepared up to 4 hours ahead.

SALT

♦

Kosher salt, the choice of many chefs, is the most delicate-tasting salt. It does not have the sharp brininess of sea salt or the iodine flavor of regular table salt. All the recipes in this book call for it, but you may use table salt if you prefer.

DELICATE HORS D'OEUVRE CHEESE PUFFS

SERVES 4 TO 6

♦

Here's a wonderful recipe from the vast repertoire of French home cooking. Extremely easy but unusual, these warm cheese puffs are light, airy, flavorful, and satisfying.

1 quart canola oil, or any other light vegetable oil
2 large egg whites
¼ pound very finely grated Emmentaler cheese
½ cup very fine fresh bread crumbs (made in a food processor), crusts removed

In a heavy-bottomed 4-quart saucepan or casserole, preheat the oil slowly, over medium heat, to 370°. Use a thermometer to check the temperature.

Beat the egg whites until stiff peaks form. Place the grated cheese in a shallow bowl, spoon the egg whites on top of the cheese, and mix gently but quickly. Form the mixture into marble-sized balls. Handling gently, roll the balls in the fine bread crumbs to cover completely, and drop about 12, one at a time, into the hot oil (370–375°). Cook only until puffed and golden-brown, about 1 minute per batch. Remove, drain on paper towels, and serve immediately.

HUMMUS

SERVES 8 TO 10; MAKES 1½ CUPS

◆

*P*ureed chick-peas, well seasoned with mint and lemon, make one of the tastiest, healthiest hors d'oeuvres. Serve as a spread for crackers or pita bread. Also good as a sandwich filling.

One 16-ounce can chick-peas, drained (reserve about ¼ cup of the liquid) and rinsed
3 to 4 tablespoons extra-virgin olive oil
4 garlic cloves, mashed to a paste (see box, page 62)
¼ cup lemon juice, or more to taste
½ teaspoon kosher salt
¼ teaspoon freshly ground black pepper
⅓ cup minced fresh parsley
3 tablespoons minced fresh mint

Put the chick-peas in a blender or food processor and process until smooth. Slowly add the olive oil until blended, then add the garlic, lemon juice, and salt and pepper, blending in the reserved liquid if the mixture is too stiff. Stir in the herbs and serve at room temperature, or refrigerate until ready to serve.

NOTE: If you wish to keep hummus in the refrigerator more than a few days (it will keep for up to 10 days), omit the herbs. You can stir them in just before serving.

MAKE AHEAD: up to 2 days; refrigerate

EASY TOMATO
AND PROSCIUTTO BRUSCHETTA

SERVES 4

◆

*B*ruschetta, the original Italian garlic toast, inspired this quick and delicious summer hors d'oeuvre. Instead of toasting or grilling the bread, then rubbing it with garlic and drizzling it with fruity olive oil, as is done traditionally, I've combined the garlic and oil with the tomatoes, basil, and prosciutto to be spread on fresh crusty bread. Try the mixture on toasted bread too!

8 thick slices from large, fresh, ripe
   tomatoes, diced
¼ cup extra-virgin olive oil
2 medium garlic cloves, mashed to a
   paste (see box, page 62)
5 leaves fresh basil, chopped
   (see box, page 88)
¼ teaspoon kosher salt
¼ teaspoon freshly ground black
   pepper
2 to 3 thin slices prosciutto, cut or
   torn into ¼ × 1-inch strips
8 large slices French baguette or
   Italian country bread, ¾ inch thick

Place the diced tomato in a small bowl. In a small saucepan, heat the olive oil over low heat for 1 minute. Turn off the heat and add the garlic and basil to infuse the oil with their flavors. Add the salt, pepper, and prosciutto to the tomato and pour the flavored olive oil over the mixture. When ready to serve, spoon the tomato mixture over the bread slices and press down with a fork.

MAKE AHEAD: prepare the tomato mixture up to 2 hours ahead; store at room temperature

PITA CRISPS WITH HERBS
SERVES 12 TO 16

♦

*T*hese are delicious served with drinks, with other hors d'oeuvres, or with soups or salads.

¼ cup minced fresh chives or finely
   chopped scallion tops
½ teaspoon kosher salt
¼ teaspoon freshly ground black
   pepper
½ cup finely chopped fresh parsley
¼ teaspoon dried oregano, or 2
   teaspoons chopped fresh oregano
¼ teaspoon dried basil, or 1
   tablespoon chopped fresh basil
½ pound (2 sticks) unsalted butter,
   softened
1 pound fresh pita bread, each pita cut
   into eighths

Preheat the oven to 375°. Combine the chives, salt and pepper, and herbs and mix into the softened butter. Taste for seasoning. Spread each pita piece with herb butter, place on baking sheets, and bake for 5 to 10 minutes, or until golden and crisped. Cool on baking racks before serving.

NOTE: Packaged pita bread can be kept in the freezer for 4 to 5 months.

MAKE AHEAD: up to 24 hours; store in a paper bag at room temperature

AMANDES GRILLÉS
SERVES 4 TO 6

◆

*T*his extremely simple preparation turns up in three-star French restaurants and hotels as a perfect accompaniment to champagne served as an apéritif. You can also use it as part of a mixed hors d'oeuvres tray.

2 tablespoons unsalted butter
1½ tablespoons virgin olive oil or light vegetable oil
1 cup whole blanched almonds
1 teaspoon kosher salt

Over medium-high heat, heat the butter and oil in a 9- or 10-inch skillet. Add the almonds and brown lightly on both sides, stirring constantly. When golden on both sides, remove and drain on paper towels. Sprinkle with salt, and let stand until cool and crisp before serving.

MAKE AHEAD: up to 24 hours; store in a covered jar at room temperature

ANCHOÏADE
(PROVENÇAL ANCHOVY TOASTS)
SERVES 4

◆

*T*his hors d'oeuvre from the south of France is one of the quickest to make and is one of my favorites. Anchovy and garlic lovers find it deliciously addictive.

4 to 8 slices crusty French bread, sliced ¾ inch thick
One 2-ounce can flat anchovies, drained, rinsed, and patted dry
3 cloves garlic
2½ tablespoons fine fresh bread crumbs (made in a food processor)
4 to 5 tablespoons extra-virgin olive oil
¼ teaspoon freshly ground black pepper
¼ teaspoon red-wine vinegar

Extra-virgin olive oil

Lightly toast the bread in a 400° oven or in a toaster oven. Pound the anchovies and garlic together in a mortar, adding the crumbs and oil gradually until you have a thick paste. Season with pepper and vinegar. Brush the toasted bread with olive oil, spread thinly with the anchovy mixture, and serve.

SMOKED TROUT MOUSSE WITH HORSERADISH AND DILL

SERVES 10

◆

*H*ere's one of the speediest and most elegant hors d'oeuvres I know, from a wonderful friend and fine cook in Brussels, Marie Claire Quittelier. Serve it as a spread on thinly sliced toast. It also makes a perfect luncheon dish, accompanied by a salad.

¾ pound smoked trout, skin and bones removed
2 shallots, chopped
2 tablespoons virgin olive oil
½ cup heavy cream or Crème Fraîche (page 210)
2 teaspoons prepared horseradish, or more to taste
2 tablespoons fresh lemon juice, or to taste
Freshly ground black pepper to taste
Sprigs of fresh dill, for garnish

Place the trout in a food processor. Add the shallot and oil, and process for 30 seconds, until well blended. Gradually add the cream and process until a thick, spreading consistency is reached. Season with the horseradish and lemon juice and pepper to taste. Place in small ramekins and refrigerate until ready to serve. Serve garnished with dill.

MAKE AHEAD: prepare up to 24 hours ahead; refrigerate

QUICK SHRIMP PÂTÉ

SERVES 6

◆

*H*ere's a delicious light appetizer. Serve it on toast, crusty French bread, or crackers.

2 cups water
Pinch kosher salt
1 pound medium shrimp in the shell
3 tablespoons fresh lemon juice

¼ cup virgin olive oil
½ teaspoon hot Hungarian paprika (see box, page 43)
½ teaspoon kosher salt

¼ teaspoon freshly ground white
   pepper
1 tablespoon minced fresh parsley or
   fresh dill, for garnish

Bring the water to a boil, add the salt, and cook the shrimp for about 3 minutes or until they curl. Drain, and plunge in a bowl of ice water to stop the cooking. When cool, peel.

Place the shrimp in a blender or food processor with the lemon juice and oil. Blend to a smooth paste, adding more oil if needed. Add the paprika, salt, and white pepper, and mix well. Spread the paste on the bottom of an 8 × 8-inch metal baking pan and chill in the refrigerator for 7 to 10 minutes, or in the freezer for 5 minutes. Serve, garnished with parsley.

NOTE: Unless the vein in shrimp is very large or dark, I generally do not devein shrimp.

MAKE AHEAD: up to 24 hours; store in a covered crock or jar in the refrigerator

GETTING THE MOST FLAVOR FROM HERBS

◆

Remember that most herbs (fresh and dried), spices, and aromatics give off a fuller flavor if they are added to a hot dish. The heat causes them to release more of their volatile oils than if they are added to a cold liquid or dish. For instance, if you are making a soup, wait until the broth comes to a simmer before adding the herbs. And be sure to bruise or crush fresh or dried herbs added to a cold dish, such as a vinaigrette or a mayonnaise or other sauce. Rub the herb firmly between your fingers or crush it in a mortar with a pestle to release the volatile oils, hence, the flavor.

SALMON CARPACCIO WITH FRESH HERBS

SERVES 8

◆

*T*his elegant appetizer or first course also makes a wonderful light spring or summer lunch dish for four served with a colorful salad of arugula and radicchio. The lime and chopped fresh herbs add a refreshing touch.

1 pound center-cut fresh salmon fillet,
    cut across the grain into eight 4 ×
    4-inch paper-thin slices (about
    ⅛ inch thick; have fishmonger do
    it or see Note)
8 heavy-duty gallon-size sealable
    plastic bags
2 limes, halved
Kosher salt
Freshly ground black pepper
2 tablespoons extra-virgin olive oil
2 tablespoons fresh chives, cut in
    2-inch pieces
2 tablespoons chopped fresh dill or dill
    sprigs
1 tablespoon fresh thyme leaves
2 tablespoons fresh Italian parsley
    leaves
2 tablespoons thinly shredded fresh
    basil (see box, page 88)

Place each slice of salmon in a plastic bag and pound it gently with a veal
pounder until very thin. Place the bags
flat in the refrigerator and chill for at
least 5 minutes, or until ready to serve.
Chill eight dinner plates.

Sprinkle the chilled plates with fresh
lime juice and a little salt and pepper and
drizzle with a little of the olive oil. Place
the salmon slices on the plates. Sprinkle
with a little more lime juice, salt, pepper,
and olive oil. Marinate for 5 minutes at
room temperature. Just before serving,
mix the herbs and sprinkle them over
each serving.

NOTE: To make the salmon easier to
slice, place it in the freezer for 20 to 30
minutes.

MAKE AHEAD: prepare up to 4 hours
ahead; cover the plates with plastic wrap
and refrigerate; remove 15 minutes before serving to take the chill off the
salmon and warm the olive oil

FRESH VERSUS
DRIED HERBS
♦

• *A general rule for substituting
dried herbs for fresh when fresh are
not available is to use a ratio of 1
dried to 2 fresh.*
• *Most fresh herbs should be added
to a dish at the last minute; if they
are cooked too long they will lose
their "fresh" quality.*
• *Dried herbs, especially thyme and
bay leaf, the most important base-
flavoring herbs, need to be added at
the beginning of cooking a dish. I like
to get two levels of flavor by adding
the dried herb to a sauce or stew at
the beginning of cooking and then
adding that same fresh herb, chopped,
just before serving for a delightful
aroma and reinforcement of flavor.
Parsley is one exception: it is often
added fresh at the beginning of a
long-cooked dish.*

CARPACCIO WITH LEMON-SHALLOT MAYONNAISE

SERVES 6

◆

*C*arpaccio, tender beef pounded paper-thin, is a welcome light appetizer or lunch dish for the hot summer months. Although this adapted Venetian dish is most often found in fine restaurants, my special method for pounding makes it very easy to prepare at home. For a simple and delicious potato salad, use the lemon-shallot mayonnaise with boiled new potatoes and fresh dill.

1 pound beef fillet, in 6 thin slices
6 heavy-duty gallon-size sealable
   plastic bags

LEMON-SHALLOT MAYONNAISE
1 large egg, at room temperature
2 tablespoons minced shallot
2 teaspoons Dijon mustard
2 tablespoons fresh lemon juice
½ teaspoon kosher salt
¼ teaspoon freshly ground white
   pepper
¾ to 1 cup virgin olive oil or
   grapeseed oil

6 leaves fresh basil or Italian parsley,
   or 6 sprigs watercress, for garnish

Put each slice of beef in the middle of one of the plastic bags and lay the bag flat on the counter. With a veal pounder, evenly flatten and spread the beef until it is very thin and fills up the bag. Lay the bags flat in the refrigerator to chill. (This is a *perfect* way to store and chill the beef if it is not to be served for a couple of hours.) Chill six large dinner plates.

Rinse the blender or food processor bowl with hot water to warm it. Dry it and combine all the mayonnaise ingredients except the oil in the blender or food processor and process for 2 minutes. Add the oil in a thin stream and process until the mayonnaise has thickened.

When ready to serve, lay the bags flat on the counter; cut off the top side of each plastic bag and discard. Invert each bag onto a dinner plate, then carefully lift off the plastic. Press the mayonnaise through the widened hole of a plastic squirt bottle or pipe it from a small pastry bag with a plain tip, to make a delicate design over the meat. Garnish with fresh basil or watercress.

MAKE AHEAD: up to 4 hours; prepare the mayonnaise and flatten the beef; refrigerate; arrange on plates just before serving

SANDWICHES

◆

THE GOURMET FRIED EGG SANDWICH
SERVES 1

◆

*T*he late Ferdinand Point, renowned chef and owner of one of French gastronomy's greatest temples, La Pyramide in Vienne near Lyon, put prospective chefs to one all-important test—correctly frying an egg. If they could perform this seemingly simple task to his standards, they were in. There is more to frying an egg than meets the eye. Although I have reduced the amount of butter Point recommended (he used several tablespoons), the technique given here is the same as his. The egg should cook *very* gently, so it doesn't toughen, as many delicate forms of protein—eggs, chicken, fish—do when cooked over too high a heat. Try this simple and delicious combination as a quick solitary snack or breakfast. Or use this method just to fry your eggs à la Ferdinand Point.

1 teaspoon unsalted butter
1 large egg, at room temperature
    (see box, page 250)
1 slice whole-wheat, rye, or French
    bread
2 large anchovies, rinsed, drained, and
    patted dry (see box)
Freshly ground black pepper

Over low heat, carefully melt the butter in a small skillet. Break the egg into the butter and cook gently over medium-low heat for about 4 to 5 minutes, or until the yolk and white have just set.

Meanwhile, toast the bread and mash the anchovies with a fork. Just before the egg is done, spread the bread with the mashed anchovies. Place the fried egg on top, evenly grind pepper over the egg (no salt is needed because the anchovies are salty), and serve immediately (with a knife and fork).

ABOUT ANCHOVIES

◆

*T*o *prepare canned anchovies for use, drain off all the oil, rinse them under cold water, and soak them in cold water or milk for 5 minutes. This removes the often unpleasant flavor of the oil in which they are canned, and it makes them less salty.*

To keep leftover anchovies, cover them with olive oil in a small jar and refrigerate for up to a month.

CROQUE MONSIEUR (FRENCH GRILLED HAM-AND-CHEESE SANDWICH)

SERVES 2

◆

*N*othing is quite as satisfying for a lunch or a late-night snack as a well-made sandwich. The key to a really good *croque monsieur* is to be sure the bread, meat, and cheese are *thinly* sliced; that way they will all be in perfect relation to one another. *Croque monsieur* loses its special character when the elements grow to gargantuan proportions. Keep all the ingredients on hand in the freezer. This is also good as an hors d'oeuvre: make several sandwiches and cut each into four canapé-size pieces. Kids love them.

4 thin slices good-quality bread
Unsalted butter, softened
Dijon mustard
2 thin slices Danish ham
2 thin slices Emmentaler cheese
2 large eggs, beaten
2 teaspoons unsalted butter
2 teaspoons virgin olive oil

Spread a slice of bread with soft butter, another with Dijon mustard. Add one slice of ham and one slice of cheese. Press the sandwich together and dip each side into the beaten egg. Repeat for the second sandwich. Melt the 2 teaspoons of butter and the oil in a small skillet and cook the sandwiches on each side over medium heat until the bread is golden and the cheese has melted. Serve hot.

VARIATION: Substitute prosciutto and Italian fontina for the Danish ham and Emmentaler for a nice variation with Italian flavor.

LEBANESE PITA SANDWICH WITH HUMMUS

SERVES 2

◆

*H*ere is a wonderfully healthful and filling sandwich. Chick-peas give a kind of "meaty" flavor, I find. Try the dressing on a cucumber, lettuce, and tomato salad or a plain green salad.

LEMON, OIL, AND YOGURT DRESSING
1 tablespoon fresh lemon juice
¼ teaspoon kosher salt
¼ teaspoon freshly ground black
    pepper
3 tablespoons extra-virgin olive oil
2 tablespoons minced fresh parsley,
    mint, or cilantro
3 tablespoons plain yogurt

Two 8-inch pita breads
⅔ cup Hummus (page 15)
1 small cucumber, thinly sliced
4 large leaves lettuce (romaine,
    oakleaf, or red leaf), washed,
    dried, and finely shredded or
sliced (see box, page 38)
1 large tomato, thinly sliced
Freshly ground black pepper

Combine the dressing ingredients thoroughly. Cut each pita bread a third of the way down from the top. Open each pita pocket and spread ⅓ cup hummus on the inside, evenly on both sides. Toss the cucumber, lettuce, and tomato with the dressing, fill the pitas, and grind a little extra pepper on top.

VARIATION: Add half a seeded, chopped jalapeño to the dressing.

◆

SOUPS, COLD AND HOT

◆

*S*oups serve many purposes: they inspire the appetite, they satisfy hunger, they fill out a meal, they soothe. A soup served as a first course sets a calming, civilized pace for a meal. Beautiful pale green Potage Dubarry adds a wonderful touch of elegance. Cold soups are delightful openers in hot summer weather, and the cold melon soup presented here also works extremely well as a refreshing and unusual dessert. A good soup can also be the centerpiece of a quick, light evening meal; for instance, the Black Bean Soup Supreme, hearty and filling, might be accompanied by tortillas or cornbread and followed by fresh fruit, a light mixed fruit salad, or a fruit sorbet. A special hearty soup can also be the focus of the meal when entertaining—Corn, Chili, and Oyster Chowder and a good crusty bread followed by a green salad and Quick Blackberry Sorbet for dessert, for example— allowing you plenty of time to enjoy your guests.

It should be emphasized that making soup is extremely

easy and not necessarily time-consuming at all. Most of the soups in this chapter take less than thirty-five minutes from start to finish. Delicious, elegant pureed vegetable soups can be made very simply. To make a broccoli soup, for instance, all you do is sauté a large chopped onion with a clove of garlic until it is soft in 2 tablespoons of butter or olive oil in a heavy-bottomed 4- to 5-quart casserole. Add 5 to 6 cups of chicken broth, bring the mixture to a simmer, and add 1 pound of chopped broccoli. When the broccoli is tender (after about 8 to 10 minutes), the soup can be seasoned and pureed, with some pieces reserved to be chopped and returned at the end to give the soup a chunkier texture, if desired. A tablespoon or two of cream, plain yogurt, or buttermilk, can be added just before serving for extra flavor. The same method can be used to make potato and leek soup, asparagus soup, carrot soup, parsnip soup, cauliflower soup, sweet potato soup, zucchini soup, and many others.

RECIPES

COLD SPICY TOMATO SOUP
WITH VODKA

SERVES 8

◆

A healthy, piquant tomato soup that is very low in fat, this packs a punch in terms of flavor. The vodka serves to enhance and heighten the tastes of the tomato and chilies. This is a perfect soup for entertaining; make it a day ahead for a crowd at a brunch or a tailgate picnic.

6 cups canned whole Italian plum
   tomatoes with juice
1 serrano chili, seeded and minced
1 cucumber, peeled, seeded, and
   chopped
1 red bell pepper, seeded and chopped
2 tablespoons fresh lemon juice
1½ tablespoons red-wine vinegar
½ teaspoon black pepper
½ teaspoon cayenne
½ teaspoon dried marjoram
½ teaspoon dried basil
1 teaspoon kosher salt
⅓ cup vodka
½ cup chopped fresh parsley
½ cup good-quality store-bought
   croutons

> ### QUICK-CHILL TECHNIQUE
>
> ◆
>
> *Here is a technique I use often in classes to chill foods quickly. Pour a hot sauce or soup into (or spread hot rice or pasta on) a large metal pan and place this pan in the refrigerator or freezer, or in front of a fan or an air conditioner, for 10 to 15 minutes or longer.*
>
> *If you have enough space in your freezer for quick chilling, this is your speediest option—it often takes only 5 to 10 minutes to chill a hot dish.*

Puree all of the ingredients except the parsley and croutons in a food processor or blender. Adjust the seasonings and chill thoroughly for at least 15 minutes (see Note 2 and box). Add the parsley and croutons just before serving.

NOTES: 1. If you don't like the hotness of the serrano, substitute an Anaheim chili, use ½ serrano for just a bit of hotness, or leave out the chili altogether.

2. Put the canned tomatoes in the refrigerator overnight to cut down the chilling time to 5 minutes.

MAKE AHEAD: prepare up to 24 hours ahead; refrigerate

QUICK COLD AVOCADO SOUP

SERVES 6

◆

*T*his ultra-speedy, ultra-delicious soup is a perfect addition to an impromptu meal or picnic. In summer, keep cans of broth refrigerated for instant cold soup. I make this quite spicy; if you prefer less heat, cut the amount of cayenne in half.

2 large ripe cold avocados, peeled
1½ cups cold low-fat buttermilk
1½ cups cold chicken broth
1 teaspoon ground cumin
1 teaspoon kosher salt
½ teaspoon cayenne, or to taste
3 tablespoons chopped fresh cilantro
    or Italian parsley
6 thin lime slices, for garnish
Cayenne, for garnish

Place all of the ingredients (except the lime slices and extra cayenne) in a blender and blend until smooth. If the ingredients are not already cold, chill the soup 5 to 10 minutes before serving. Check for seasoning, garnish with thin lime slices and a sprinkling of cayenne, and serve cold.

NOTE: I prefer the blender for this soup because it purees the avocado more finely than the food processor. See box, page 32.

QUICK COLD MELON SOUP

SERVES 2

◆

*S*peedy, light, and refreshing, this soup from La Verl Daily of Le Panier Cooking School in Houston is a great beginning for a spicy meal. For a stunning two-color effect, make one recipe with cantaloupe and one with honeydew and place the chilled soups in two separate pitchers. To serve, pour the two soups at the same time into individual soup bowls.

Pulp of 1 perfectly ripe, cold
    cantaloupe or honeydew melon

(about 1¼ pounds), coarsely chopped

¼ cup fresh lemon juice
¼ cup fresh lime juice
Grated rind of ½ lemon
2 sprigs fresh mint, for garnish
2 nasturtium flowers, for garnish
   (optional; see box)

Place the chopped melon in a food processor or blender with the juices and lemon rind and puree until smooth. Chill for about 15 minutes if the melon is not cold. Serve cold, with mint and nasturtium garnish.

NOTE: If the melon needs more flavor, add ¼ teaspoon ground ginger to the recipe.

MAKE AHEAD: up to 6 hours; refrigerate

EDIBLE FLOWERS

◆

Provided they have not been treated with chemicals, many flowers of spring, summer, and early fall are edible: chive blossoms, violets, begonias, calendulas, chrysanthemums, and nasturtiums, whose leaves are also delicious in salads. Pick the flowers, rinse them lightly, and use them the same day. They make beautiful garnishes but are each surprisingly tasty as well, especially the peppery nasturtium and the lemony begonia. Edible flowers are often available at specialty markets and are usually displayed with the fresh herbs.

EASY BROCCOLI SOUP

SERVES 6 TO 8

◆

*U*se this as a basic recipe for wonderfully simple and healthy soups made with different vegetables, such as cauliflower, potato, carrot, sweet potato, zucchini, or asparagus. Simply substitute about 1 to 1½ pounds of any of these vegetables for the broccoli.

1 to 2 tablespoons sweet butter or
   vegetable oil
1 large onion, chopped
2 garlic cloves, mashed to a paste (see
   box, page 62)
1 bunch broccoli (about 1½ pounds),

   trimmed and coarsely chopped
6 to 7 cups chicken broth
Kosher salt
Freshly ground black pepper
½ cup heavy or light cream (optional)

In a heavy-bottomed 4- to 5-quart saucepan, heat the butter until foaming. Add the onion and cook until soft; then add the garlic, broccoli, and broth. Simmer, *uncovered,* until the broccoli is tender, 8 to 10 minutes. Puree with a hand blender in the saucepan, or in a blender or food processor, until smooth (see box, page 32). Season to taste with salt and pepper. Add the cream if you wish—the soup is also delicious without it.

MAKE AHEAD: make puree up to 24 hours ahead; refrigerate; reheat gently and add the cream (if using) just before serving

> ### ABOUT STOCK AND BROTH
>
> ◆
>
> **H**omemade stock will always give a richer flavor and more body to a soup than canned broth. If you are in the habit of making stock and freezing it to have it on hand, that is wonderful. But the soups and other recipes in this book were designed to taste very good with canned broth or bouillon cubes (see page 4) as well, so that they can be made quickly. The new unsalted canned broths are quite acceptable in flavor.

CANNELLINI BEAN SOUP WITH GREENS AND PARMESAN

SERVES 4 TO 6

◆

*T*his hearty soup makes a perfect meal served with crusty country bread. Greens cooked quickly like this are a great way to add calcium and other nutrients to your diet.

6 cups chicken broth
2 tablespoons extra-virgin olive oil
1 large yellow or white onion, minced
1 large garlic clove, mashed to a paste
   (see box, page 62)
1 small bunch spinach, young tender
   mustard or turnip greens, kale, or
   Swiss chard, stemmed, washed,

and sliced into thin shreds
One 12-ounce can cannellini beans,
   drained and rinsed
¼ teaspoon kosher salt, or to taste
½ teaspoon freshly ground black
   pepper, or to taste
½ cup freshly grated Italian Parmesan,
   for serving

Put the broth on to simmer. Heat the olive oil in a 4-quart casserole or stockpot. Over medium heat, cook the onion and garlic until soft, about 8 minutes. Stir in the greens and cook, uncovered, until wilted. Add the hot chicken broth and the beans and simmer for 5 minutes. Season with salt and pepper, making it quite peppery. Serve hot, with Parmesan to sprinkle over the top.

MAKE AHEAD: up to 1 hour; leave in pan and reheat gently

ROMAINE SOUP WITH PARMESAN
SERVES 4 TO 6

I created this soup from the memory of an unusual country soup I once had in a small town near Parma. Other lettuces (except iceberg) can be substituted and are as subtly delicious as romaine. It makes a delicate first course.

2 tablespoons unsalted butter
10 scallions, sliced
1 large head romaine lettuce, washed, dried, and finely sliced
6 cups chicken broth
½ teaspoon kosher salt
½ teaspoon freshly ground black pepper
2 tablespoons minced fresh parsley, for garnish
½ cup freshly grated Italian Parmesan, for serving

Melt the butter in large saucepan. Add the scallion and lettuce, and cook for 4 to 5 minutes, until the lettuce is wilted. Add the chicken broth and simmer, uncovered, for 10 minutes. Add the salt and pepper and puree the soup with a hand blender or in a blender or food processor (see box, page 32). Taste for seasoning, garnish with the parsley, and serve hot, with Parmesan cheese to sprinkle over the top.

VARIATIONS: Thin strips of prosciutto or Danish ham, cooked garbanzo beans or rice, or raw orzo or other pasta could be added with the chicken broth. Or, add julienned zucchini, carrots, or green beans with the broth to make a hearty, main-course soup.

MAKE AHEAD: up to 1 hour; leave in pan and reheat gently

MINTY PEA SOUP

SERVES 6

◆

*T*his delightful soup makes a perfect first course for a spring dinner of lamb or salmon. It's also excellent and filling enough for lunch or supper, accompanied by bread and salad.

4 cups chicken broth
Two 10-ounce packages frozen peas
2 medium carrots, peeled and diced or
    shredded
5 lettuce leaves, washed
¼ cup chopped shallot or scallion
½ teaspoon dried chervil (optional)
3 tablespoons finely chopped fresh
    parsley
⅛ teaspoon freshly ground white
    pepper
2 tablespoons sweet butter
½ teaspoon kosher salt, or more to
    taste
1 teaspoon sugar, or more to taste
2 tablespoons chopped fresh mint, or
    1 teaspoon dried mint and
    2 tablespoons fresh parsley
¼ cup heavy or light cream, for
    garnish

Bring the broth to a simmer. Place all of the remaining ingredients except the cream in a large saucepan. Pour in the hot broth and simmer, partly covered, for about 10 minutes, or until the carrots are tender. Puree with a hand blender in the saucepan, or in a blender or food processor, until smooth (see box). Taste for seasoning. Serve hot, or chill for at least 30 minutes and serve cold. Just before serving, pour the cream into the soup and swirl into patterns using a skewer or fork.

PUREEING SOUPS

◆

*M*ost French soups are pureed. If you prefer a chunkier soup, puree only one-half to three-quarters of the soup and vegetables, then mix in the rest for a nicely blended but textured soup.

The easiest and safest way to puree any amount of soup is to use the mini-pimer or hand blender, a gadget that is a kind of "blender on a stick." Although relatively new to the American marketplace, it is standard equipment in most French kitchens. To use it, simply submerge the blenderlike blade beneath the surface of the hot soup in the saucepan and move it in a circular motion until all the large chunks of vegetables have been pureed. This eliminates the complicated procedure of ladling the steaming-hot soup in stages into a blender or food processor. Both the mini-pimer *and a regular blender do a better job of pureeing soups than a food processor.*

MAKE AHEAD: up to 24 hours; refrigerate; reheat gently

CREAMY MUSHROOM SOUP

SERVES 4 TO 6

◆

*F*or me, this replaces Mom's chicken soup for comfort, but it is elegant enough to serve to guests and is excellent for winter meals, either as a first course or as the main course of a light supper.

4 tablespoons (½ stick) sweet butter
¾ pound fresh white mushrooms, stems left on but trimmed, cleaned, and chopped
2 shallots or 3 scallions, chopped
1 small garlic clove, mashed to a paste (see box, page 62)
3 tablespoons all-purpose flour
½ teaspoon kosher salt
¼ teaspoon freshly ground black pepper
Pinch freshly ground nutmeg
4½ cups chicken broth, or 2¼ cups broth and 2¼ cups milk
½ cup light or heavy cream, heated to a simmer
3 tablespoons minced fresh parsley
Thin lemon slices, or 2 tablespoons minced fresh parsley, thyme, or dill, for garnish

In a 3-quart saucepan, melt the butter and cook the mushroom, shallot, and garlic over medium-high heat until most of the liquid has evaporated, about 5 minutes. Add the flour and cook for 2 minutes, stirring with a whisk. Add the seasonings and broth and whisk vigorously. Simmer, uncovered, for about 10 minutes. Taste for seasoning, add the hot cream, and puree with a hand blender or in a blender or food processor (see box, opposite page). Serve hot, garnished with lemon slices or minced herbs.

VARIATION: Use different mushrooms, such as fresh shiitakes, porcini, oysters, or morels, depending on availability.

MAKE AHEAD: up to 24 hours; refrigerate; reheat gently

ZUPPA PRIMAVERA

SERVES 6

◆

I love the clean, clear taste of this simple but sophisticated soup. Its light, delicate flavor makes it a perfect first course for a spring dinner.

6 cups homemade or canned light chicken broth
½ pound fresh asparagus, peeled (see box), trimmed, and cut into ¼-inch slices on the diagonal
½ pound fresh peas, sugar snap peas, or snow peas, cut into ½-inch slices on the diagonal
1 small head Boston lettuce, washed, dried, and sliced into thin shreds
1 tablespoon unsalted butter
Kosher salt
Freshly ground black pepper
12 to 15 whole leaves Italian parsley

Heat the broth in a 4- to 5-quart casserole until simmering. Add the asparagus, peas, and lettuce and cook for 2 to 3 minutes. Stir in the butter, salt and pep-

per to taste, and the parsley. Serve hot.

VARIATION: Add 1 teaspoon of finely chopped or grated fresh ginger and 2 teaspoons of Oriental sesame oil to give this soup an Oriental character.

ASPARAGUS: TO PEEL OR NOT TO PEEL

Pencil-thin fresh asparagus does not need peeling, but older asparagus with thicker stalks benefits from peeling since the skin is quite tough. Use a swivel-bladed vegetable peeler and lightly peel up to the purplish heads.

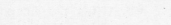

BLACK BEAN SOUP SUPREME
SERVES 6

*T*his soup from Austin, Texas, chef Larry Osborne is supremely good, and it's hearty enough to be almost a meal in itself. I've altered the recipe, using canned black beans for convenience, but if you prefer, use 1 pound dried black beans and cook them covered with water for about 60 minutes or until they are tender. Don't worry about the chili being too hot—here it serves to spark the flavor of the beans.

½ pound bulk breakfast sausage
1 large yellow onion, chopped
1 large garlic clove, mashed to a paste (see box, page 62)

1 serrano chili, minced
1 imported bay leaf
⅓ cup fresh cilantro leaves (if unavailable, use Italian parsley)

¼ teaspoon cayenne
¼ teaspoon freshly ground black
    pepper
32 ounces canned black beans,
    drained and rinsed
Kosher salt to taste
⅓ to ½ cup whole milk

In a large heavy-bottomed casserole, break up the sausage and cook with the onion over medium-high heat until the sausage is fully cooked and the onion is golden, about 10 minutes. Add the garlic and gently cook for about ½ minute. Add all of the remaining ingredients except the milk, stir, partially cover, and simmer for 10 minutes, or until very hot. Puree the soup with a hand blender or in a food processor or blender (see box, page 32). If you wish, strain through an ordinary strainer for an even finer consistency. Thin the soup if necessary with the milk. Taste for seasoning, add salt if needed, reheat, and serve.

MAKE AHEAD: up to 24 hours; refrigerate; reheat gently

ROASTING CHILIES AND BELL PEPPERS

◆

To roast a whole pepper, stick a fork firmly into the stem end and hold it over a gas flame, or place the pepper 4 inches under the flame of a broiler or 4 inches over the coals on a grill. Turn the pepper as soon as one side is fully charred or blackened (use tongs if roasting in a broiler or on a grill); if you roast it for too long (more than 3 or 4 minutes on each side), the pulp will simply disappear. When the pepper is completely charred, place it on a plate, wrap it immediately in a cold, damp paper towel, and let it sit for a few minutes to allow the steam to loosen the charred skin.

Then remove the skin: Hold the pepper in the paper towel with both hands with the stem facing you. Starting from the top, push down the paper towel firmly with both thumbs, pushing off the blackened skin and turning it to the inside and rolling it up in the paper towel. One continuous firm movement is better than a dabbing one. Discard the paper towel. Don't rinse the pepper or you will lose or dilute the flavorful juices. When the skin is off and all the black bits have been removed, cut out the stem and seeds.

Peppers can be roasted, peeled, and seeded and kept refrigerated for 24 hours. It is not quite as easy to roast peppers evenly over an electric ring or filament, but it is possible. Use medium to medium-high heat and watch to see that the peppers don't get too black.

CORN, CHILI, AND OYSTER CHOWDER

SERVES 6

◆

*T*his hearty chowder has the wonderful spicy zip of southwestern and Mexican cuisine. You may omit the cayenne and/or the poblano chili if you prefer a milder chowder. Serve with lots of crusty bread or tortilla chips as a main course.

2 tablespoons unsalted butter
3 leeks, slit, well washed, and thinly
    sliced, or 8 scallions or 1 large red
    onion, finely chopped
3 medium new potatoes, cut into
    1-inch cubes
1 red bell pepper, roasted, peeled,
    seeded, and chopped (see box,
    page 35)
1 large poblano chili or 2 small,
    roasted, peeled, seeded, and
    chopped (see box), or, if
    unavailable, 1 green bell pepper,
    roasted, peeled, seeded, and
    chopped
3 cups chicken broth
4 cups whole milk
1 teaspoon kosher salt
1 teaspoon freshly ground black pepper
½ teaspoon cayenne
Kernels from 3 ears sweet corn, or
    16 ounces frozen corn kernels,
    unthawed
1 pint fresh oysters with their juices
½ cup minced fresh Italian parsley
    (use regular parsley if Italian is
    not available)

Melt the butter in a heavy-bottomed 3- to 4-quart casserole. Add the leek, potato, bell pepper, and poblano, and cook gently for 5 to 7 minutes.

Add the broth and cook until the veg-

POBLANO CHILIES

◆

*S*ome poblanos are hotter than others. One way to tell is to look at the tip: A poblano with a pointed end will probably be hotter than one with a more rounded end. Poblanos have a dense smoky flavor and are not as hot as serranos or jalapeños. The hot taste of a poblano comes more as an aftertaste.

etables are soft, about 7 minutes. Add the milk, seasonings, and corn, and cook for another 5 minutes, or until piping hot. Taste, and adjust seasonings.

Just before serving, poach the oysters in the hot soup, off the flame, for 2 to 3 minutes. Stir in the parsley and serve immediately.

VARIATIONS: Substitute fresh chopped clams or fresh flaked crabmeat for the oysters.

MAKE AHEAD: prepare (up to the point of adding the oysters) up to 24 hours ahead; refrigerate; reheat gently before adding oysters

POTAGE DUBARRY

SERVES 8

◆

Cauliflower tastes marvelous in soup. This is an elegant first-course winter soup, one that beautifully graces a table with its delicate pale-green color.

3 quarts water
3½ to 4 teaspoons kosher salt
2 medium heads cauliflower, trimmed, cut into florets
1 cup thinly sliced leek or yellow onion
4 tablespoons (½ stick) unsalted butter
3 tablespoons all-purpose flour
3 cups chicken broth
1 cup whole milk
About 2 packed cups fresh parsley or watercress
1½ to 2 teaspoons kosher salt
¼ teaspoon freshly ground white pepper
½ cup light or heavy cream
Sprigs of watercress or parsley, for garnish

Bring the water to a boil, add 2 teaspoons of the salt, and cook the cauliflower for 5 minutes. Drain, reserving 2 cups of the cooking liquid. Meanwhile, in a 4-quart saucepan, cook the leek gently in the butter until soft, about 5 minutes. Stir in the flour and cook for 3 minutes over low heat.

Combine the broth, milk, and reserved cooking liquid, and heat to a simmer. Pour this all at once over the *roux,* and whisk until smooth. Add the cauliflower, parsley, and salt and pepper, and simmer gently for about 10 minutes. Puree the soup with a hand blender, or in a blender or a food processor (see box, page 32). Just before serving, add the cream. Taste for seasoning, garnish with watercress, and serve very hot.

MAKE AHEAD: make puree up to 24 hours ahead; refrigerate; reheat gently and add cream just before serving

LEMONY GREEN SOUP WITH POACHED SCALLOPS

SERVES 4

◆

Oriental in style, subtly flavored yet filling, this soup makes a wonderful, delicate lunch or supper entrée or first course.

3 tablespoons unsalted butter
3 scallions, finely minced
2 shallots, minced
½ tablespoon minced fresh ginger
1 head Boston lettuce, washed, dried,
   and finely shredded *en chiffonade*
   (see box)
5 ounces fresh spinach, washed, dried,
   stemmed, and finely shredded *en
   chiffonade* (see box)
4 cups chicken broth
Kosher salt
Freshly ground white pepper
Dash Tabasco
Squeeze of fresh lemon juice
½ pound sea or bay scallops, cleaned
   of sand but not rinsed (see box,
   page 68)
¼ pound fresh shiitake, chanterelle,
   oyster, or enoki mushrooms, or if
   these are not available, ½ pound
   very thinly sliced fresh white
   mushrooms
4 paper-thin lemon slices, for garnish

Melt 2 tablespoons of the butter in a
4- or 5-quart casserole. Add the scallion,
shallot, ginger, lettuce, and spinach, and
gently cook until the greens wilt and the
scallion is soft, 5 to 7 minutes. Add the
chicken stock and simmer, uncovered, for
10 minutes. Cool slightly and then puree
the soup with a hand blender or in a
blender or food processor (see box, page

SHREDDED GREENS

Chiffonade, *French for "little rags
or shreds," refers to lettuce or other
greens or herbs that have been sliced
or shredded very finely, across the
grain. This is an excellent way to cut
lettuce that is fresh but not beautiful
to use in a salad, and the best way
to prepare lettuce to be added to
soups or cooked as a vegetable. Flat-
leaved herbs like basil look wonderful* en chiffonade, *piled on top of a
salad or a sauce as a garnish.*

32). Season to taste with salt, pepper, Tabasco, and lemon juice.

Just before serving, heat the remaining 1 tablespoon of butter in a heavy skillet. Add the scallops and mushrooms, and
cook over high heat for 2 minutes. Add to
the hot soup and serve immediately, garnished with lemon slices.

VARIATIONS: Substitute ½ pound small
peeled shrimp, cleaned lump crab or
thinly sliced squid for the scallops.

MAKE AHEAD: prepare soup base up to
24 hours ahead; refrigerate; reheat gently
before adding scallops

◆

POULTRY, FISH, AND MEAT ENTRÉES

◆

*A*gain and again my students tell me plaintively that they are tired of plain broiled, grilled, or sautéed chicken breasts, steaks, chops, and fish and ask whether there isn't some way to jazz up these old standbys without having to spend hours in the kitchen. In fact, there are *many* quick and easy ways to brighten and sharpen the tastes of familiar cuts of chicken, fish, and meat, as I show in the out-of-the-ordinary selection of entrées in this chapter.

I have included more chicken and fish than meat entrées because consuming less meat seems to be a very widespread trend. I use a lot of boneless chicken breast because it cooks so quickly and is so versatile. (Buy it already boned, or have the butcher bone and skin it for you.) Organic free-range chicken is available in better markets; its only drawback is a higher price.

I have used a wide range of seasonings to make these entrées stand out with exceptional flavor. Many of the seasoning ideas in these dishes can be applied to other foods, greatly expanding your use of the recipes. The mint pesto for the lamb chops, for example, also works beautifully with grilled or sautéed chicken or turkey breast, or a salmon or redfish fillet. And the Chicken Sauté with Red and Green Peppers could be done equally well with thin strips of tender beef or veal. The Halibut with Scallions and Ginger en Papillote works beautifully with many other fish and shellfish, from redfish to scallops and shrimp.

Flavors here range from the sharp zing of jalapeños, peppercorns, garlic, Hungarian paprika, and vinegars to the milder, subtler flavors of sesame seeds, hazelnuts, grapes, walnut oil, and mint. I love the tastes of all these seasonings; they delight and satisfy and sharpen the palate. And I find that having an entrée with distinctive flavors lets you "off the hook" for the other dishes—they *can* be very, very simple, so they don't conflict with the main course. Plain rice and a simple green dinner salad could accompany the wonderfully garlicky Scallops Provençal, for example. Fettucine tossed in a little butter or cream would go very nicely with the Salmon Fillets with Toasted Hazelnuts and Dill. This is helpful when you are in a hurry and only have time to prepare one recipe.

There are a few dishes here that go in the oven, but most are top-of-the-stove dishes that cook in minutes as you stir or watch them.

Menus and beverage suggestions are given for all of the main-dish recipes in the book, and they begin in this chapter. These menus are intended as guidelines to indicate which foods go well together, not as strict prescriptions. Most of them make wonderful dinner-party menus. All of the recipes listed in the menus are included in this book.

HOW TO TRUSS A BIRD FOR ROASTING

♦

The purpose of trussing any bird (chicken, squab, quail, duck, or Cornish hen) is to make it look better and stay moist. For a 3- to 3½-pound roasting chicken use a yard of kitchen or linen trussing string. Place it underneath the upper third of the bird, with both ends pulled up to equal lengths. Cross the ends over the breast and tighten so that the wings are pulled snug to the body. Then loop each end of the string under and around each leg, tighten, and pull the legs close to the body. Finally, tie the ends of the string tightly underneath the tail to make a knot or bow, and seal up the cavity. Remove the string with scissors before carving.

POULTRY

FISH

MEAT

POULTRY

◆

HUNGARIAN PAPRIKA CHICKEN

SERVES 4 TO 6

◆

*H*ungarian paprika is a wonderful aromatic seasoning that combines marvelously with chicken. Serve this over wide noodles, such as pappardelle, tossed in
butter.

⅓ cup all-purpose flour
2 tablespoons sweet Hungarian
    paprika (see box, opposite page)
2 teaspoons kosher salt
½ teaspoon freshly ground black
    pepper
6 skinless, boneless chicken breast
    halves, washed, trimmed of fat,
    patted dry, and cut into 1-inch
    diagonal strips
2 tablespoons virgin olive oil
2 tablespoons unsalted butter
1 large white onion, minced
⅓ cup chicken broth
¾ cup sour cream
Finely grated rind of 1 large lemon
Kosher salt
Freshly ground black pepper

Combine the flour, 1 tablespoon of
the paprika, and the salt and pepper on a
plate and dredge the chicken pieces in
the mixture. Heat the oil and butter in
large sauté pan and sauté the chicken
over medium-high heat, not more than 4
minutes. Remove to a plate, cover, and
keep warm.

Add the remaining tablespoon of paprika and the onion to the skillet and
gently cook until golden. Mix in the broth,
return the chicken to the pan, cover, and
simmer for about 5 minutes. Stir in the
sour cream and lemon peel, and heat
gently for a few minutes, but do not boil.
Season carefully to taste with salt and
pepper and serve on a heated platter.

MAKE AHEAD: make up to point of adding sour cream up to 24 hours ahead; refrigerate; reheat gently before adding the
sour cream

MENU
◆
℘℘

HUNGARIAN PAPRIKA CHICKEN

PAPPARDELLE

APPLE, FENNEL,
AND WATERCRESS SALAD

CHOCOLATE CAKE

◆

RIESLING, VOUVRAY,
CHENIN BLANC

ABOUT PAPRIKA

◆

A sprinkle of paprika on a dish as a garnish doesn't do justice to the great flavor of this spice. Like curry powder, paprika needs to be cooked for a few minutes for its true flavor to develop. And to get the full rich flavor of paprika, use it liberally; several teaspoons will nicely flavor a chicken sauté for 4 to 6.

Paprika is actually the Hungarian word for "pepper." The spice paprika is ground from a pepper grown in Central Europe, where it is a predominate seasoning. The paprika from Hungary is considered the world's finest. In fact, Hungarian paprika pepper harvests are graded for quality like wine vintages—with good and better years! Hungarian paprika is available in both hot and sweet varieties. Hot Hungarian paprika is surprisingly pungent; "sweet" really means "less hot." Store Hungarian paprika in the refrigerator in a tin or jar. It will keep for 6 to 8 months stored this way.

CHICKEN SAUTÉ WITH RED AND GREEN PEPPERS

SERVES 2 TO 4

◆

Here is a delightfully colorful chicken dish that takes only 20 minutes to prepare.

2 tablespoons virgin olive oil
1 green bell pepper, seeded and cut into ½ × 4-inch strips
1 red bell pepper, seeded and cut into ½ × 4-inch strips
¼ teaspoon kosher salt
¼ teaspoon freshly ground black pepper
⅛ teaspoon cayenne
½ teaspoon dried thyme

⅓ cup all-purpose flour
1 pound skinless, boneless chicken breast, washed, trimmed of fat, patted dry, and cut into 1 × 3-inch strips
2 tablespoons chopped fresh parsley, marjoram, thyme, or basil, for garnish
½ lemon or lime, for serving (optional)

M E N U

❧

CHICKEN SAUTÉ WITH RED
AND GREEN PEPPERS

COUSCOUS WITH CARROTS
AND MINT

APPLES, GRAPES, AND WALNUTS
(AS SALAD OR DESSERT)

◆

CHARDONNAY,
SAUVIGNON BLANC

Heat the oil in a large skillet. Add the peppers and sauté over medium-high heat until soft, 8 to 10 minutes. Remove and hold. Mix the seasonings with the flour, and just before cooking, toss the chicken strips in the seasoned flour to flavor. Add a little more oil to the skillet if needed and sauté the chicken over medium-high heat until lightly browned, 3 to 4 minutes. Add the peppers and mix together. Serve garnished with parsley, and squeeze lemon or lime over all if desired.

CHICKEN SAUTÉ WITH SHALLOTS, MUSHROOMS, AND WHITE WINE

SERVES 6

◆

*S*autés are, by definition, quick. Enjoy this sophisticated, speedy version of a French classic.

½ tablespoon unsalted butter
½ tablespoon virgin olive oil
2 slices slab bacon, cut in thin strips
8 small shallots or boiling onions, peeled and finely chopped
2 carrots, finely chopped
6 skinless, boneless chicken breast halves, washed, trimmed of fat, and patted dry, each cut diagonally into 4 long pieces
½ teaspoon kosher salt
¼ teaspoon freshly ground black pepper
1 tablespoon all-purpose flour
1 cup sliced fresh mushrooms

¾ cup dry white wine
Sprigs of fresh parsley, for garnish

M E N U

❧

CHICKEN SAUTÉ
WITH SHALLOTS, MUSHROOMS,
AND WHITE WINE

ORZO

THE ORIGINAL CAESAR SALAD

COLD CHERRIES IN BRANDY

◆

CHARDONNAY, MÂCON BLANC

Heat the butter and oil in a large skillet. Brown the bacon, about 5 minutes, and set aside. Lightly brown the vegetables, about 8 minutes, and set aside. Add the chicken to the skillet and stir-fry for 2 minutes. Remove and set aside. Return the bacon and browned vegetables to the skillet, add the salt, pepper, flour, and mushrooms, and cook for 3 to 4 minutes. Add the wine and simmer until the sauce thickens nicely. Add the chicken and cook for another 5 minutes, or until the sauce and chicken are well blended. Taste for seasoning. Serve on a hot platter, garnished with parsley.

VARIATIONS: Substitute a light red wine such as a Beaujolais or a Pinot Noir for the white wine.

Add 10 ounces canned or frozen artichoke hearts with the bacon and vegetables.

THE BEST WAY TO COOK BONELESS CHICKEN BREAST

Boneless chicken breast is not only delicious, it is one of the quickest, easiest dishes to cook. With this simple recipe you can make a great variety of fabulous quick meals simply by adding different sauces and/or side dishes.

Cut away the chicken skin and any fat and discard it. Remove the tenderloin, the slightly separated smaller strip behind the breast, and cook it separately if you like. Place the chicken breast in a gallon-size, sealable plastic bag and flatten it with a veal pounder to a thickness of ¼ inch for quick and even cooking. (For even quicker cooking, cut each breast half on the diagonal into five or six ½-inch strips.)

Melt a couple of teaspoons of oil or butter in a heavy skillet and stir-fry the chicken over high heat for 5 to 6 minutes, or until the juices of the chicken run clear when pierced with a knife. Don't be tempted to cook it any longer or the chicken will become rubbery. (Alternatively, bake the chicken in a baking dish in a preheated 400° oven for about 8 to 10 minutes—8 minutes for strips. Use a few tablespoons of chicken broth or sauce to moisten while cooking.)

Serve plain or with a sauce (see chapter 9), or use in a salad or pasta dish. With larger pieces of cooked chicken, let the meat sit for about 5 minutes to allow the juices to settle back into the tissue, before slicing.

QUICK AND FRAGRANT INDIAN CHICKEN

SERVES 2

◆

*I*ndian cooking is known for its brilliant use of a wide range of spices. Here is a delicate and delicious combination of the spices most likely to be on hand in your kitchen. Two teaspoons of curry powder can be substituted for the combination of cumin, coriander, turmeric, cloves, and cinnamon. This dish can also be made with turkey breast or fish fillets, and the sauce is excellent over roasted chicken or Cornish hens. Multiply the recipe for serving more.

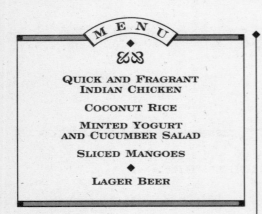

MENU

◆

ॐॐ

QUICK AND FRAGRANT
INDIAN CHICKEN

COCONUT RICE

MINTED YOGURT
AND CUCUMBER SALAD

SLICED MANGOES

◆

LAGER BEER

YOGURT SAUCE

1½ tablespoons vegetable oil
1 medium yellow onion, finely chopped
2 large garlic cloves, mashed to a
   paste (see box, page 62)
1 tablespoon finely chopped fresh
   ginger
1 teaspoon hot Hungarian paprika
¼ teaspoon cayenne
½ teaspoon ground cumin
1 teaspoon ground coriander
¼ teaspoon turmeric
2 whole cloves
⅛ teaspoon ground cinnamon
¼ teaspoon kosher salt
½ cup plain low-fat yogurt

½ tablespoon vegetable oil (safflower,

peanut, canola, or grapeseed)
10 ounces skinless, boneless chicken
   breast, washed, trimmed of fat,
   and patted dry
⅓ cup raw cashews
¼ cup raisins
¼ cup fresh coriander or fresh mint,
   for garnish

First, make the sauce. Heat the 1½ tablespoons of oil in a 9-inch skillet or sauté pan. Add the onion, garlic, and ginger. Stir in all the spices and cook over medium-high heat for about 6 to 7 minutes, or until the onion is soft, stirring occasionally. Pour the onion-and-spice mixture into a blender, add the salt and yogurt, and blend for 30 seconds. Keep warm by keeping the lid on the blender.

Wipe the skillet with a paper towel and heat the ½ tablespoon oil. Pound the chicken lightly a few times between sheets of plastic wrap with a large knife or veal pounder to flatten to ½-inch thickness, then add to the skillet along with the cashews and raisins. Cook 3 to 4 minutes on one side, turn, and cook 3 to 4 minutes on the other side, being careful not to overcook and toughen the chicken.

The cashews will brown lightly and the raisins will soften. Remove to a warm plate, pour the warm yogurt sauce over the chicken, garnish with coriander or mint, and serve immediately.

VARIATION: Add ½ cup canned unsweet-ened coconut milk (the best brands are Thai) to the skillet to cook with the spices and onion.

MAKE AHEAD: prepare the sauce up to 6 hours ahead (refrigerate); reheat gently just before serving

CHICKEN BREASTS WITH SAGE AND ROSEMARY

SERVES 8

◆

ere's a terrific entrée of Tuscan inspiration that's as easy as it is delicious. It's especially helpful if you are cooking for a crowd since it uses few dishes or utensils and comes to the table in its baking dish. I like the rustic look of earthenware oval gratin dishes, but any baking dish will do.

SAGE AND ROSEMARY MARINADE
3 tablespoons extra-virgin olive oil
¼ cup fresh lemon juice
2 garlic cloves, mashed to a paste
    (see box, page 62)
1 ounce prosciutto, chopped
2 teaspoons fresh rosemary, finely
    chopped (see box, page 71)
4 fresh sage leaves, chopped
1 teaspoon freshly grated lemon rind
½ teaspoon kosher salt
¼ teaspoon freshly ground black
    pepper

8 skinless, boneless chicken breast
    halves, washed, trimmed of fat,
    and patted dry

Fresh rosemary and sage sprigs, for garnish

MENU

◆

◆◆

CHICKEN BREASTS
WITH SAGE AND ROSEMARY

SUMMER POTATOES
FROM THE VAUCLUSE

ITALIAN GREEN SALAD
WITH BASIL-OIL DRESSING

RICOTTA AND RUM DESSERT

◆

PINOT GRIGIO

Combine the marinade ingredients in a large bowl; add the chicken breasts, and coat well. Arrange the chicken breasts neatly in a large baking dish and roast in a preheated 375° oven for 15 to 20 minutes, or in a 400° oven for about 10 to 12 minutes, until the juices run clear.

MAKE AHEAD: marinate chicken breasts in the refrigerator, covered, up to 24 hours ahead

PAILLARD OF CHICKEN BREAST WITH PARMESAN

SERVES 2

◆

*T*his is a fabulously tasty recipe—quick and elegant, too. Serve with fettuccine for a perfect Italian supper.

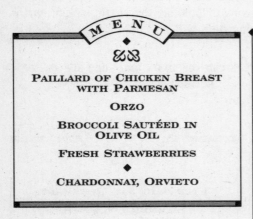

MENU

&&

PAILLARD OF CHICKEN BREAST WITH PARMESAN

ORZO

BROCCOLI SAUTÉED IN OLIVE OIL

FRESH STRAWBERRIES

◆

CHARDONNAY, ORVIETO

2 skinless, boneless chicken breast
    halves, washed, trimmed of fat,
    and patted dry
Fresh lemon juice
¼ cup flour mixed with a dash of
    kosher salt, a grinding of black

pepper, and a pinch of dried thyme
1 large egg, lightly beaten
¼ cup fine fresh white bread crumbs
    made in food processor, mixed
    with ¼ cup grated Italian
    Parmesan and ¼ teaspoon dried
    basil
1 tablespoon olive oil or clarified
    butter
Chopped Italian parsley, for garnish
Lemon wedges, for garnish

Place each breast in a quart-sized sealable plastic bag and pound with a mallet or veal pounder to a thickness of ¼ inch. Sprinkle with lemon juice. Put the seasoned flour mixture, the beaten egg, and the bread-crumb mixture on separate plates. While heating the oil in a large skillet, dredge the chicken breasts in the seasoned flour, then dip in the beaten egg and the crumbs. Cook over medium-high heat about 3 to 4 minutes on each side or until lightly browned. Serve immediately, garnished with parsley and lemon.

BAKED MUSTARD-TARRAGON CHICKEN
SERVES 4
◆

*M*ustard and tarragon flavor chicken very nicely in this homey, easy dish.

1 tablespoon unsalted butter
½ teaspoon cayenne
¾ teaspoon dried tarragon, or
    1 tablespoon chopped fresh
    tarragon
1 teaspoon balsamic vinegar
3 tablespoons Dijon mustard, Cajun
    mustard, or grainy mustard
½ teaspoon kosher salt
½ teaspoon freshly ground black
    pepper
4 pieces (1 pound) skinless, boneless
    chicken breast, washed, trimmed
    of fat, patted dry

Preheat the oven to 375°. Melt the butter and stir in all the seasonings. Dip the chicken in this mixture, place the coated breasts in a buttered baking dish, and bake 15 minutes, uncovered, or until the juices of the chicken run clear when pricked with a fork.

VARIATIONS: Add 1 tablespoon rinsed and drained capers or 2 tablespoons toasted mustard seeds (see box, page 67) to the coating mixture.

Use skinless, boneless chicken thighs instead of the breasts, and bake for 25 minutes.

MAKE AHEAD: up to 1 hour; cool at room temperature and reheat in a 350° oven for 10 minutes

M E N U
🙰

BAKED MUSTARD-TARRAGON
CHICKEN

BOILED NEW POTATOES
WITH PARSLEY

ROMAINE AND CHERRY TOMATO
SALAD WITH
CREAMY CAESAR DRESSING

RIPE PEARS
◆
BEAUJOLAIS

BREAST OF CHICKEN
IN JALAPEÑO-CITRUS MARINADE
SERVES 4 TO 6
◆

*T*errifically simple, this healthy, delicious, mildly spicy chicken recipe goes very well with corn and tomatoes for a quick summer supper. You can also use the marinade with fish fillets, lamb, beef, pork, or turkey. Don't be put off by the chilies—they do flavor the dish but don't overwhelm it.

MENU
◆
&⫯&

QUICK COLD AVOCADO SOUP

BREAST OF CHICKEN IN JALAPEÑO-CITRUS MARINADE

HOMINY WITH SWEET CORN, POBLANO, AND CILANTRO

CANTALOUPE AND FRESH BLUEBERRIES

◆

SAUVIGNON BLANC, CHENIN BLANC

1½ pounds skinless, boneless chicken breast, washed and patted dry

Puree the marinade ingredients in a food processor or blender. Put the chicken and marinade in a plastic bag and refrigerate for at least 15 minutes.

Remove the chicken from the marinade, but do not wipe. Grill, broil, or sauté the chicken, or bake it at 375°—it will take a maximum of 10 minutes, with a little variation for each method. If broiling, be careful not to overcook.

MAKE AHEAD: marinate the chicken in refrigerator up to 24 hours ahead

JALAPEÑO-CITRUS MARINADE
2 to 3 jalapeño or serrano chilies, seeded
4 medium garlic cloves
Juice of 1 lemon
2 tablespoons extra-virgin olive oil
¼ cup chopped fresh Italian parsley or cilantro
½ teaspoon freshly ground black pepper
½ teaspoon kosher salt
1 teaspoon ground cumin

COLD CIRCASSIAN CHICKEN

SERVES 6 TO 8

◆

A great addition to picnics or make-ahead meals, this intriguing dish from northern Turkey and the republic of Georgia is very easy to prepare. The paprika and nuts give fabulous flavor as they sauce the chicken. This recipe, adapted from Roy Andries de Grootes's wonderful book, *A Feast for All Seasons,* has long been a part of my summer repertoire.

3 cups chicken broth
6 skinless, boneless chicken breast
    halves (1½ pounds), washed,
    trimmed of fat, and patted dry
1 teaspoon dried thyme
2 tablespoons chopped fresh parsley
2 yellow onions, finely chopped
3 tablespoons virgin olive oil
4 thin slices white bread
½ cup whole milk
1 cup blanched almonds
1 scant cup hazelnuts
1 cup walnuts
1 tablespoon hot Hungarian paprika
1 tablespoon sweet Hungarian paprika
1 teaspoon kosher salt, or more to
    taste
¼ teaspoon cayenne
Sweet Hungarian paprika, for garnish

In a heavy-bottomed 4-quart saucepan bring the broth to a simmer, add the thyme and parsley, and poach the chicken breasts for 6 to 7 minutes, until just barely cooked. Remove the chicken and let cool. Reserve the broth. Sauté the onion in the olive oil until very soft. Soak the bread in the milk, and squeeze dry.

In a food processor, finely chop all the nuts and place in a large mixing bowl. To this, add the onion, bread, and seasonings and mix well. Slowly add a little reserved chicken broth, until the mixture has a thick, saucelike consistency. Cut the cooled poached chicken into ½-inch-wide strips and toss with the sauce, coating well. Chill in the refrigerator for at least 10 minutes. To serve, place on a platter and garnish with a light sprinkling of paprika for color.

MAKE AHEAD: prepare up to 24 hours ahead; refrigerate

MENU

◆

ℰℬ

COLD CIRCASSIAN CHICKEN

CLASSIC GREEK SALAD

QUICK BLACKBERRY SORBET

◆

BEAUJOLAIS,
CALIFORNIA CHARDONNAY,
SAUVIGNON BLANC

POULET AU VINAIGRE

SERVES 4

◆

*T*his simple chicken dish, with its exquisite flavor, derives from old-fashioned French *cuisine bourgeoise*—so simple, but so memorable. I love the very subtle flavor of the vinegar in this dish.

🙰 TO COOK A SMALL BIRD

◆

Small birds like squab, quail, dove, poussin, and Cornish hens sauté or braise more evenly and quickly if they are split into two pieces and then slightly flattened. Using sharp kitchen scissors or poultry shears, cut through the bird close to one side of the backbone. Or, if you wish, cut out the backbone completely. Flatten by firmly applying the weight of both hands on the halves until they spread out a bit. Or lightly pound with a veal pounder or mallet.

---

3 tablespoons unsalted butter
One 2½-pound frying chicken, cut into
    8 pieces
Kosher salt
Freshly ground black pepper
⅓ cup water or dry white wine
2 tablespoons finely chopped scallion
    or red onion
2 tablespoons minced fresh parsley
¼ cup red-wine vinegar or Spanish
    sherry wine vinegar
¼ cup water or dry white wine

¼ cup minced fresh parsley, for
    garnish

Heat the butter in a large skillet and brown the chicken pieces on all sides. Season with salt and pepper, add the ⅓ cup water or wine, and simmer, covered, for about 15 minutes. Add the scallion and parsley, cover, and cook for another 10 minutes. Remove the chicken.

Add the vinegar to the pan and bring to a boil, scraping up the browned pieces and juices and stirring. When the sauce is cooked down and looks syrupy, add the ¼ cup water and stir. Return the chicken to the pan, reheat, garnish with parsley, and serve hot.

M E N U

◆

🙰

POULET AU VINAIGRE

**OAKLEAF LETTUCE,
GREEN BEAN, WALNUT,
AND ROQUEFORT SALAD**

COEUR À LA CRÈME

◆

BEAUJOLAIS, PINOT NOIR

CHICKEN LIVER SAUTÉ WITH MADEIRA

SERVES 4 TO 6 AS AN ENTRÉE, 8 TO 10 AS AN HORS D'OEUVRE

◆

*H*ere's a delicious quick entrée or warm hors d'oeuvre. Madeira gives the best flavor, but port, dry sherry, or dry white wine work as well. This is also good as a sauce for noodles or pasta. Or, chop the livers and fill an omelet with them.

MENU

◆

CHICKEN LIVER SAUTÉ WITH MADEIRA

RICE

PROVENÇAL SPINACH SALAD

SLICED ORANGES AND STRAWBERRIES WITH GRAND MARNIER

◆

BEAUJOLAIS, MÂCON BLANC, CHARDONNAY

GARLIC TOAST
6 or more slices French bread
3 cloves garlic, split in half

4 shallots or scallions, minced
4 tablespoons (½ stick) unsalted
    butter
1 pound very fresh chicken livers (see
    box, page 70), trimmed of fat and
    any green matter, cut in half,
    rinsed, drained, and patted dry
3 tablespoons Sercial (dry) Madeira
½ teaspoon kosher salt
¼ teaspoon freshly ground black
    pepper

½ teaspoon dried thyme or tarragon
2 tablespoons finely chopped fresh
    parsley

First, make the garlic toast. Toast the bread in a preheated 350° oven until dried out, about 8 minutes, then rub each piece with the cut side of the raw garlic slices. Keep the toast warm.

In a large skillet, cook the shallot gently in the butter until soft, about 3 minutes. Add the chicken livers and cook over medium heat for 3 minutes. Scoop the chicken livers (they should still be pink inside) into a bowl and cover to keep warm. Add the Madeira and the seasonings to the skillet, and cook for 1 to 2 minutes over high heat, until a glaze remains. Taste for seasoning. Stir in the cooked chicken livers and spread the mixture on the garlic toast.

VARIATIONS: For a richer dish, add ½ cup of one or more of the following along with the shallot: thin strips of ham, sliced fresh mushrooms, homemade chicken broth.

SPLIT QUAIL
WITH JUNIPER BERRIES AND GIN
SERVES 2
◆

Here is an easy technique for quail that also keeps it moist. If you are not a hunter, look for farm-raised quail in specialty meat markets and fine grocery stores. The juniper berries and gin nicely complement dove, guinea hen, partridge, or chicken breasts.

MENU
◆
🙰🙰

SPLIT QUAIL WITH JUNIPER BERRIES AND GIN

ANGEL HAIR PASTA PANCAKES

GREEN SALAD WITH WALNUT-OIL VINAIGRETTE

RUSTIC PEAR AND APPLE CLAFOUTIS
◆
RIESLING, MUSCADET, MÂCON BLANC, CHARDONNAY

4 small (4-ounce) or 2 large (8-ounce) quail, split down the back and flattened (see box, page 52)
¼ cup flour mixed with ¼ teaspoon kosher salt, ⅛ teaspoon freshly ground black pepper, and ½ teaspoon dried thyme
1½ tablespoons unsalted butter
2 shallots, minced
8 juniper berries, crushed
¼ cup dry gin
⅓ cup dry white wine

⅓ cup heavy cream
Kosher salt
Freshly ground black pepper
2 tablespoons finely chopped fresh parsley, for garnish
½ tablespoon chopped fresh thyme, for garnish (optional)

Dredge the split quail in the flour mixture. Melt the butter in a large skillet. When it foams, add the quail and sauté for 2 to 3 minutes on each side over medium-high heat. Add the shallot and stir. Add the juniper berries, gin, and white wine and simmer gently for about 10 minutes, or until only 3 tablespoons of liquid remain. Add the cream and cook until the sauce thickens and the quail are tender, about 5 to 10 minutes (larger quail will take longer to cook). Season with salt and pepper to taste, and serve sprinkled with parsley and thyme.

MAKE AHEAD: up to 24 hours; reheat gently

ROAST CORNISH HENS RUBBED WITH CORNMEAL AND CAYENNE

SERVES 2

◆

*T*he warm flair of Southwestern seasonings gives new life to these little "company" birds. Cornmeal makes the skin very crisp. A poussin, whole chicken breast, or half a chicken or turkey breast can also be used. (Timing will vary a little for each.)

MENU

◆

ROAST CORNISH HENS RUBBED WITH CORNMEAL AND CAYENNE

GRILLED PEPPERS AND ONIONS

COLD LEMON RICE

◆

TEXAS OR CALIFORNIA SAUVIGNON BLANC

Two 1-pound Cornish hens, rinsed and dried
½ teaspoon dried sage, or 2 sprigs fresh sage
8 sprigs fresh parsley
¼ cup finely ground yellow cornmeal
1 teaspoon cayenne
½ teaspoon kosher salt
¼ teaspoon freshly ground black pepper
Kitchen string, for trussing (optional)

Preheat the oven to 400°. Stuff the cavities of the hens with sage and parsley. Mix the cornmeal and seasonings together. Rub the skin with the mixture and truss if desired (see box, page 40). Place on a rack in a small roasting pan or baking dish and roast for 45 minutes, or until the hens are golden-brown and the juices from the breast or thigh run clear when pierced.

CAYENNE

◆

*C*ayenne that has turned from a bright color to a dark red has probably gotten too old and will be bitter in flavor. Buy cayenne in small quantities and check for color change or a bitter aroma before using. It's always best to store herbs and spices away from heat and light. Cayenne, properly stored, should last about one year.

FISH

♦

INDIAN FISH IN SPICY MARINADE

SERVES 4 TO 6

♦

*T*his marinade would be just as good with chicken or lamb. Despite the presence of chilies, the flavor here is really more aromatic than hot.

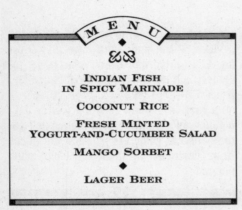

MENU

**INDIAN FISH
IN SPICY MARINADE**

COCONUT RICE

**FRESH MINTED
YOGURT-AND-CUCUMBER SALAD**

MANGO SORBET

♦

LAGER BEER

1 pound fresh swordfish, red snapper, redfish, or halibut

SPICY MARINADE
2 tablespoons virgin olive oil
5 tablespoons fresh lemon juice
3 garlic cloves, mashed to a paste (see box, page 62)
½ small yellow onion, chopped
1½ tablespoons chopped fresh ginger
2 small jalapeño or serrano chilies, or ½ teaspoon cayenne

¾ teaspoon ground turmeric
½ teaspoon freshly ground black pepper

1 lemon, cut into thin wedges, for garnish
Fresh cilantro leaves, for garnish

Wipe the fish with a damp cloth and place it in a bowl or sealable plastic bag. Puree the marinade ingredients in a blender, pour over the fish, and marinate in the refrigerator for about 15 minutes or up to 2 hours. Remove the fish from the marinade and broil or grill, or bake in a preheated 400° oven, for about 10 minutes per inch of thickness. Serve garnished with lemon and cilantro.

VARIATION: Substitute 1½ pounds of large shrimp for the fin fish. Peel them, marinate, and cook as described above.

MAKE AHEAD: marinate fish in refrigerator up to 2 hours ahead

HALIBUT WITH SCALLIONS AND GINGER EN PAPILLOTE

SERVES 4

◆

*T*his dish satisfies both the gourmet and the dieter as it is very low in calories and fat but has a rich, complex flavor. Red snapper, redfish, monkfish, trout, lingcod, bluefish, cod, or pike also work well.

Four 15 × 15-inch sheets parchment paper
1 to 1¼ pounds halibut fillet, 1 inch thick, skinned, and cut into 4 equal portions
12 scallions with 3 inches of green left on, cut into fine 3-inch-long julienne
¼ cup peeled, finely grated fresh ginger
8 large fresh shiitake mushrooms, cut into quarters (or use 4 carrots, thinly sliced on the diagonal)
¼ cup soy sauce mixed with 2 tablespoons virgin olive oil
½ cup coarsely chopped fresh cilantro leaves

Preheat the oven to 425°. Fold each piece of parchment paper in half, open, and lightly oil or butter the center of one side. Place one piece of halibut on this side, then top with a quarter of the scallion, ginger, and mushrooms and sprinkle with 1 tablespoon mixed soy sauce and oil. Top with 2 tablespoons cilantro leaves. Fold the parchment over the halibut, crimping and folding the edges all the way around the fish, but leaving a 2-inch space between the folded edge and the fish. Be sure there are no cut edges exposed. Continue with the remaining three portions.

Arrange the *papillotes* on two baking sheets so they do not overlap, and bake for 7 to 9 minutes. When done, the parchment will be puffed out and lightly browned. Cut a large X with a pair of scissors in the top of the *papillote* and serve immediately.

MAKE AHEAD: Fill and seal *papillotes* up to 8 hours ahead; refrigerate

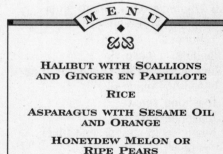

MENU

◆

HALIBUT WITH SCALLIONS AND GINGER EN PAPILLOTE

RICE

ASPARAGUS WITH SESAME OIL AND ORANGE

HONEYDEW MELON OR RIPE PEARS

◆

SAUVIGNON BLANC, CHENIN BLANC

REDFISH À LA NIÇOISE

SERVES 4

◆

*T*he cuisine of the French Riviera abounds in anchovy-flavored dishes. Anchovies add a distinctive richness and depth of flavor to any fish dish. Try the anchovy butter as a quick sauce over grilled fish or shellfish. If you are pressed for time, substitute a good-quality marinara sauce for the homemade tomato sauce.

MENU

◆

୫ଓ

REDFISH À LA NIÇOISE

ZUCCHINI, SCALLION AND
THREE-PEPPER
SAUTÉ

MESCLUN SALAD WITH
GOAT CHEESE CROUTONS

PROVENÇAL ORANGE CAKE

◆

ORVIETO, MÂCON BLANC

TOMATO SAUCE
Two 28-ounce cans Italian plum
   tomatoes, peeled, seeded, and
   chopped
2 shallots, minced
1 large garlic clove, mashed to a paste
   (see box, page 62)
½ teaspoon sugar
½ teaspoon kosher salt
½ teaspoon freshly ground black
   pepper
½ teaspoon dried basil
2 tablespoons extra-virgin olive oil

ANCHOVY BUTTER
2 anchovies, rinsed and patted dry, or
   ½ tablespoon anchovy paste

1 tablespoon unsalted butter
½ teaspoon grated lemon rind

½ tablespoon extra-virgin olive oil
1 pound redfish or red snapper fillets
½ cup all-purpose flour seasoned with
   ¼ teaspoon each kosher salt and
   freshly ground black pepper, and a
   pinch dried basil
Lemon wedges, for garnish

Place the tomatoes and all of the sauce seasonings in a 2½-quart saucepan. Cook over medium heat for about 10 minutes, until the liquid is reduced and the flavors concentrated.

While the tomato sauce is cooking, make the anchovy butter. In a mortar, pound the anchovies into a paste. Mash in the butter, add a few drops of lemon juice and the grated lemon rind, and combine thoroughly.

Heat the olive oil in a large sauté pan. Dredge the fish in the seasoned flour, shake off excess, and sauté over medium-high heat for 5 minutes per inch of thickness, until the fish is brown on both sides and milky-white all the way through. Spoon hot tomato sauce over the fish, dot with anchovy butter, and serve very hot.

MAKE AHEAD: prepare tomato sauce and anchovy butter up to 24 hours ahead; refrigerate

CURRIED SHRIMP WITH MANGO

SERVES 4 TO 6

◆

*T*he sauce is excellent with lobster, scallops, or sautéed fish fillets.

3 tablespoons light vegetable oil (olive, canola, or safflower)
1 large yellow onion, finely chopped
2 garlic cloves, mashed to a paste (see box, page 62)
1 red bell pepper, seeded and finely diced
1 tablespoon grated fresh ginger
1 tablespoon curry powder
2 tablespoons orange liqueur, or 2 tablespoons wine and 1 teaspoon grated orange rind
1⅓ cups chicken broth
⅔ cup light cream
1 to 2 tablespoons fresh lime juice
Kosher salt
Freshly ground black pepper
1 tablespoon olive oil
1 pound medium shrimp, peeled, tails left on
1 fresh mango, finely diced, or 1¼ cups canned mango slices, rinsed
Fresh lime juice

2 tablespoons fresh cilantro leaves, left whole
Pinch sugar

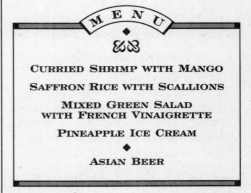

MENU

❧❧

CURRIED SHRIMP WITH MANGO

SAFFRON RICE WITH SCALLIONS

MIXED GREEN SALAD WITH FRENCH VINAIGRETTE

PINEAPPLE ICE CREAM

◆

ASIAN BEER

Heat the 3 tablespoons oil in a large skillet and add the onion, garlic, pepper, and ginger. Cook over medium-high heat until the vegetables are soft, about 5 minutes. Add the curry powder and cook for

2 to 3 minutes. Add the orange liqueur, broth, and cream and simmer for about 8 minutes, or until reduced by half. Season with the lime juice and add salt and pepper to taste if needed.

Heat the 1 tablespoon oil in a second skillet and quickly sear the shrimp until they curl, about 3 minutes. Add them to the sauce. Combine the mango, lime juice, sugar, and cilantro and sprinkle over the top of the dish.

MAKE AHEAD: prepare sauce up to 24 hours ahead; refrigerate; reheat gently

SALMON FILLETS
WITH TOASTED HAZELNUTS AND DILL
SERVES 4

◆

*T*oasted hazelnuts add a rich and subtle flavor in this simple, quick entrée. Redfish, red snapper, halibut, amberjack, or trout fillets can also be used. Substitute pecans if you don't have time to toast the hazelnuts.

COOKING FISH RARE
◆

Salmon, tuna, and swordfish are so much better when left a little rare in the middle. When cooked through completely, the flesh loses its delicacy and becomes dry. Test the fish as it is cooking, using the tip of a sharp knife to check the center of the fillet or steak for doneness. Be sure to leave a thin line of translucence in the middle. For a 1-inch-thick fillet or steak, for instance, leave a ⅛-inch center line that is slightly rare.

½ cup hazelnuts, toasted, skinned, and chopped (see box, page 120)
½ cup Crème Fraîche (page 210)
1 large egg yolk
Juice of ½ lemon
½ teaspoon kosher salt
¼ teaspoon freshly ground black pepper
¼ cup chopped fresh dill, or if unavailable, Italian parsley
1 pound fresh salmon fillet, skinned and cut into 4 equal portions

Toast the nuts, then turn the oven up to 400°. Combine the *crème fraîche*, egg yolk, lemon, salt, pepper, and dill and set aside. Place the salmon pieces in a buttered baking dish, spoon 2 tablespoons of sauce on each piece of salmon, and sprinkle with the hazelnuts. Bake for 8 to 10 minutes, leaving the salmon a little undercooked in the middle (see box, opposite page).

VARIATION: For a fancier presentation, bake the salmon *en papillote* or in phyllo. Seal each portion, with sauce on top, in parchment paper (see directions, page 57) or wrap in several leaves of phyllo, each brushed with melted butter, and bake for 8 to 10 minutes, or until the phyllo is golden. The *papillotes* can be prepared up to 8 hours ahead, but the phyllo-wrapped fish cannot be done ahead, as the phyllo gets soggy.

MAKE AHEAD: up to 8 hours (unless wrapped in phyllo); refrigerate

MENU

❧

SALMON FILLETS WITH TOASTED HAZELNUTS AND DILL

WILD AND WHITE RICE WITH LEEKS AND MUSHROOMS

PROVENÇAL SPINACH SALAD

WARM BLUEBERRY CRISP

◆

GRAVES, CHARDONNAY, SAUVIGNON BLANC

TUNA AU POIVRE

SERVES 2

◆

*F*or pepper lovers, here is a snappy, quick way to enjoy a nice thick fish steak or fillet. This recipe calls for tuna, but the pepper complements any fatty fish, such as salmon, swordfish, amberjack, or mahi mahi, very well indeed. For a discussion of peppercorns, see box, page 77.

½ tablespoon black peppercorns
½ tablespoon white peppercorns
½ tablespoon freeze-dried green peppercorns
½ tablespoon freeze-dried pink peppercorns (optional)
10 to 12 ounces fresh tuna steak, cut

into 2 portions, each 1 inch thick
½ tablespoon virgin olive oil
Pinch kosher salt

Crush all the peppercorns together in a mortar with a pestle. Rub the tuna with

MENU

TUNA AU POIVRE

FETTUCCINE WITH LEMON
AND VODKA SAUCE

SIMPLE FRENCH
MUSHROOM SALAD

FRESH STRAWBERRIES

◆

CHILLED BEAUJOLAIS

the oil on both sides and press the crushed peppercorns into both sides. Grill, broil 4 to 5 inches from the flame, or sauté the tuna in olive oil over medium-high heat for about 3 to 4 minutes on each side, leaving the center just a little rare (see box, page 60).

VARIATION: Before cooking, sprinkle the tuna with ½ tablespoon ginger juice, squeezed from 2 to 3 tablespoons freshly grated ginger (see box, page 154).

BUYING, STORING, AND USING GARLIC

◆

*B*e *sure to buy heads of garlic that are very firm to the touch, with tightly clustered cloves. Avoid garlic that is soft or discolored. Store in a cool, airy place, but don't refrigerate.*

To remove garlic skin, crush a whole clove with a pestle in a mortar (or with a sharp blow with the flat side of a chef's knife), then peel. This allows you to remove the skin quickly, usually in one piece. Always remove the indigestible and slightly bitter green sprout from the center of older garlic cloves.

Rather than chopping garlic, the best way to prepare it is to pound the cloves to a paste in a big wooden mortar with a wooden pestle that has a flat-

tened end. Or use the tip of a chef's knife or the tines of a fork to mash it, and add a little salt to absorb the garlic juices. The mashed garlic will disintegrate in cooking, but chopped garlic can often be perceived as a distinct little nodule on your tongue, which can give a sudden unpleasant sharp flavor. Mashed garlic also gives more flavor than chopped garlic because the crushing releases more of the oils.

For subtle garlic flavor, blanch whole garlic cloves in boiling water for 10 minutes, then chop or puree to use. To make garlic juice, use only a stainless-steel garlic press, as aluminum presses give garlic an odd flavor.

SUMMER SAUTÉ
OF CRAB, FRESH CORN, RED PEPPER, AND SCALLIONS

SERVES 6

◆

*T*his delightful, easy dish is extremely versatile. Serve it as a dinner entrée, or for lunch or brunch. It is wonderful with Cornmeal Madeleines (page 221). Peeled crawfish can be used instead of crabmeat.

2 tablespoons unsalted butter
1 bunch scallions, white and green, all finely chopped
2 shallots, finely chopped
1 large red bell pepper, seeded and diced
Kernels cut from 3 large ears sweet corn, or 16 ounces frozen corn
12 ounces fresh lump crabmeat
½ cup heavy cream or Crème Fraîche (page 210)
½ teaspoon kosher salt
¼ teaspoon cayenne
½ teaspoon freshly ground black pepper
½ tablespoon chopped fresh thyme
1 tablespoon chopped fresh parsley or basil, for garnish

Melt the butter in a large skillet. Add the scallion and shallot and cook gently until soft, about 3 minutes. Add the red pepper and corn; cook for 5 minutes. Add the crab and cook for 2 minutes to heat through, then add the cream and bring to a simmer over medium heat. Add all of the remaining ingredients except the parsley and cook for 2 to 3 more minutes, until the sauce thickens slightly and the flavors are blended. Do not overcook. Garnish with parsley and serve hot.

MAKE AHEAD: prepare up to 1 hour ahead; refrigerate; reheat quickly until hot and serve immediately

M E N U
◆
❧❧

SUMMER SAUTÉ OF CRAB, FRESH CORN, RED PEPPER, AND SCALLIONS

ANGEL HAIR PASTA PANCAKES

CHUNKY GAZPACHO SALAD

THE BEST AND EASIEST FRENCH CHOCOLATE CAKE

◆

CHARDONNAY

SCALLOPS PROVENÇAL
SERVES 4

◆

*T*his wonderfully garlicky sauce is an ode to Provence. Try it over ravioli, fettuccine, or other pasta, or just dip chunks of crusty French bread in it. Shrimp, squid, monkfish, or lobster can be used instead of scallops.

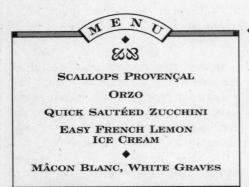

MENU

❧❧

SCALLOPS PROVENÇAL

ORZO

QUICK SAUTÉED ZUCCHINI

EASY FRENCH LEMON ICE CREAM

◆

MÂCON BLANC, WHITE GRAVES

¼ cup extra-virgin olive oil
3 large garlic cloves, mashed to a
    paste
2 large shallots, minced
3 large tomatoes, skinned, seeded, and
    finely chopped
½ tablespoon tomato paste
2 teaspoons fresh lemon juice
½ teaspoon kosher salt
¼ teaspoon freshly ground black
    pepper
½ teaspoon dried thyme, or
    2 teaspoons fresh thyme
Pinch crushed rosemary or 1 sprig
    fresh rosemary

1 to 2 teaspoons olive oil
¾ pound bay or sea scallops, cleaned of sand but not rinsed, quartered if large (see box, page 68)
⅓ cup finely chopped fresh parsley
¼ cup very thin strips fresh basil

Heat the ¼ cup of olive oil in a large skillet. Gently cook the garlic and shallot until soft but not browned, about 5 minutes. Add the tomato, tomato paste, lemon juice, salt and pepper, and spices. Stir, and cook over high heat until the mixture is thickened and well blended, about 5 minutes.

Heat another skillet until very hot. Add the 1 to 2 teaspoons olive oil and heat until almost smoking. Add the scallops and sear on both sides about 1 minute a side, or until slightly browned. Add the seared scallops to the hot tomato mixture. Taste for seasoning, stir in the parsley and basil, and serve immediately.

SCALLOP SAUTÉ
WITH WINTER VEGETABLES

SERVES 2 TO 4

◆

*T*his is a wildly colorful dish that is rich in texture as well as flavor. An elegant stir-fry dish, it is perfect to prepare with friends keeping you company in the kitchen. You can use a food processor to chop, slice, and shred the vegetables if you like, but remember, all the ingredients in stir-fry dishes must be very thinly and uniformly sliced to cook evenly in less than a minute. Small peeled shrimp, cooked lobster slices, or monkfish may be substituted for the scallops.

4 tablespoons sunflower, safflower, or peanut oil

One 1-inch knob unpeeled fresh ginger, thinly sliced

4 garlic cloves, mashed to a paste (see box, page 62)

1 small red bell pepper, seeded and sliced very thinly, each slice cut into 3-inch pieces

White part of 1 leek, well washed (see box, page 136) and very thinly sliced

2 small carrots, finely grated

¼ head red cabbage or 1 head radicchio, very thinly sliced or shredded

2 heads Belgian endive or ½ head curly endive (white part only), very thinly sliced, or 1 bunch watercress, chopped

One 2-inch knob fresh ginger, peeled and finely chopped

1 tablespoon dark Oriental sesame oil (see box)

½ pound scallops, cleaned of sand but not rinsed (see box, page 68), each scallop cut into 4 to 6 thin slices

---

ORIENTAL SESAME OIL

◆

*P*lease note that Oriental sesame oil, a dark red oil made only from toasted *sesame seeds, is never used for cooking because of its low smoking point, but for flavoring dishes. Its inimitable flavor enhances cooked seafood, vegetables, and salad dressings. Available in Asian markets, it must be stored in the refrigerator.*

Unroasted sesame seeds are also pressed to yield a mild, clear, golden oil, available in health-food stores, which can be used for cooking or salads but is not interchangeable with the darker oil.

Recipes occasionally call for a chili-sesame oil, which is the dark red sesame oil with hot red chili peppers added to it. If your palate can tolerate a lot of heat, try this oil.

Heat a dry wok, heavy skillet, or sauté pan for 1 to 2 minutes, then add 1 tablespoon of the oil. Heat over a high flame until hot but not smoking, about 1 to 2 minutes. Place the sliced ginger and half of the garlic in the hot oil, stir, and remove after 1 minute. (This step flavors the oil.) With a fine mesh skimmer, discard the ginger and garlic.

Add another tablespoon of the oil; heat. Stir in half of all the vegetables, mixed together, stir-fry for 30 seconds to 1 minute, and remove. Reheat the oil and stir-fry the remaining vegetables. Remove and hold.

Add the chopped ginger and the remaining garlic and cook for 1 minute. Add the sesame oil and the scallops and stir-fry for about 1 minute. Add the vegetables; toss to reheat and mix the in-

gredients evenly. Taste for seasoning, adding salt and pepper to taste. Serve immediately.

MAKE AHEAD: chop, slice, and shred all the vegetables and refrigerate in plastic bags up to 24 hours ahead

MENU

MINTY PEA SOUP

SCALLOP SAUTÉ
WITH WINTER VEGETABLES

GOAT CHEESE,
GRAPES, AND WALNUTS

VOUVRAY

CHINESE STIR-FRIED SCALLOPS WITH SESAME SEEDS AND ASPARAGUS

SERVES 4

◆

I find that stir-frying, besides being quick, enhances the flavors of certain foods: Asparagus, for example, retains much more flavor when it is not cooked in water, and this is the perfect way to cook scallops.

2 tablespoons canola, grapeseed, sunflower, or safflower oil
1 bunch asparagus, ends trimmed, cut in 1½-inch pieces
1 garlic clove, mashed to a paste
3 tablespoons finely julienned fresh ginger

4 scallions with 3 inches of green left on, julienned
½ red bell pepper, seeded and very thinly sliced
1 pound fresh scallops, cleaned of sand but not rinsed (see box, page 68)

1 tablespoon dry sherry or dry white
   wine
1 tablespoon Oriental sesame oil
2 tablespoons sesame seeds, toasted
   (see box)
Kosher salt to taste
⅓ cup fresh cilantro leaves or fresh
   parsley, for garnish

Heat a dry wok over high heat for 1 minute. Carefully add the oil and heat until very hot. Add the asparagus, stir-fry for 2 minutes, and remove. Add the garlic, ginger, scallion, and red pepper and stir-fry for 30 to 40 seconds. Add more oil if needed. Add the scallops and stir-fry for about 1 minute. Add the sherry and

sesame oil and the toasted sesame seeds. Taste for seasoning, adding salt to blend the flavors. Garnish with cilantro and serve immediately.

MENU

CHINESE STIR-FRIED SCALLOPS WITH SESAME SEEDS AND ASPARAGUS

RICE

EXOTIC FRUIT SALAD

◆

CHINESE BEER

TOASTING SEEDS

◆

Sesame seeds, mustard seeds, and cumin seeds need a little heat to release their oils and bring out their flavors. Grocery stores specializing in Mediterranean foods often sell a wonderful small metal sauté pan with a movable screen/cover for toasting seeds, but any small skillet with a lid will do. Place the seeds in a dry skillet with the lid nearby, and heat over medium-low heat. When most of the seeds start to pop and are golden-brown, they are ready. Immediately put the lid on to keep the seeds from jumping out of the pan, and remove from the heat. Toasting seeds takes only a minute or two. Don't walk away from the pan, as the seeds burn quickly!

SEARED SCALLOPS WITH WALNUT PERSILLADE

SERVES 4 TO 6

◆

A persillade is nothing more than a mixture of parsley and minced garlic added to a dish at the last minute to give a little boost of fresh flavor. With the addition of walnuts and butter it becomes a quick sauce. Try it on salmon, red-fish, bluefish, grouper, tuna, or mahi mahi. It's also very good on pasta.

WALNUT PERSILLADE
4 garlic cloves, mashed to a paste (see box, page 62)
⅔ cup coarsely chopped walnuts
⅓ cup minced fresh parsley
4 tablespoons (½ stick) unsalted butter
Kosher salt
Freshly ground black pepper

½ tablespoon extra-virgin olive oil
1 pound fresh sea scallops, cleaned of sand but not rinsed (see box)

MENU

SEARED SCALLOPS
WITH WALNUT PERSILLADE

COUSCOUS WITH CARROTS
AND MINT

GRILLED SCALLIONS
IN BASIL OIL

FRESH NECTARINES
AND BLUEBERRIES

♦

PINOT GRIGIO, CHARDONNAY,
CHENIN BLANC

Combine the *persillade* ingredients in a food processor and process 1 minute.

HOW TO CLEAN SCALLOPS

♦

Pull off the firm muscular hinge that is attached to one side of large sea scallops and discard. Rinsing scallops under cold water to wash off sand or grit doesn't always work. The sand can lodge more deeply in the crevices, and the scallops always lose some of their delicate flavor because the juices are rinsed away.

To remove small specks of sand, look the scallops over carefully in good light, and use the tip of a small knife to flick out offending particles. You may also wipe them with a cold damp paper towel if you wish. Pat dry before sautéing.

Heat a nonstick skillet until very hot. Add the oil and sear the scallops quickly, 1 minute or less on each side, or until lightly browned. Add the sauce to the scallops in the hot skillet, mix well, and serve immediately.

MAKE AHEAD: prepare the *persillade* up to 24 hours ahead; refrigerate

MEAT

◆

LAMB CHOPS WITH
MINT PESTO

SERVES 2

◆

*M*int has a pungency similar to that of basil and makes a great variation on the traditional basil pesto. Use the pesto on grilled chicken breasts or fish fillets such as salmon, trout, redfish, or amberjack, or toss it with hot pasta.

MINT PESTO
1 packed cup fresh mint leaves
¼ cup fresh Italian parsley
4 fresh basil leaves
1 clove garlic
¼ cup pine nuts
½ cup virgin olive oil
⅓ cup freshly grated Italian Parmesan
¼ teaspoon kosher salt
⅛ teaspoon freshly ground black
     pepper

2 teaspoons virgin olive oil
Four 4-ounce lamb chops, 1 inch thick,
     trimmed of fat
Kosher salt
Freshly ground black pepper

Prepare the mint pesto by blending all the ingredients until smooth in a blender or food processor. Heat the olive oil in a 9- or 10-inch skillet. Sauté the lamb chops over medium-high heat for 3 to 4 minutes on each side. (They should still be pink inside.) Season with salt and pepper and serve immediately, topped with pesto.

MAKE AHEAD: make the pesto up to 4 hours ahead; refrigerate; bring to room temperature before using

MENU

🙰🙰

LAMB CHOPS WITH MINT PESTO

**FETTUCCINE WITH LEMON AND
VODKA SAUCE**

CLASSIC GREEK SALAD

RED BERRY GRATIN

◆

RIOJA, MERLOT

CALF'S LIVER WITH SHALLOTS, GRAPES, AND BALSAMIC VINEGAR

SERVES 2

◆

*E*ven as a child, I always loved calf's liver. This subtle combination of ingredients will surprise you with its fabulous flavor. And it makes a very quick dinner for friends who share this taste.

MENU

◆

ZUPPA PRIMAVERA

CALF'S LIVER WITH SHALLOTS, GRAPES, AND BALSAMIC VINEGAR

GREEN SALAD WITH MUSTARD-CAPER VINAIGRETTE

WARM CARAMEL PEARS

◆

SAUVIGNON BLANC, CHENIN BLANC, JULIENAS

½ tablespoon light vegetable oil (canola or grapeseed)

6 large shallots, chopped
⅓ pound calf's liver (see box), sliced thin
Kosher salt
Freshly ground black pepper
½ tablespoon balsamic vinegar
⅓ cup seedless red grapes, cut in half

    Heat the oil in a 9-inch skillet. Add the shallot, and cook until soft over medium-high heat. Add the liver, sprinkle lightly with salt and pepper, and cook for 3 minutes on each side. Add the vinegar and grapes and cook for 2 minutes.

TO PREPARE CALF'S LIVER OR CHICKEN LIVERS FOR COOKING

◆

*T*o be sure liver is very fresh, buy it from a good butcher. It should smell fresh and not too strong. At home, rinse the liver in cold water. Then cover it with milk or buttermilk, cover, and refrigerate overnight if possible. Soaking it for even 15 minutes to 1 hour is helpful—it softens the strong liver flavor that some people find objectionable.

NOISETTES OF LAMB WITH ROSEMARY AND THYME

SERVES 2

◆

*T*his is what I prepare when I have a craving for lamb but don't have time to roast a whole leg. Increase the number of chops if they are very small. I serve this often for small dinner parties.

MENU

◆

**NOISETTES OF LAMB
WITH ROSEMARY AND THYME**

**LEMON-GARLIC POTATOES
WITH SPINACH**

**LEEK SALAD IN MUSTARD-
CAPER VINAIGRETTE**

CRÈME AUX FRAISES

◆

HAUT-MÉDOC OR VOLNAY

MARINADE
2 tablespoons virgin olive oil
1 garlic clove, mashed to a paste
   (see box, page 62)
½ teaspoon finely crushed or rubbed
   fresh or dried rosemary (see box)
½ teaspoon dried thyme
¼ teaspoon kosher salt
¼ teaspoon freshly ground black
   pepper
½ tablespoon fresh lemon juice

Four 1-inch-thick lamb loin chops,
   boned and tied (ask your butcher
   to do this)
½ tablespoon virgin olive oil

6 large or 12 small fresh mushrooms,
   washed and sliced, with stems
   left on
1 shallot, minced
Kosher salt to taste
Freshly ground black pepper to taste
1 tablespoon finely chopped fresh
   thyme (if unavailable, use chopped
   fresh parsley)
2 teaspoons virgin olive oil
Sprigs of fresh thyme or Italian
   parsley, for garnish

Combine all of the marinade ingredients thoroughly. Place the lamb in the marinade so that it is completely covered,

ROSEMARY

◆

*D*ried rosemary is hard to eat even after cooking because its leaves have the texture of pine needles. So crush or pulverize dried rosemary with a mortar and pestle before adding it to a dish. Fresh rosemary is softer, but it does need to be finely chopped before using.

and marinate at room temperature for about 15 minutes. Meanwhile, heat the ½ tablespoon olive oil in a small skillet. Add the mushrooms and shallot, and cook for 2 to 3 minutes over medium-high heat. Season with salt and pepper, add the thyme, and stir. Cover and keep warm.

Remove the lamb from the marinade and pat dry with paper towels. Heat the 2 teaspoons olive oil in a sauté pan and

sauté the lamb quickly over high heat 3 to 4 minutes on each side. (The lamb should be lightly browned on the outside and pink on the inside.) Arrange the lamb chops on a heated platter and spoon mushrooms and shallot on top of each one. Garnish with fresh thyme and serve immediately.

MAKE AHEAD: marinate lamb up to 8 hours ahead; refrigerate

VEAL CHOPS WITH MUSHROOM-TARRAGON CREAM
SERVES 2
◆

*E*legant, simple, and quick, this is a perfect entrée for a small dinner party.

MENU

VEAL CHOPS WITH MUSHROOM-TARRAGON CREAM

ANGEL HAIR PASTA PANCAKES

BROILED TOMATOES WITH BASIL OIL

FRESH STRAWBERRIES AND RASPBERRIES

◆

CHARDONNAY

¼ pound large fresh button, shiitake, or oyster mushrooms
½ cup dry white wine
½ cup homemade veal or chicken stock (if unavailable, use canned chicken broth)
⅓ cup heavy cream or Crème Fraîche (page 210)
Kosher salt
Freshly ground black pepper
1 tablespoon chopped fresh tarragon (if unavailable, use fresh parsley or ½ tablespoon fresh thyme)

1 tablespoon unsalted butter
2 pounds veal loin chops

Melt the butter in a heavy-bottomed skillet or sauté pan. Add the veal chops and brown lightly over medium-high heat, 5 minutes on each side. Add the mushrooms and stir until they take on color. Add the wine and stock and simmer, uncovered, for 20 to 25 minutes, or until the veal is tender. Remove the chops to a warm serving plate, and cover.

Reduce the sauce over high heat until only ¼ cup remains. Stir in the cream and cook over medium-high heat until the sauce has the consistency of heavy cream. Season to taste with salt and pepper, add the tarragon, pour the sauce over the chops, and serve immediately.

VEAL SCALLOPS WITH OREGANO AND FONTINA

SERVES 4

◆

$\mathcal{V}$eal scallops make one of the quickest entrées, and the superb flavor of Italian fontina adds a memorable savory touch.

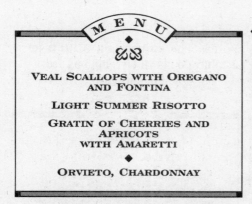

MENU

&&

VEAL SCALLOPS WITH OREGANO AND FONTINA

LIGHT SUMMER RISOTTO

GRATIN OF CHERRIES AND APRICOTS WITH AMARETTI

◆

ORVIETO, CHARDONNAY

Eight 2-ounce veal scallops, pounded thin
⅓ cup all-purpose flour mixed with ¼ teaspoon kosher salt,

¼ teaspoon freshly ground black pepper, and ½ teaspoon dried oregano
3 tablespoons unsalted butter
¼ teaspoon dried oregano, or 1 teaspoon chopped fresh oregano
About ¼ pound Italian fontina, sliced very thin
⅓ cup dry white wine
1 lemon, cut in wedges, for garnish
Sprigs of fresh oregano, for garnish

Dredge the veal in the seasoned flour. Heat the butter in a large skillet, add the ¼ teaspoon oregano, and sauté the veal over medium-high heat for about

2 minutes on each side. Place the fontina slices on top of the veal, add the wine, and bring to a boil. Lower the heat and cook about 3 minutes more. Taste for seasoning. Serve on a hot platter, garnished with lemon and fresh oregano.

VARIATIONS: Mix grated Parmesan and grated Emmentaler and press lightly onto the veal instead of the fontina.

Use a thin slice of prosciutto on each scallop in addition to the cheese.

STEAK AU POIVRE
SERVES 2

◆

*T*his is one of my favorite beef dishes when I am in a "meat and potatoes" state of mind. This recipe can easily be doubled and prepared in two skillets. No advance preparation is necessary, but it does require an advance warning: Peppercorns in this quantity often cause a strange reaction—expect tiny beads of sweat to form just above your upper lip. Since spices and chilies are used sparingly in French cooking, this is one of the few classic French dishes that can be called hot.

2 tablespoons black peppercorns, or a mix of black, white, and freeze-dried green peppercorns (see box, page 77)

2 tablespoons virgin olive oil

Two 1-inch-thick New York strip steaks (6 to 8 ounces each), trimmed of fat, at close to room temperature

1½ tablespoons brandy

¼ cup minced shallot

⅓ cup dry white wine

½ cup heavy or light cream or Crème Fraîche (page 210)

1½ teaspoons Dijon mustard

½ teaspoon dried tarragon, or
    1 teaspoon chopped fresh tarragon

¼ teaspoon kosher salt, or to taste

2 tablespoons finely chopped fresh parsley, for garnish

MENU

STEAK AU POIVRE

QUICK POTATO GRATIN

GREEN SALAD
WITH RED-WINE VINAIGRETTE

STRAWBERRY SORBET
WITH CASSIS

◆

CABERNET SAUVIGNON

Crack or crush the peppercorns in a sealable plastic bag with a rolling pin, or in a mortar with a pestle, but do not grind finely. Press them into both sides of the trimmed steaks. Heat the oil in a heavy sauté pan and sauté the steaks over medium-high heat 3 to 4 minutes per side for medium-rare, 7 to 10 for well done. Push the steaks to one side of the pan, add the brandy, and flame. Remove the steaks to a hot platter and cover with foil.

Add the shallot to the sauté pan and cook over low heat until soft, 1 to 2 minutes. Add the wine, turn up the heat, and bring to a boil. Add the cream and simmer, scraping up the pan juices, for 2 to 3 minutes, or until the sauce has thickened. Stir in the mustard, tarragon, and salt. Pour the sauce over the steaks, sprinkle them with parsley, and serve immediately.

VENISON STROGANOFF

SERVES 6 TO 8

◆

*V*enison tenderloin is perfectly suited to Stroganoff, a classic usually made with beef tenderloin. Hunters and hunters' wives will welcome this elegant entrée. Venison is significantly lower in fat than beef and is available in specialty meat markets year-round, but if you can't find it, use beef tenderloin instead. Serve the Stroganoff over wide noodles, fettuccine, or spätzle.

2 tablespoons virgin olive oil
2 tablespoons unsalted butter
1½ pounds venison tenderloin, trimmed, sliced ¼ inch thick
¼ cup flour mixed with ½ teaspoon kosher salt, ¼ teaspoon freshly ground black pepper, and ½ teaspoon hot or sweet Hungarian paprika
½ pound small fresh mushrooms, quartered
1 tablespoon unsalted butter
1 large yellow onion, finely chopped

2 shallots, finely chopped
1 teaspoon hot or sweet Hungarian paprika
2 teaspoons chopped fresh thyme, or ½ teaspoon dried thyme
1 cup chicken broth or thin beef broth
1 cup light sour cream
½ teaspoon kosher salt
¼ teaspoon freshly ground black pepper
¼ cup minced fresh parsley, for garnish

Heat the oil and butter in a large skillet. Lightly dust the venison slices with the seasoned flour. Sauté the meat quickly for 30 seconds on each side; remove and hold. (Venison, like tenderloin, becomes tough if cooked too long.)

Add the mushrooms to the skillet and cook over high heat for about 3 minutes to brown lightly, then remove. Add the butter, onion, shallot, and paprika and cook over medium heat until soft, 6 to 7 minutes. Add the thyme and broth and simmer until only ½ cup sauce remains. Just before serving, stir in the sour cream and season with salt and pepper. Cook over low heat until very hot but not boiling, then add the venison and reheat gently. Garnish with parsley and serve.

MAKE AHEAD: make sauce up to 24 hours ahead; refrigerate; sauté meat and deglaze pan with a little broth just before serving; add the deglazed pan juices to the sauce along with the sour cream and reheat gently until hot; then add meat

MENU

VENISON STROGANOFF

FETTUCCINE

SIMPLE FRENCH
MUSHROOM SALAD

WARM CARAMEL PEARS

HAUT-MÉDOC, BAROLO

MAKING A SIMPLE PAN SAUCE FOR MEAT, CHICKEN, OR FISH

An easy way to "jazz up" simply cooked meat, chicken, or fish is to make a pan sauce. In the skillet in which the meat, chicken, or fish has been browned or sautéed (leaving dark crispy bits stuck to the pan), add ½ cup broth, white wine, or water to deglaze, or loosen and dissolve, the bits of meat from the pan. If you are cooking fish, add ½ tablespoon of white vinegar or champagne vinegar. Stir constantly over high heat until the dissolved bits flavor and darken the liquid. At this point you can add a few tablespoons of minced shallot and cook until soft, or omit the shallot and add ⅓ to ½ cup heavy cream. Continue to cook over high heat a few minutes more to reduce the volume and concentrate the flavors. Add salt, pepper, and minced fresh parsley, tarragon, basil, or other herbs to season the sauce.

HAM STEAKS IN CIDER SAUCE

SERVES 4

◆

*T*he cooking of Normandy inspired this hearty entrée. It is delicious served with Quick Potato Gratin (page 166) for dinner or with Sautéed Corn Cakes (page 156) for brunch. The Cider Sauce also complements redfish, red snapper, and halibut.

2 tablespoons unsalted butter
Four ½-inch slices ham steak

CIDER SAUCE
1 teaspoon cider vinegar
2 to 3 shallots, minced
1 cup alcoholic French or Spanish
　　cider
½ cup heavy cream
Freshly ground white or green pepper
　　to taste

2 tablespoons minced fresh parsley, for
　　garnish

＆Ↄ

HAM STEAKS IN CIDER SAUCE

QUICK POTATO GRATIN

**GREEN SALAD WITH WALNUT
OIL–MUSTARD VINAIGRETTE**

SAUTÉED APPLES

◆

**FRENCH ALCOHOLIC CIDER,
RIESLING, MUSCADET**

Heat the butter in a large skillet or sauté pan. Add the ham, two slices at a time, and lightly brown over medium-high heat a few minutes on each side. Remove from the pan and cover tightly to keep warm. Add the vinegar, shallot, and cider to the pan and reduce by half over high heat (2 to 3 minutes). Add the cream and continue cooking on high until the sauce thickens, 4 to 5 minutes. Check the seasoning, adding freshly ground white or green pepper to taste. Arrange the ham slices on a warm platter, pour the sauce over them, and garnish with parsley.

VARIATION: Substitute slices of pork or veal tenderloin for the ham.

＆Ↄ

PEPPERCORNS

◆

*P*eppercorns are a staple in my kitchen. I have five or six pepper mills so I can have several different types and combinations readily available. Black peppercorns are dried before they ripen, which causes the skin to shrivel and turn black. Black pepper can be quite hot if used in sufficient quantity. White peppercorns are fully ripened, then picked and skinned before drying, which results in a lighter color and milder flavor. Green peppercorns are picked green, then freeze-dried to preserve the flavor. Their flavor is quite mild.

＆Ↄ

SAUSAGE COOKED THE FRENCH WAY

SERVES 2 TO 4

◆

*S*ausage takes on a more refined flavor when cooked this way.

3 cups light beef or chicken broth
1 cup dry white wine
½ teaspoon dried thyme
1 imported bay leaf
1 pound cooked or uncooked
    sausage (Italian, Cajun, German,
    or French)

Bring the broth and wine to a simmer in a 2½-quart saucepan or a 10-inch skillet; add the herbs. Prick the sausage once on each side and add to the broth. Cover and simmer for 20 minutes. Remove, drain, and serve. Or, after poaching, let the sausage brown lightly on each side in a skillet over medium-high heat before serving.

MENU

◆

SAUSAGE COOKED
THE FRENCH WAY

FRENCH MASHED POTATOES
WITH GARLIC AND CREAM

GREEN SALAD WITH MUSTARD-
SHALLOT VINAIGRETTE

APPLES, GRAPES, AND WALNUTS
AS SALAD OR DESSERT

◆

BELGIAN BEER, LAGER BEER,
MÂCON BLANC

◆

PASTA
AND
GRAINS

◆

Pastas and grains are among the healthiest foods we can eat. They are filling and delicious, as well as quick and easy to prepare. And they lend themselves readily to improvisation—an excellent pasta sauce or risotto can often be made from ingredients on hand. Fettuccine topped with out-of-the-cupboard garlic, anchovy, and olive oil sauce, or goat cheese, walnut, and parsley sauce has pleased many a drop-in guest. Other quick pasta-sauce combinations from the pantry or refrigerator include tomatoes, shallots, and basil; capers, parsley, black pepper, melted butter, and Parmesan; clams with garlic, oil, and parsley; green peas, prosciutto, cream, and Parmesan; and garlic, shallots, and dried and fresh mushrooms.

Risotto is a classic northern Italian seasoned rice dish

with a wonderful chewy texture. I adore risottos—they call out for *creativity*. Some of my favorite risotto additions (stirred in five minutes before the dish is done) are green peas, prosciutto, and cream; sautéed cultivated or wild mushrooms such as chanterelles, porcini, or morels with lots of fresh herbs (chives, parsley, thyme); cooked julienned carrots, broccoli florets, and strips of leftover pork roast, chicken, or lamb. Create your own risottos with your favorite ingredients. Although many American cookbooks call dishes made with ordinary long-grain rice *risottos,* classic northern Italian risottos are made with arborio rice, a starchy short-grain rice grown in northern Italy that absorbs more liquid, is meatier, chewier, and more filling than any other rice. It is available in many large supermarkets and in most gourmet stores. A whole meal can be made of a risotto, although in Italy it is most often served as a separate first course.

A number of the pasta dishes in this chapter are whole-meal dishes too. These are especially welcome for entertaining. Try the Angel Hair Pasta Salad with Basil, Tomatoes, and Sliced Grilled Steak in summer; and the Spaghetti with Italian Sausage, Sun-Dried Tomatoes, and Oregano in winter.

Pasta and rice are probably most commonly used as starchy side dishes to accompany meat, chicken, or fish entrées. Simple buttered rice or noodles make a perfect bed for an entrée cooked with a sauce or for cooked vegetables. For more interesting accompaniments for simply cooked entrées, try Pasta con Aglio e Olio, Spinach Fettuccine with Tomato-Mint Sauce, Saffron Rice with Scallions, or Coconut Rice. Other less commonly used grains or grain products such as couscous and hominy make unusual, flavorful, and nutritious side dishes with great texture.

PASTAS

GRAINS

ABOUT RISOTTO

The texture of a true northern Italian risotto is at once creamy and chewy; no other rice but Italian arborio achieves this texture. (If you can't find arborio you can make a risotto recipe with long-grain rice and it will taste good, but it will have a totally different texture and thus will not be a true risotto.) Classic Italian risottos are made with a distinctive technique: the liquid (usually homemade broth and some wine) is added a little bit at a time instead of all at once, and stirred constantly, which allows the rice to cook gently and absorb a lot of liquid so that when done, the rice grain is tender on the outside and still a little firm in the center. This technique requires a bit of time and energy on your part—most risottos take 20 to 25 minutes to cook—but the results are definitely worth it. Extra broth or sometimes cream is added just before serving to lighten and loosen the risotto.

PASTA

◆

PASTA CON AGLIO E OLIO
(PASTA WITH OLIVE OIL AND GARLIC)

SERVES 4 AS A MAIN COURSE, 6 TO 8 AS A SIDE DISH

◆

*G*arlic and extra-virgin olive oil make a perfect sauce for pasta. Add a little red pepper, black pepper, and herbs and enjoy a richly satisfying but light pasta dish.

4 quarts water
2 tablespoons kosher salt
1 pound bow-tie pasta, linguini,
    capellini, or fettuccine
4 tablespoons extra-virgin olive oil
3 large cloves fresh garlic, mashed to a
    paste (see box, page 62)
Pinch dried red-pepper flakes
Kosher salt
Freshly ground black pepper
⅓ cup minced fresh parsley

MENU

PASTA CON AGLIO E OLIO

**MIXED GREEN SALAD
WITH GOAT CHEESE
AND TOASTED PINE NUTS**

GRAPES AND COOKIES

◆

CHIANTI

Heat the water to boiling, add the salt, and cook the pasta at a rapid boil until *al dente,* 5 to 10 minutes. While the pasta cooks, heat the oil in a skillet and cook the garlic gently over low heat until it is pale golden. Add the red-pepper flakes and salt and pepper to taste, then toss with the hot pasta, mixing thoroughly. Add the parsley, toss again, and serve hot on warmed plates.

VARIATIONS: Add 4 to 6 rinsed, drained, mashed anchovies to the hot oil.

Add 2 tablespoons fresh chopped basil or 1 tablespoon fresh oregano to the parsley.

PENNE WITH OLIVES, TOMATOES, RED PEPPER, AND PARSLEY

SERVES 4 TO 6 AS A MAIN COURSE, 6 TO 8 AS A SIDE DISH

◆

*N*ot every pasta needs the addition of Parmesan cheese. Here the distinctive flavor of the olives and red pepper dominate. This sauce is excellent with any tubular or ridged pasta.

4 quarts water
2 tablespoons kosher salt
1 pound dry penne (quills) or medium rigatoni or radiatore

SAUCE
2 tablespoons extra-virgin olive oil
1 teaspoon dried red-pepper flakes
3 large garlic cloves, mashed to a paste (see box, page 62)
2 pounds fresh tomatoes or canned Italian plum tomatoes or Italian boxed tomato chunks, seeded and chopped
1 tablespoon imported concentrated Italian tomato paste (if unavailable, use canned tomato paste)
½ pound imported black olives, pitted
¼ teaspoon kosher salt, or to taste
½ teaspoon freshly ground black pepper, or to taste

¼ cup chopped fresh parsley, for garnish

Bring the water to a boil, add the salt, and cook the pasta at a rapid boil until *al dente*, about 10 to 12 minutes. Drain. While the pasta cooks, prepare the sauce. Heat the olive oil in a large skillet and gently cook the red-pepper flakes and garlic over low heat for 1 minute. Do not let the garlic brown. Add the tomato and tomato paste and cook over medium-high heat for 13 to 15 minutes, or until the mixture is slightly thickened. Add the olives, and salt and pepper to taste. Toss the hot drained pasta with the sauce in a warmed shallow pasta bowl, sprinkle with parsley, and serve immediately.

MAKE AHEAD: prepare sauce up to 24 hours ahead; refrigerate; reheat gently while cooking the pasta

MENU

&

PENNE WITH OLIVES, TOMATOES, RED PEPPER, AND PARSLEY

ITALIAN GREEN SALAD WITH BASIL-OIL DRESSING

RICOTTA AND RUM DESSERT

◆

ORVIETO, CHARDONNAY, MÂCON BLANC

FETTUCCINE WITH LEMON AND VODKA SAUCE

SERVES 4 AMPLY AS A MAIN COURSE, 6 AS A FIRST COURSE

◆

*T*his is a particularly delicious and subtle dish. Vodka heightens the flavor of anything acidic, which makes the sauce very lemony. This is one recipe in which there is no substitute for cream, but divided among six portions, the amount is modest.

4 quarts water
2 tablespoons kosher salt
1 pound fettuccine

LEMON AND VODKA SAUCE
2 large lemons, rind washed
1 cup heavy cream
¼ cup vodka

½ teaspoon freshly ground black pepper

¼ cup chopped fresh parsley, for garnish
¾ cup freshly grated Italian Parmesan, for serving

Bring the water to a boil, add the salt, and cook the pasta at a rapid boil until *al dente,* 8 to 10 minutes. Drain. While the pasta cooks, prepare the sauce. Finely grate the rind of 1 lemon, then squeeze the juice of this lemon and reserve. Combine the cream and vodka in a 10-inch skillet and simmer for 5 minutes, or until the sauce thickens a little. Add the lemon juice and rind to the hot sauce and cook for 1 minute, stirring. Add the drained hot pasta to the sauce and toss. Season with pepper, garnish with parsley, and serve immediately on warmed plates. Serve the Parmesan separately.

VARIATION: To make a whole-meal dish, add cooked scallops and/or cooked asparagus, cut into 1-inch pieces, to the sauce, just before tossing with the pasta.

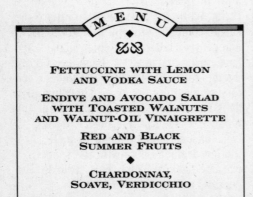

MENU

◆

❧

FETTUCCINE WITH LEMON AND VODKA SAUCE

ENDIVE AND AVOCADO SALAD WITH TOASTED WALNUTS AND WALNUT-OIL VINAIGRETTE

RED AND BLACK SUMMER FRUITS

◆

CHARDONNAY, SOAVE, VERDICCHIO

SPINACH FETTUCCINE WITH TOMATO-MINT SAUCE

SERVES 4 TO 6 AS A MAIN COURSE, 6 TO 8 AS A SIDE DISH

◆

*H*ere's a fabulous pasta dish with no fat. The combination of fresh mint and lemon adds a delightful new dimension to a tomato sauce. This is excellent as a main course or as an accompaniment to a fish or chicken entrée.

4 quarts water
2 tablespoons kosher salt
1 pound dry spinach fettuccine

TOMATO-MINT SAUCE
3 minced shallots or ½ minced red
   onion
1½ pounds fresh tomatoes or canned
   Italian plum tomatoes, peeled,
   seeded, and chopped
1 bunch fresh mint, leaves only, finely
   chopped
Pinch kosher salt
¾ teaspoon freshly ground black
   pepper

Grated rind of 1 lemon, for garnish

Bring the water to a boil, add the salt, and cook the pasta at a rapid boil until *al dente,* 4 to 7 minutes. Drain.

MINT

◆

*M*int's delicately pungent freshness adds a cooling distinction to a wide variety of foods. It not only stimulates the palate and the appetite but also tames spicy dishes and nervous stomachs as well. Called "yerba buena," the good herb, in Mexico, mint especially enhances the flavors of tomatoes, cucumbers, eggplant, lamb, peas, chicken soup, and Mediterranean salads of grains and vegetables. Look for spearmint with bright green leaves, the main culinary mint. Peppermint, with dark stem and darker leaves, is too strong for cooking.

While the pasta cooks, prepare the sauce. Put the shallot and tomato in a large skillet, bring to a simmer, and cook for 3 to 4 minutes. Stir in the mint, salt, and pepper. Toss the hot drained pasta with the sauce, place on a heated serving platter, garnish with the lemon rind, and serve hot.

MAKE AHEAD: prepare sauce up to 4 hours ahead; refrigerate; reheat gently while cooking the pasta

MENU

SPINACH FETTUCCINE
WITH TOMATO-MINT SAUCE

TOASTED GOAT CHEESE
IN GREEN VINAIGRETTE

PROVENÇAL ORANGE CAKE

◆

SAUVIGNON BLANC

Spinach Fettuccine
with Walnut-Gorgonzola Sauce

SERVES 4 AMPLY AS A MAIN COURSE, 6 AS A FIRST COURSE

◆

*H*ere's a deliciously rich pasta entrée. Serve small portions and accompany with a crisp salad and a light dessert.

4 quarts water
2 tablespoons kosher salt
1 pound dry spinach fettuccine or
    linguini

WALNUT-GORGONZOLA SAUCE
4 tablespoons (½ stick) unsalted
    butter
1 large garlic clove, mashed to a paste
    (see box, page 62)
1¼ cups chopped walnuts
½ pound torta di Gorgonzola cheese
    (layered Gorgonzola and
    mascarpone), or ¼ pound
    Gorgonzola and ¼ pound ricotta,

cream cheese, or Crème Fraîche
    (page 210), mixed together
½ teaspoon freshly ground black
    pepper

¾ cup freshly grated Italian Parmesan
¼ cup minced fresh parsley, for
    garnish

Bring the water to a boil, add the salt, and cook the pasta at a rapid boil until *al dente,* about 10 minutes. Drain.

While the pasta cooks, prepare the sauce. Melt the butter in a large skillet, add the garlic and walnuts, and cook, stirring, over medium-high heat for 3 to 4 minutes. Add the cheese and pepper to the sauce and toss to melt. Remove the pan from the heat. Toss the hot drained pasta with the walnut sauce and the Parmesan. Garnish with parsley and serve immediately on warmed plates.

MAKE AHEAD: prepare sauce up to 1 hour ahead; hold in pan; reheat gently while cooking the pasta

MENU

◆
೮೩

Spinach Fettuccine with
Walnut-Gorgonzola Sauce

Apple, Fennel,
and Watercress Salad

Pineapple-Mint Sorbet

◆

Beaujolais, Pinot Noir

SPAGHETTI WITH ITALIAN SAUSAGE, SUN-DRIED TOMATOES, AND OREGANO

SERVES 6 AMPLY AS A MAIN COURSE

◆

*H*ere's a terrific thirty-minute main-course pasta dish full of hearty Italian flavor.

4 quarts water
1½ tablespoons extra-virgin olive oil
1 pound fresh sweet or hot Italian
    fennel sausage
1 yellow onion, finely chopped
1 large garlic clove, mashed to a paste
    (see box, page 62)
1 cup dry white wine
½ cup dry-packed, sun-dried tomatoes,
    plumped in hot water (see box,
    page 95), drained, and chopped
1 tablespoon chopped fresh oregano,
    or 1½ teaspoons dried oregano
Kosher salt
Freshly ground black pepper
2 tablespoons kosher salt
1 pound dry spaghetti or tagliarini
¼ cup chopped fresh parsley
½ cup freshly grated Italian Parmesan,
    for serving

MENU

☙☙

**SPAGHETTI WITH ITALIAN
SAUSAGE, SUN-DRIED
TOMATOES, AND OREGANO**

GRILLED FENNEL

SLICED NECTARINES AND FIGS

◆

ORVIETO, CHARDONNAY

Put the water on to boil for the pasta. Heat the olive oil in a large skillet. With scissors or a knife, cut off the sausage casings and crumble the sausage into the oil. Cook, breaking up the sausage, until lightly browned, 4 to 5 minutes. Remove the sausage, leaving the oil and fat in the skillet. Add the onion and garlic, and gently cook until soft, 5 to 7 minutes. Add the wine, bring to a boil, and reduce by half over high heat. Then add the sun-dried tomatoes, cooked sausage, and oregano and simmer for 10 minutes, until the flavors are blended. Season with salt and pepper to taste.

While the sauce is cooking, add the 2 tablespoons of salt to the rapidly boiling water and cook the pasta until *al dente,* about 10 minutes. Toss the hot drained pasta with the sauce and parsley. Place in a hot serving bowl and serve immediately. Pass the Parmesan cheese.

MAKE AHEAD: prepare the sauce up to 24 hours ahead; refrigerate; reheat gently while cooking the pasta

SPAGHETTI ALLA BELLINI

SERVES 4 AS A MAIN COURSE, 6 AS A FIRST COURSE

◆

*T*his pasta, of Sicilian origin, is particularly delicious. The grilled eggplant, tomatoes, and basil combine beautifully with the spaghetti and Romano cheese.

MENU

◆

SPAGHETTI ALLA BELLINI

THE ORIGINAL CAESAR SALAD

COLD CHERRIES IN BRANDY

◆

ORVIETO, VERDICCHIO, SOAVE, CHARDONNAY, GRAVES

4 quarts water

2 tablespoons kosher salt

1 pound dry spaghetti, spaghettini, or linguine

4 cups canned Italian plum tomatoes pureed in a food processor

1 large eggplant, peeled, thinly sliced, ¼ to ½ inch thick

¼ cup olive oil or flavored oil (basil, garlic, or fennel oil—see box, page 150)

¼ cup fresh basil leaves, finely chopped

½ cup freshly grated Romano cheese

Preheat the broiler. Bring the water to a boil, add the salt, and cook the pasta at a rapid boil until *al dente*, about 10 minutes. Drain. While the pasta cooks, heat the tomato puree to a simmer and prepare the eggplant.

Generously brush a large baking sheet with oil. Place the eggplant slices on the sheet, brush them with the ¼ cup oil, and broil 4 inches under the flame on one side only until lightly browned and soft, about 5 minutes. Remove, chop the eggplant, and keep warm. Toss the hot drained pasta with 1 cup of the tomato puree and the eggplant and basil. Serve on heated plates with extra tomato puree and Romano cheese on the side.

MAKE AHEAD: prepare the eggplant and tomato puree up to 4 hours ahead; refrigerate; reheat the tomato puree while cooking the pasta

BASIL

◆

*B*asil turns an unattractive black when cut and exposed to air for too long. Shred or chop fresh basil leaves just before using to keep them from darkening. Or chop leaves and cover with olive oil and freeze.

ANGEL HAIR PASTA SALAD WITH BASIL, TOMATOES, AND SLICED GRILLED STEAK

SERVES 6 AS A MAIN COURSE

◆

*T*his gorgeous main-course salad was inspired by leftovers. It's a perfect one-dish meal.

MARINADE

1 pound ripe tomatoes, peeled, seeded, and chopped

3 large garlic cloves, or 1 large clove elephant garlic, mashed to a paste (see box, page 62)

2 cups fresh basil, stemmed and chopped (see box, opposite page)

½ teaspoon kosher salt

½ teaspoon freshly ground black pepper

2 tablespoons virgin olive oil

½ tablespoon balsamic vinegar

½ pound New York strip steak, rib-eye, or sirloin, cut 1 inch thick

3 to 4 quarts water

1 teaspoon virgin olive oil

1 tablespoon kosher salt

1½ pounds angel hair pasta, broken into 4-inch pieces

Sprigs of fresh basil, for garnish

In a large bowl, combine the tomato, garlic, basil, ½ teaspoon salt, pepper, 2 tablespoons olive oil, vinegar, and steak. Cover and marinate for at least 10 minutes or up to 2 hours at room temperature.

Put the water for the pasta on to

MENU

◆

QUICK COLD AVOCADO SOUP

ANGEL HAIR PASTA SALAD WITH BASIL, TOMATOES, AND SLICED GRILLED STEAK

WARM BLUEBERRY CRISP

◆

BEAUJOLAIS, PINOT NOIR

boil. Heat the 1 teaspoon olive oil in a skillet. Remove the steak from the tomato mixture, reserving the mixture, and sear on both sides over high heat, then cook about 4 minutes on each side, until the steak is medium-rare. Let stand 5 minutes, then slice thinly.

Add the 1 tablespoon salt to the boiling water and cook the pasta until *al dente*, 4 to 5 minutes. Drain, place in a serving bowl, and toss well with the tomato mixture. Arrange the steak slices on top, garnish with basil, and serve at room temperature.

VARIATION: Substitute arugula for the basil.

ANGEL HAIR PASTA PANCAKES

SERVES 4 TO 6 AS A SIDE DISH

◆

*T*hese crispy pasta "pancakes" make an unusual and wonderful base for serving shrimp curry, Hungarian goulash, or Thai and Chinese stir-fry entrées, or a delicious side dish served with butter or a sauce, such as a spicy Thai peanut sauce. This is an excellent way to use up leftover angel hair pasta.

3 quarts water
1 tablespoon kosher salt
½ pound dry angel hair pasta, cut into
    3-inch lengths (or about 2 cups
    leftover cooked pasta)
2 large eggs, beaten
½ teaspoon kosher salt
¼ teaspoon freshly ground black
    pepper
Virgin olive oil or clarified butter

BROWN EGGS

◆

*F*arm-raised brown eggs most often have a darker-colored yolk, which I find preferable in many dishes because of a richer flavor.

Bring the water to a boil, add the salt, and cook the pasta until *al dente*, 4 to 5 minutes. Drain. Mix the eggs and seasonings in a bowl, add the hot drained pasta, and combine thoroughly.

Heat a nonstick skillet over medium-high heat, brush with oil, and add 1 tablespoon of the pasta-egg mixture. Spread the batter out with a spatula until thin and cook until golden-brown, 1 to 2 minutes. Turn and cook on the other side. Keep the pancakes warm on a baking sheet in a 350° oven. Do not stack or cover or they will lose their crispness. Serve warm.

VARIATION: Substitute any fine, thin pasta noodles, such as vermicelli, for the angel hair pasta.

MAKE AHEAD: up to 1 hour; refrigerate, reheat 10 minutes in 350° oven

GRAINS

◆

SPRING RISOTTO WITH ASPARAGUS AND BAY SCALLOPS

SERVES 4 TO 6 AS A MAIN COURSE, 6 TO 8 AS A FIRST COURSE

◆

*N*orthern Italian rice dishes, called risottos, are elegant, filling, and satisfying. This one is really a whole meal in one dish, and it's very simple to make while talking to guests in the kitchen.

6 to 8 cups chicken broth
3 tablespoons unsalted butter
1 red or yellow onion, finely chopped
1 bunch pencil-thin asparagus,
    trimmed and cut into 2-inch pieces
½ pound bay scallops, cleaned of sand
    but not rinsed (see box, page 68)
1½ cups arborio rice
½ cup dry white wine
Kosher salt
Freshly ground black pepper
2 tablespoons heavy cream
½ cup freshly grated Italian Parmesan

MENU
◆
&

**SPRING RISOTTO WITH
ASPARAGUS AND BAY SCALLOPS**

**ROMAINE AND CHERRY TOMATO
SALAD WITH A CREAMY
CAESAR DRESSING**

**BAKED CHOCOLATE
AND HAZELNUT MOUSSE**

◆

**ORVIETO, CALIFORNIA
CHARDONNAY, WHITE GRAVES**

Heat the broth to boiling. In a separate heavy-bottomed 2½-quart saucepan, melt the butter. Add the onion and cook over low heat until the onion is soft, about 5 minutes. While the onion is cooking, bring 2 inches of water to a boil in a skillet, and cook the asparagus for 2 to 3 minutes. Remove, drain, and keep warm. Poach the scallops in lightly salted water at a simmer for 1 minute. Remove, drain, and keep warm.

Add the rice to the onion and stir until the rice is coated with butter and opaque, about 3 minutes. Add the wine to the rice and cook over medium-high heat, stirring constantly, until the liquid is absorbed. Add ½ cup of the hot broth or just enough to cover the rice; continue stirring, and cook until it is absorbed. Continue to add the broth, ½ cup at a time, stirring after each addition until absorbed, until the rice is tender, about 20 to 25 minutes. The grains of rice will be a little firm in the center but softer on the outside.

When the rice is done, season to

taste with salt and pepper, then stir in the cream and cheese and about ⅓ cup of the broth so the risotto is creamy and light, not dry and stiff. Stir in the hot asparagus and scallops just before serving.

VARIATIONS: Substitute squid or shrimp and/or broccoli for the scallops and asparagus.

Substitute sautéed mushrooms for the asparagus.

SOUTHWESTERN RISOTTO
SERVES 4 AS A MAIN COURSE, 6 TO 8 AS A FIRST COURSE

◆

*T*his recipe gives a spicy American twist to the classic Italian risotto. Stir in a cup of thinly sliced cooked chicken, shrimp, beef, or lamb just before serving and you'll have a whole meal.

MENU

❧

SOUTHWESTERN RISOTTO

SIMPLE MIXED GREEN SALAD
WITH FRENCH VINAIGRETTE

STRAWBERRY SORBET
WITH CASSIS

◆

CHENIN BLANC

2 tablespoons unsalted butter, or olive, canola, or grapeseed oil
¼ teaspoon cayenne
½ cup pecan halves
1 medium red onion, minced
3½ to 4¼ cups chicken or beef broth
1½ cups arborio rice
1 small poblano chili, roasted (see box, page 35), peeled, seeded, and

chopped, or 1 to 2 jalapeños, seeded and minced
½ teaspoon kosher salt
¼ teaspoon freshly ground black pepper
Kernels cut from 2 large ears sweet corn or 1 cup frozen corn kernels
½ cup finely grated Monterey Jack cheese
1 cup thinly sliced cooked chicken, shrimp, beef, or lamb (optional)

Melt the butter or heat the oil in a heavy-bottomed 2-quart saucepan. Add the cayenne, pecans, and onion and cook over medium heat until the onion is soft, about 6 minutes. Meanwhile, in another 2-quart saucepan heat the broth to boiling. Add the rice to the pecan-onion mixture and stir until all the grains are coated with butter and are opaque, about 2 to 3 minutes. Add the chili.

Add ½ cup of the hot broth and the salt and pepper and cook, stirring, over medium-high heat until the broth is absorbed. Continue to add the broth, ½ cup at a time, stirring after each addition until absorbed, until only ¾ cup broth is left. At this point, add the corn, cheese, and ½ cup broth and finish cooking. The rice is done when it is tender but slightly chewy. If the risotto seems too dry and stiff, add 2 to 4 tablespoons more broth. The risotto should have a creamy consistency. Stir in the cooked meat just before serving, if desired.

LIGHT SUMMER RISOTTO

SERVES 4 AS A MAIN COURSE, 6 TO 8 AS A FIRST COURSE OR SIDE DISH

◆

*T*his colorful fresh-vegetable risotto is a delicious and healthy summer entrée.

3½ to 5 cups chicken broth
3 tablespoons unsalted butter or virgin olive oil
1 bunch scallions, with 3 inches green left on, chopped
⅛ pound prosciutto, thinly sliced, cut into ½-inch dice
1½ cups arborio rice
½ cup dry white wine
1 tablespoon unsalted butter or virgin olive oil
2 large tomatoes, each cut into 8 wedges, seeds drained in a colander
1 large or 2 small zucchini, very thinly sliced or shredded
½ teaspoon kosher salt
½ teaspoon freshly ground black pepper
8 large leaves fresh basil, finely shredded (see box, page 88)

2 tablespoons chopped fresh Italian parsley
Grated rind of 1 lemon
2 tablespoons light or heavy cream
¼ cup freshly grated Italian Parmesan

Heat the broth to boiling. Melt the 3 tablespoons of butter in a heavy-bottomed 2½-quart saucepan. Add the scallion and

M E N U

◆

CARPACCIO WITH
LEMON-SHALLOT MAYONNAISE

LIGHT SUMMER RISOTTO

COLD LIME MOUSSE

◆

BEAUJOLAIS, CHARDONNAY

prosciutto and cook over low heat until the scallion is soft, 1 to 2 minutes. Add the rice and stir until all the grains are coated with butter and opaque. Stir in the wine and cook over medium-high heat until it is absorbed. Then begin adding hot broth, ½ cup at a time, stirring after each addition until it is absorbed. Continue until the rice is done—it should be tender but just a little chewy on the inside. The amount of broth used will vary.

While the rice is cooking, heat the 1 tablespoon of butter in a large sauté pan or skillet. Add the tomato and zucchini and cook for 2 to 3 minutes. Stir into the risotto along with all of the remaining ingredients and serve immediately.

SAUSAGE AND SUN-DRIED TOMATO RISOTTO

SERVES 4 AS A MAIN COURSE

◆

*T*his is a hearty, satisfying dish! Keep the sausage on hand in your freezer and the rice and sun-dried tomatoes in your pantry.

3 tablespoons unsalted butter
1 red onion, minced
1 garlic clove, mashed to a paste
    (see box, page 62)
1 pound hot Italian fennel sausage,
    crumbled
3 to 4 cups chicken broth
1½ cups arborio rice
½ cup dry white wine
½ teaspoon dried oregano
½ teaspoon kosher salt
½ teaspoon freshly ground black
    pepper
⅓ cup dry-packed sun-dried tomatoes,
    plumped in hot water (see box,
    opposite page), drained, and
    chopped
1 tablespoon chopped fresh oregano or
    basil
⅓ cup chopped fresh parsley

MENU
◆

SAUSAGE AND SUN-DRIED
TOMATO RISOTTO

TOASTED GOAT CHEESE
IN GREEN VINAIGRETTE

BLUEBERRY CRISP

◆

PINOT GRIGIO, ORVIETO,
CHARDONNAY

In a heavy-bottomed 2-quart saucepan, melt the butter and add the onion and garlic. Cook over medium heat until the onion is soft, about 5 minutes. In a skillet, cook the crumbled sausage until lightly browned, about 5 minutes. Meanwhile, heat the broth to boiling and plump the sun-dried tomatoes. Add the sausage to the onion, then add the rice and stir until it is coated with butter and is opaque.

Add the wine and cook until it is absorbed. Then add ½ cup of the hot broth with the dried oregano, salt, and pepper.

Cook, stirring, until the broth is absorbed. Continue to add the broth, ½ cup at a time, stirring after each addition until absorbed, until the rice is done—it will be tender but slightly chewy. Stir in the sun-dried tomatoes and fresh herbs, and taste for seasoning. Stir in about ⅓ cup of broth so that the risotto is creamy and light.

ABOUT SUN-DRIED TOMATOES

Sun-dried tomatoes stored in oil vary a great deal in flavor. Some are really too strong because of the quality of the oil they are in; they also tend to be quite expensive. I prefer to use sun-dried tomatoes without oil, since they have a better flavor, are more modestly priced, and can be quickly softened by soaking in hot water to cover for 10 minutes, then draining, or micro-waving on high for 1 to 2 minutes. The Sonoma brand is consistently excellent in flavor.

You can make your own sun-dried tomatoes in oil by softening the dry-packed tomatoes, patting them dry, and then adding a good-quality extra-virgin olive oil. This makes a marvelously flavored oil for salads or grilling.

RISOTTO ROSSA

SERVES 4 TO 6 AS A SIDE DISH

◆

I've adapted this spectacular-looking dish—a beet-red risotto—which I first tasted as part of a special meal prepared by Matt Kenney, a talented young chef in New York City. It is a perfect and filling accompaniment to small roasted birds or chicken breasts.

2 quarts water
3 medium-large fresh beets, scrubbed
    and chopped
3 cups chicken broth
3 tablespoons unsalted butter
1 medium yellow onion, minced
1 shallot, minced
1½ cups arborio rice
½ cup dry red wine
1½ teaspoons balsamic vinegar
2 tablespoons port
½ teaspoon kosher salt
⅛ teaspoon freshly ground black
    pepper

In a 3- to 4-quart saucepan, bring the water to a boil. Add the beets and boil on high heat, uncovered, until soft, about 20 minutes. When cool enough to handle, peel and puree in a food processor.

While the beets are cooking, heat the broth to boiling. Melt the butter in a heavy-bottomed 1½-quart saucepan and cook the onion and the shallot over low heat until soft, 8 to 10 minutes. Add the rice and cook over medium heat, stirring, about 5 minutes. Add the wine, vinegar, and port and cook, stirring, for 2 to 3 minutes, until the liquid has been absorbed.

Add 1½ cups of the hot chicken broth to the pureed beets and begin to add this to the rice, ½ cup at a time, stirring after each addition until the liquid has been absorbed. Continue until the beet mixture, and then the remaining 1½ cups of broth, are all used up and the rice is tender. Season with the salt and pepper and serve hot.

COCONUT RICE

SERVES 2 AS A SIDE DISH

♦

*R*ice prepared with the exotic flavors of India is a special treat and makes an unusually good side dish for roasted or grilled lamb, chicken, or fish. Basmati rice comes from the Himalayas; it has a delicately perfumed odor and a milky flavor. It is sold in gourmet grocery stores.

1 tablespoon unsalted butter
⅓ cup pistachios, toasted
Seeds removed from 10 cardamom
    pods and crushed in a mortar with
    a pestle
4 whole cloves
2 cinnamon sticks

1¼ cups basmati rice (if unavailable,
    use long-grain rice)
1¼ cups canned unsweetened coconut
    milk (if unavailable, use whole
    milk)
1¼ cups water
¾ teaspoon salt

Melt the butter over medium heat in a heavy-bottomed 2-quart saucepan. Add the pistachios, crushed cardamom seeds, cloves, and cinnamon and stir for 1 or 2 minutes. Add the rice and stir until all the grains are coated with the butter. Add the coconut milk, water, and salt. Stir the rice, cover, leaving the lid ajar, and simmer over medium-low heat for about 15 minutes, or until the rice is tender and all the liquid has been absorbed.

MAKE AHEAD: up to 30 minutes; let stand in pan; reheat gently

SAFFRON RICE WITH SCALLIONS

SERVES 2 TO 4 AS A SIDE DISH

◆

*T*his lovely dish, with its wonderful yellow color and subtle saffron flavor, goes well with many foods—pork, fish, shellfish, beef, lamb, veal, and chicken.

½ teaspoon saffron threads
2 cups hot chicken broth or water
½ tablespoon unsalted butter
4 scallions with 3 inches of green
    left on, chopped
1 cup long-grain rice
½ teaspoon kosher salt
¼ teaspoon freshly ground white
    pepper
Pinch dried thyme

In a ½-cup measure, steep the saffron threads in 2 tablespoons of the hot broth for 2 minutes (see box, page 98). Melt the butter in a heavy-bottomed 2-quart saucepan. Add the scallion and cook over medium-high heat until soft, about 2 minutes. Add the rice and the remaining ingredients, including the saffron. Stir, bring to a boil, and cook, covered, at

THE SIMPLEST WAY TO COOK LONG-GRAIN RICE

◆

*T*here are many ways to cook long-grain rice, but this one is the simplest of all. Use two parts liquid to one part rice. Heat the water or broth to boiling, add a pinch of salt, ½ tablespoon of butter, and rice; stir, reduce the heat to a simmer, and cook, uncovered, for 15 to 20 minutes, until the rice is fluffy and dry. Do not stir during cooking—this releases the starch and makes the rice gummy. Small holes appearing on the surface indicate that the rice is done.

a gentle simmer for 15 to 20 minutes, or until all the liquid is absorbed and the rice is tender. Do not stir the rice except when you add it. It will become very starchy and soggy if you stir it during or after cooking.

VARIATION: For a main-course dish, add ⅓ pound sautéed shrimp or roast lamb to the rice just before serving.

MAKE AHEAD: up to 1 hour; let stand in pan; reheat gently

ABOUT SAFFRON

Saffron is one of the world's most expensive spices, but take comfort in the fact that a small amount packs a lot of flavoring power. This pungent bright orange-red threadlike spice, which gives an exquisite yellow color to the dishes it is cooked with, is the dried stigmas of a crocus flower. Never buy powdered saffron as it can be adulterated and does not give the best flavor. Spain is the major producer and exporter of saffron,

and Spanish saffron is considered the best. Its subtle flavor is central to paella and bouillabaisse.

To use saffron threads, pour hot or boiling water, stock, or sauce over them in a small bowl and let them steep for a few minutes. Press the saffron against the sides of the bowl with a spoon or a small pestle to extract the flavor. Then pour the threads and the soaking liquid into the dish and stir to distribute the flavor.

WILD AND WHITE RICE WITH LEEKS AND MUSHROOMS

SERVES 8 TO 10 AS A SIDE DISH

◆

*H*ere's an elegant, easy rice dish that complements a winter company dinner of roast turkey, beef, or pork. It's also very good as a leftover rice salad with a raspberry vinaigrette.

6 cups chicken stock
2 cups wild rice, well rinsed
2 imported bay leaves

2½ teaspoons kosher salt
2 cups water
1 cup long-grain rice

5 tablespoons unsalted butter
4 large leeks, white only, well cleaned
    (see box, page 136), thinly sliced
2 teaspoons dried thyme, or
    1½ tablespoons fresh thyme
¾ pound fresh mushrooms, thinly
    sliced or quartered
Kosher salt
Freshly ground black pepper
½ cup chopped fresh parsley

Bring the stock to a simmer. Add the wild rice; cook, uncovered, with 1 of the bay leaves and 2 teaspoons of the salt, until the rice is tender and the stock has evaporated, about 30 minutes. Do not stir the rice. Remove the bay leaf. At the same time, bring the water to a simmer and cook the long-grain rice with the remaining bay leaf and ½ teaspoon salt by the same method.

While the rice is cooking, melt the

USING WILD-RICE LEFTOVERS

Leftover wild rice can be added to a plain pancake or muffin batter with delicious, chewy results. It also makes a wonderful addition to Creamy Mushroom Soup (page 33), any of the green salads with walnuts (pages 124, 129, 138, 145), or the vinaigrette of the Winter Pork Loin, Apple, and Hazelnut Salad (page 119).

butter in a large casserole. Add the leek and thyme, cover, and cook until soft, about 5 minutes. Add the mushrooms, season, and cook for 5 minutes. Stir in the rice and cook over low heat until the mixture has absorbed all moisture. Season to taste and stir in the parsley.

COUSCOUS WITH CARROTS AND MINT
SERVES 4 TO 6 AS A SIDE DISH

Couscous is a light and delicious Moroccan grain product made from coarsely ground durum or semolina wheat that has been precooked. It is very practical for quick meals, as it needs only 5 to 8 minutes to absorb hot broth and seasonings. I love its nutty flavor and often serve it in place of rice with fish or as a bed for steamed or sautéed vegetables. It's also delicious cold, tossed with a vinaigrette, and served as a salad. (Couscous is also the name of a traditional North African one-dish meal consisting of the cooked grain with cooked carrots, tomatoes, zucchini, spices, and fish or meat.)

1½ cups chicken broth
1 tablespoon virgin olive oil
4 whole scallions, finely chopped
3 large carrots, peeled, quartered, and
    very thinly sliced
¼ teaspoon *each* ground cumin,
    cinnamon, cardamom, and
    turmeric (or 1 teaspoon curry
    powder)
1¼ cups couscous
About ½ cup chopped fresh mint
    leaves

⅓ cup slivered or sliced almonds

Bring the broth to a boil. Meanwhile, heat the olive oil in a 2½-quart saucepan and cook the scallion and carrot until soft, about 5 minutes. Add all the seasonings and cook a few more minutes. Add the boiling broth, the couscous, and the mint and almonds. Stir, cover, and let stand off the heat until the couscous has absorbed all the liquid, about 7 or 8 minutes. Uncover and serve immediately.

QUICK GRITS, SOUTHERN STYLE

SERVES 4 AS A SIDE DISH

◆

*G*rits, also called hominy grits or corn grits, are a staple of southern cuisine. Milled from dried hominy, grits are traditionally served plain for breakfast along with ham, biscuits, and red-eye gravy, or for lunch or dinner with fried chicken and gravy. This version finds its way to the Thanksgiving table in many southern homes.

2¾ cups water
⅛ teaspoon kosher salt
¾ cup quick white hominy grits
1 tablespoon unsalted butter
1 garlic clove, mashed to a paste (see
    box, page 62)
¼ pound cheddar cheese, grated
    (optional)
Freshly ground black pepper to taste

Bring the water to a boil, add the salt, and slowly stir in the grits. Reduce the heat and cook for 5 minutes, stirring occa-

sionally, until very thick. Remove from the heat, cover, and let sit for 2 minutes.

While the grits are cooking, heat the butter in a separate pan and sauté the garlic for 1 minute, or until fragrant. Mix the garlic butter, cheese (if using), and pepper into the grits, stirring until combined or until the cheese has melted. Taste for seasoning.

MAKE AHEAD: up to 3 days; refrigerate; reheat gently

HOMINY WITH SWEET CORN, POBLANO, AND CILANTRO

SERVES 6 AS A SIDE DISH

◆

*H*ominy, dried whole corn kernels that have been soaked to remove the skin and plump them up, is used in southern and Mexican cooking. The addition of fresh corn here reiterates the corn flavor in a different texture, and the deep, smoky flavor of the poblano chili adds a nice rich counterpoint to this wholesome dish. Hominy is available both canned and dried, but I use canned hominy here, as the dried takes a very long time to cook.

2 tablespoons unsalted butter
Kernels from 1 or 2 ears of corn
1 poblano chili, roasted, peeled, and chopped (see box, page 35), or if unavailable, 1 jalapeño or serrano chili, minced (see Note)
One 29-ounce can white or golden hominy, rinsed and drained
Kosher salt
Freshly ground black pepper
A few leaves fresh cilantro or parsley, for garnish

Melt the butter in a 2-quart saucepan. Add the corn kernels and cook over low heat for 5 minutes while roasting the poblano. Add the chopped poblano and the hominy and cook over medium heat for 4 to 5 minutes, or until hot. Season with salt and pepper to taste. Garnish and serve hot.

MAKE AHEAD: up to 24 hours; refrigerate; reheat gently

CHILIES

◆

*Y*ou can cut off and taste the end of a chili to see how hot it is. Depending upon growing conditions, some chilies are not as hot as they should be. If a chili isn't as hot as you wish, simply leave in the seeds and ribs. To get a mildly hot flavor from a hot chili, such as a jalapeño, simply make two or three slits in the chili and add it whole to a simmering soup or dish. Then retrieve the chili before serving. It will have added a subtle but not-too-hot touch of flavor.

NOTE: If you don't like hot chilies, use 1 small red or green bell pepper, chopped.

Kasha with Mushrooms and Onions
SERVES 4 TO 6 AS A SIDE DISH

◆

A classic Russian side dish, kasha deserves to be better known. Kasha is another name for roasted buckwheat groats, a very flavorful grain. It is cooked just like rice after an initial (and necessary) toasting with egg, which seals in the starch. Kasha goes well with all meat and chicken dishes.

1 cup kasha
1 large egg, lightly beaten
5 tablespoons unsalted butter
1 yellow onion, minced
3 whole scallions, finely chopped
1 garlic clove, mashed to a paste
    (see box, page 62)
2 cups beef broth
Kosher salt
Freshly ground black pepper
½ pound fresh mushrooms, chopped
3 tablespoons chopped fresh parsley
2 tablespoons sour cream

Mix the kasha and egg in a bowl. Transfer to a dry skillet and stir the mixture gently over medium heat for 3 to 4 minutes to dry and separate the grains.

In a 2½-quart saucepan heat 3 tablespoons of the butter. Add the onion, scallion, and garlic and cook gently until soft, 7 to 8 minutes. Add the kasha and broth to the onion mixture, season to taste with salt and pepper, and simmer, covered, for 15 minutes.

Meanwhile, heat the remaining 2 tablespoons of butter in a small skillet and cook the mushrooms until all the liquid has evaporated. When the kasha is tender, stir in the cooked mushrooms, parsley, and sour cream, and serve hot.

MAIN-COURSE, LUNCHEON, AND ACCOMPANIMENT SALADS

◆

*T*his chapter presents something relatively new in menu planning—the main-course salad. Popularized, perhaps, by the trend toward lighter foods and the recent interest in spa cooking, main-course salads creatively combine protein, vegetable, and carbohydrates into one light and delicious meal. My versions feature combinations you may never have considered—for example, the Oakleaf Lettuce Salad with Turkey, Cantaloupe, and Roasted Pecans, or the Warm Asparagus and Pasta Salad with Hazelnuts, Prosciutto, and Balsamic

Vinaigrette, which makes a delightful summer meal. Create your own versions as well—main-course salads are a great outlet for creativity since they allow you to combine so many foods, including leftovers (meat and/or rice from last night's dinner, melon from breakfast, cooked asparagus, and so on). You will find that great combinations can be made from whatever happens to be on hand (in your refrigerator or garden).

Another advantage of these salads is that most can be partially or completely prepared in advance. And they are always beautiful, because of the varied colors, shapes, and sizes of the ingredients. I like to present these whole-meal salads in a nontraditional way. Instead of heaping all the ingredients in a deep salad bowl, I toss them with the dressing and then spread them out on a large flat platter (the bigger the better), which makes a stunning presentation. A turkey platter, if you have one, is useful for this.

This chapter also includes a category of salads I refer to as "luncheon salads"—not quite as hearty as the main-course salads, not necessarily containing all of the elements required for a whole meal (protein, vegetables, carbohydrates), but substantial enough for a lunch or a light supper. For example, there is Romaine and Cherry Tomato Salad with Creamy Caesar Dressing, a salad with lots of flavor and crunch. Of course, these categories are not absolute; any of the main-course salads can be eaten for lunch, and a luncheon salad can be served as an accompaniment to a regular meal.

Finally, this chapter includes some of my favorite accompaniment salads, giving you many interesting variations of the classic green salad from which to choose. These salads can take their rightful places as palate cleansers after the main course and before the dessert. Or they can be used as the hearty second course of a simple soup-and-salad meal. There are some wonderful combinations here—the Winter Salad Greens with Cranberry-Orange Vinaigrette for your holiday meals; the Apple, Fennel, and Watercress Salad, which perfectly accompanies a pâté or hearty meat dish; the Simple French Mushroom Salad, which makes a nice change from greens; the deliciously aromatic Provençal Spinach Salad, and the Autumn Salad of Bitter Greens, Sweet Pears, and Goat Cheese. There is also an excellent recipe for a basic green salad with a classic vinaigrette.

Many of the dressings that accompany the salads can be used in different ways: on different greens and salad combinations, as dressings for cooked vegetables, or as marinades. Try the Sesame Oil Dressing (page 117) on broccoli or asparagus, for example, or use it as a marinade for grilled chicken or fish. Most of the dressings can be made at least a day ahead.

MAIN-COURSE OR LUNCHEON SALADS

LUNCHEON OR ACCOMPANIMENT SALADS

ACCOMPANIMENT SALADS

WASHING AND STORING SALAD GREENS

Salad greens are best washed in a large bowl of cold water. Cut off the core of the lettuce; if you're using romaine, cut off about 4 inches of the stalk. Separate the leaves, plunge them into the water, and swish them around to loosen any dirt clinging to the folds. Lift the greens out of the water and place them in a colander. Rinse under cold water and let drain a few minutes. Then put a couple of handfuls of greens into a salad spinner. (The best ones have a pull cord.) Spin off as much water as possible. Remove the lettuce to a sealable plastic bag and pour off the excess water. Repeat until all the greens are spun dry. Salad greens will keep crisp in the sealable plastic bags for up to three days in the refrigerator. When storing, leave the greens in large pieces and tear them just before serving; cut or torn edges tend to discolor slightly.

My preference, unless otherwise stated in a recipe, is to leave the salad greens in larger pieces, say 4 inches by 4 inches. I use a knife and fork to eat salad and prefer the visual effect of the larger pieces to postage-stamp-size pieces. Tiny pieces wilt more quickly than large ones, too.

MAIN-COURSE
OR LUNCHEON SALADS

◆

COLD ORIENTAL NOODLE SALAD
WITH SPICY PEANUT SAUCE

SERVES 6 AS A MAIN COURSE

◆

*T*his salad, healthy and rich in flavor, is particularly satisfying as a meal in it-self. Try the spicy peanut sauce with roast pork or chicken.

3 to 4 quarts water
1 pound linguine, spaghettini, or *soba* (buckwheat) noodles
1 tablespoon kosher salt
1 tablespoon vegetable oil
1 tablespoon Oriental sesame oil (see box, page 65)

SPICY PEANUT SAUCE
⅓ cup chunky peanut butter
2 tablespoons champagne or rice-wine vinegar
½ tablespoon soy sauce
2 teaspoons sugar
2 teaspoons vegetable oil
1½ teaspoons Oriental sesame oil
3 scallions with greens, chopped
½ teaspoon dried red-pepper flakes or cayenne
⅔ cup yogurt
1 inch fresh ginger, peeled
1 garlic clove
¼ teaspoon kosher salt

2 carrots, peeled and thinly sliced
1 red bell pepper, seeded and cut in 3 × ¼-inch slices

Chopped fresh cilantro or chives, for garnish

Bring the water to a boil. Add the noodles, salt, and vegetable oil, and cook until *al dente*, 8 to 10 minutes. Drain the noodles and toss with the sesame oil. Place the noodles on a metal baking sheet and refrigerate, uncovered, for 10 to 15 minutes, or until well chilled.

While the noodles are cooking, place all of the sauce ingredients in a blender or food processor and blend until smooth. Chill. Toss the noodles and the raw vege-

MENU

❧❧

QUICK COLD MELON SOUP

COLD ORIENTAL NOODLE SALAD
WITH SPICY PEANUT SAUCE

BANANA-GINGER SORBET

◆

DARK BEER

tables with the chilled sauce, place in a large bowl or on a platter, garnish with the cilantro, and serve.

VARIATIONS: Toss with the salad ½ cucumber, seeded and thinly sliced, ½ cup cooked chopped broccoli, and ¼ cup toasted sesame seeds (see box, page 67).

For a main-course salad, add 8 ounces beef fillet or steak, grilled medium-rare and thinly sliced, or 8 ounces roasted or grilled lamb or pork arranged on top of tossed noodles.

MAKE AHEAD: up to 24 hours; refrigerate; add garnish just before serving

SHELL PASTA SALAD WITH SPINACH AND ARTICHOKES

SERVES 8 AS A MAIN COURSE

◆

*P*asta always makes a satisfying main-course salad; seasonings and additions are really a matter of personal choice. This combination is very good, but feel free to add or subtract according to what's in your refrigerator and pantry.

3 to 4 quarts water
1 tablespoon kosher salt
1 tablespoon olive oil
1 pound dry medium-sized shell pasta, radiatore, or bow-tie pasta
1 bunch fresh spinach, well washed, stems removed (see box, page 106)
One 1-pound can artichoke hearts, drained and halved
1 large red onion, thinly sliced, cut in 2-inch lengths
1 *each* green and red bell pepper, seeded and very thinly sliced in 2-inch lengths
⅓ cup imported black olives (Niçoise or Kalamata)
¼ cup fresh basil, very finely shredded (see box, page 88)

½ cup drained crumbled feta or goat cheese

PARMESAN VINAIGRETTE
2½ tablespoons Spanish sherry wine vinegar
1 teaspoon kosher salt
½ teaspoon freshly ground black pepper
1 tablespoon Dijon mustard
2 tablespoons freshly grated Italian Parmesan
About ⅔ cup virgin olive oil
1 tablespoon capers, drained and rinsed
1 teaspoon dried basil

Put the water on to boil. Meanwhile,

MENU

❧

**EASY TOMATO AND
PROSCIUTTO BRUSCHETTA**

**SHELL PASTA SALAD
WITH SPINACH AND
ARTICHOKES**

**RED AND BLACK SUMMER
FRUITS**

♦

BEAUJOLAIS, CÔTES DU RHÔNE

prepare the salad ingredients and combine the vinaigrette ingredients. Add the salt and oil to the boiling water and cook the pasta until *al dente,* about 10 minutes. Drain but do not rinse. Toss with half the vinaigrette and chill for 10 minutes.

Just before serving, toss the pasta with the remaining salad ingredients and the remaining vinaigrette. Taste for seasoning. You may need to add a bit more oil, vinegar, and black pepper.

VARIATIONS: Use other salad greens, such as arugula or oakleaf lettuce, in place of or in addition to the spinach. More fresh herbs could be added as well.

Add thin slices of cold roast pork, beef, or lamb.

MAKE AHEAD: cook pasta and make dressing up to 24 hours ahead; refrigerate (toss pasta with enough dressing to keep it from sticking); assemble salad just before serving

CHICK-PEA, ITALIAN SALAMI, AND OLIVE SALAD

SERVES 6 AS A MAIN COURSE

♦

*I*f you like Italian antipasti, you'll enjoy this colorful salad—perfect lunch or picnic fare.

BALSAMIC VINAIGRETTE
2½ tablespoons balsamic vinegar
6 tablespoons extra-virgin olive oil
2 tablespoons water
½ teaspoon kosher salt
½ teaspoon black pepper

1 pound canned chick-peas, drained and rinsed well, sprinkled with lemon juice

½ pound Italian hard salami, thinly sliced, each slice cut into quarters
4 to 6 scallions, thinly sliced
1 red bell pepper, seeded and chopped
1 cup imported black olives, pitted
1 tablespoon fresh oregano, chopped
1 head red leaf or oakleaf lettuce, washed, dried, and cut into 3-inch pieces
½ cup chopped fresh Italian parsley

Whisk together the vinaigrette ingredients. In a large serving dish, combine all of the salad ingredients and toss with the dressing.

VARIATIONS: Substitute thinly sliced New York strip steak, cooked medium-rare, for the salami.

Substitute freshly cooked green beans for the chick-peas.

MAKE AHEAD: prepare except for greens up to 24 hours ahead; refrigerate;

add lettuce and parsley and toss again just before serving

MENU

❧

CHICK-PEA, ITALIAN SALAMI,
AND OLIVE SALAD

CRUSTY TUSCAN BREAD

GRATIN OF CHERRIES
AND APRICOTS WITH AMARETTI

◆

ORVIETO, CHIANTI

WARM JALAPEÑO CHICKEN ON A BED OF GREENS AND ROASTED PEPPERS

SERVES 6 TO 8 AS A MAIN COURSE

◆

*T*his is an especially attractive salad, with warm colors and flavors. Try the Tomato-Cumin Vinaigrette over cucumbers, blanched sliced zucchini, or green beans.

MENU

◆
❧

GOAT CHEESE, SHALLOT, AND
FRESH HERB TOASTS

WARM JALAPEÑO CHICKEN
ON A BED OF GREENS
AND ROASTED PEPPERS

SUMMER PLUM COMPOTE

◆

CHENIN BLANC, MEXICAN BEER

1 recipe Breast of Chicken in Jalapeño-Citrus Marinade (page 50)
1 *each* red, yellow, and green bell pepper

TOMATO-CUMIN VINAIGRETTE
3 tablespoons Spanish sherry wine vinegar
½ teaspoon kosher salt
¼ teaspoon freshly ground black pepper
⅛ teaspoon cayenne

½ teaspoon ground cumin
1 small tomato, seeded and finely
    chopped
½ cup virgin olive oil

1 large head red leaf or oakleaf
    lettuce, washed, dried, and torn
1 large bunch spinach, stemmed,
    washed, dried, and torn (see box,
    page 106)
2 tablespoons finely chopped fresh
    cilantro or parsley, for garnish

Marinate the chicken for at least 15 minutes. While the chicken is marinating, roast the peppers, then peel, seed, and thinly slice them (see box, page 35), or slice the peppers and use them uncooked. Whisk together the vinaigrette ingredients.

Just before serving, remove the chicken from the marinade and sauté in a skillet for 4 or 5 minutes, slice, and keep warm. Toss the lettuce and spinach with the dressing and arrange on a large platter. Alternate the chicken and peppers in a decorative pattern on top of the greens, garnish with cilantro or parsley, and serve.

MAKE AHEAD: marinate chicken, roast peppers, and make dressing up to 24 hours ahead; refrigerate; sauté chicken just before serving

---

HANDLING FRESH CHILIES

◆

Handle all chilies with care—the seeds and the inner ribs are the hottest parts and may irritate your skin. When preparing chilies, don't touch your face or eyes with your hands! If your skin is sensitive, wear rubber gloves.

OAKLEAF LETTUCE SALAD WITH TURKEY, CANTALOUPE, AND ROASTED PECANS

SERVES 2 AS A MAIN COURSE

◆

*A*ll of these ingredients happened to be in my refrigerator one summer Saturday. The unexpected arrival of a friend from New York inspired me to assemble these native Texas foodstuffs into an interesting and refreshing midday meal.

1 tablespoon unsalted butter or oil
2 teaspoons sweet or hot Hungarian
    paprika, or 1 teaspoon of each
⅓ cup whole pecan halves
2 tablespoons all-purpose flour
⅛ teaspoon kosher salt
¼ teaspoon sweet or hot Hungarian
    paprika
⅛ teaspoon dried oregano
¼ pound skinless turkey tenderloin,
    sliced across the grain in thin
    strips

SPANISH SHERRY VINAIGRETTE
1 tablespoon Spanish sherry vinegar
½ teaspoon kosher salt
¼ teaspoon freshly ground black
    pepper
4 tablespoons virgin olive oil,
    grapeseed oil, or canola oil
⅛ teaspoon dried oregano

1 head oakleaf lettuce, washed and
    dried, left in large pieces
⅓ small cantaloupe, chopped into
    ½-inch pieces or cut into long thin
    slices

Heat ½ tablespoon of the butter in a
9-inch nonstick skillet. Add the 2 teaspoons paprika and the pecans, and stir
over medium heat for 2 to 3 minutes, or
until the pecans are starting to brown
lightly. Remove and hold. Wipe out the
skillet. In the same skillet, melt the remaining ½ tablespoon butter. On a plate,
combine the flour, salt, ¼ teaspoon paprika, and oregano and toss the turkey
strips lightly in the seasoned flour. Stir-
fry the turkey over high heat for only
about 1 minute, or until cooked through.
Remove and hold.

Combine the vinaigrette ingredients
in the bottom of a large bowl. Add the lettuce, cooked turkey, and roasted pecan
halves, and toss. Gently stir in the cantaloupe. Arrange the salad on a large platter and serve.

VARIATION: Substitute slices of roasted
or grilled pork tenderloin or sautéed,
grilled, or roasted chicken for the turkey.

MAKE AHEAD: make vinaigrette and
cook turkey up to 24 hours ahead; refrigerate; toast pecans and toss the salad
just before serving

MENU

COLD SENEGALESE SOUP

OAKLEAF LETTUCE SALAD
WITH TURKEY, CANTALOUPE,
AND ROASTED PECANS

ESPRESSO CAKE

FUMÉ BLANC

CILANTRO-CHILI
CHICKEN SALAD

SERVES 6 TO 8 AS A MAIN COURSE

◆

*T*his vinaigrette is also delicious combined with medium-rare cooked steak, thinly sliced, or with peeled shrimp, simmered for 2 minutes and served cold, or with squid, simmered for 1 minute.

3 quarts water
1 tablespoon kosher salt
2½ pounds chicken pieces (thighs and
    breasts)

CILANTRO-CHILI VINAIGRETTE
1 large bunch fresh cilantro, finely
    minced
4 large garlic cloves, finely minced
1½ inches fresh ginger, peeled and
    finely minced, to yield 1
    tablespoon
2 jalapeño or serrano chilies, seeded
    and finely minced
½ teaspoon kosher salt
Juice of 1½ large lemons, or more to
    taste
⅓ cup virgin olive oil

3 stalks bok choy (ribs and leaves) or
    celery, thinly sliced
1 red bell pepper, seeded and thinly
    sliced, for garnish

MENU

&&

CILANTRO-CHILI
CHICKEN SALAD

CORNBREAD WITH
GOAT CHEESE AND
SUN-DRIED TOMATOES

MELONS AND FRESH FIGS

◆

SAUVIGNON BLANC,
DRY CHENIN BLANC

In a 6-quart stockpot, bring the water to a boil. Add the salt and simmer the chicken pieces for about 20 minutes, or until tender. Remove and drain. When cool, remove the skin and bone and chop the chicken meat very fine.

While the chicken is simmering, blend the vinaigrette ingredients in a blender or a food processor and let sit at room temperature to blend the flavors. Toss the chicken and bok choy with the vinaigrette, garnish with the red pepper, and serve at room temperature.

MAKE AHEAD: prepare up to 24 hours ahead; refrigerate; bring to room temperature before serving

COBB SALAD WITH LOBSTER

SERVES 6 AS A MAIN COURSE

◆

*H*ere's an elegant rendition of an old American favorite. This makes a perfect weekend luncheon dish for friends.

3 large eggs, at room temperature
1 pound frozen lobster tail in the shell, thawed
5 slices bacon

RED-WINE VINAIGRETTE
1 cup virgin olive oil
⅓ cup red-wine vinegar

2 teaspoons Dijon mustard
1 teaspoon cognac or white wine
Kosher salt
Freshly ground black pepper
½ teaspoon dried basil

1 small bunch of spinach, 1 small head red leaf lettuce, 1 small head romaine, and 1 head Boston lettuce, all washed, dried, and cut *en chiffonade* (see box, page 38)
2 avocados, peeled and thinly sliced
8 cherry tomatoes, halved
4 whole scallions, finely chopped
4 ounces Roquefort cheese, crumbled
1 large bunch fresh chives, chopped

THE BEST WAY TO HARD-BOIL EGGS

◆

*R*un very warm water over cold refrigerated eggs in a bowl for a few minutes until they are at room temperature. Meanwhile, in a small saucepan, bring to a boil enough water to cover the eggs. Pierce the large end of each egg with a pin (this keeps shells from cracking), lower them gently into the water, and simmer for 12 minutes. Remove the eggs and immediately place them in a bowl of ice water to loosen the shells. (Running cold water from the tap over the eggs does not have the same effect. Plunging the hot eggs into ice water creates steam, which helps to separate the shell from the cooked white.) Leave them in ice water for 7 to 10 minutes. The shells will come off perfectly.

Hard-boil the eggs according to the directions in the box to the left. At the same time, cook the lobster tail: Bring 4 inches of water to a boil in a large saucepan, add the lobster tail in its shell, and cook for about 12 minutes, or until the lobster is cooked through. Remove, let cool, remove the shell, and chop the lobster meat. Chill until ready to toss the salad.

While cooking the eggs and lobster, cook the bacon in a large heavy skillet until lightly browned. Drain on a paper towel and crumble. Whisk together the vinaigrette ingredients.

When ready to serve, toss the greens

with the vinaigrette and spread them on a large platter. Arrange all the remaining ingredients except the chives in individual heaps on top of the lettuce to make a colorful pattern. Sprinkle with the chives and serve. Or, if you prefer, toss all the ingredients together and serve.

VARIATION: Substitute 1 pound cooked flaked crab or 1 pound cooked small shrimp for the lobster.

NOTE: The Red-Wine Vinaigrette is a classic dressing for a simple green salad.

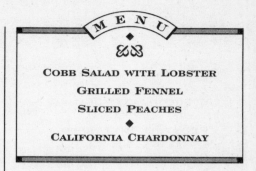

M E N U

ঙঙ

COBB SALAD WITH LOBSTER

GRILLED FENNEL

SLICED PEACHES

CALIFORNIA CHARDONNAY

MAKE AHEAD: cook eggs, lobster, and bacon and prepare dressing up to 24 hours ahead; refrigerate; arrange salad just before serving

NORMANDY POTATO, MUSHROOM, AND SCALLOP SALAD

SERVES 4 TO 6 AS A MAIN COURSE

◆

Crème fraîche and lemon come together here to create an unusually delicate salad dressing. In Normandy you'll also find this dressing tossed with tender spring salad greens, as in Green Salad from Normandy (page 136). This salad is also delicious with steamed mussels instead of scallops.

6 large new potatoes, quartered
¼ pound bay scallops, cleaned of sand but not rinsed (see box, page 68)

CRÈME FRAÎCHE DRESSING
½ cup Crème Fraîche (page 210) or heavy cream
3 tablespoons fresh lemon juice
¼ teaspoon kosher salt, or to taste
¼ teaspoon freshly ground black pepper

1 large head Boston lettuce, washed, leaves left whole
3 thin slices Danish ham, cut in thin strips
8 large fresh mushrooms, stems left on but trimmed, quartered
2 celery stalks, thinly sliced on the diagonal
2 tablespoons minced fresh parsley and/or chives, for garnish

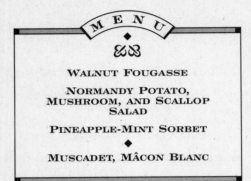

M E N U

❦

WALNUT FOUGASSE

NORMANDY POTATO, MUSHROOM, AND SCALLOP SALAD

PINEAPPLE-MINT SORBET

◆

MUSCADET, MÂCON BLANC

1 minute in simmering salted water, then drain and pat dry.

Combine the dressing ingredients. Just before serving, line a platter with the lettuce. In a separate bowl toss the potatoes, scallops, ham, mushrooms, and celery with the dressing to coat well. Spoon the salad onto the lettuce and garnish with herbs. Serve at room temperature or lightly chilled.

Boil the potatoes until tender but still firm, about 15 minutes. Cool and slice, leaving the skins on. While the potatoes are cooking, poach the scallops gently for

MAKE AHEAD: cook potatoes up to 24 hours ahead; refrigerate; toss with scallops and dressing just before serving

LARRY'S FRIED OYSTER AND ROMAINE SALAD

SERVES 2 AS A MAIN COURSE, 4 AS AN ACCOMPANIMENT

◆

*L*arry Osborne, a talented private chef in Austin, dreamed up this fabulous combination of ingredients. I've enjoyed many of his refined creations over the years.

MUSTARD-HONEY DRESSING
2 tablespoons balsamic vinegar
½ teaspoon kosher salt
¼ teaspoon freshly ground black
    pepper
½ teaspoon Dijon mustard
1 teaspoon honey
⅛ cup canola or virgin olive oil

3 tablespoons unsalted butter or
    vegetable oil

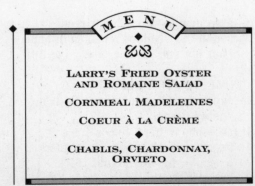

M E N U

❦

LARRY'S FRIED OYSTER AND ROMAINE SALAD

CORNMEAL MADELEINES

COEUR À LA CRÈME

◆

CHABLIS, CHARDONNAY, ORVIETO

10 to 12 large oysters or 24 small,
    drained and patted dry
1 cup finely crushed saltines
1 large head romaine, washed,
    dried, and thinly sliced
    (see box, page 131)
1 pink or ruby red grapefruit, peeled
    and cut into sections, pith removed
1 large avocado, thinly sliced

Whisk together the dressing ingredients. Heat the butter in a 9-inch skillet. Dredge the oysters in the cracker crumbs and sauté over medium heat for about 4 to 5 minutes, or until the oysters are golden-brown on both sides. Drain on paper towels.

Toss the lettuce with three-quarters of the dressing, place on a large platter, and arrange the grapefruit, avocado, and oysters on top. Drizzle with the remaining dressing and serve.

MAKE AHEAD: prepare dressing up to 24 hours ahead; refrigerate

FRIED RICE SALAD WITH SHRIMP, SNOW PEAS, AND SESAME OIL

SERVES 6 AS A MAIN COURSE

◆

*T*he nutty flavor and fragrance of toasted sesame oil lends distinction to this easy cold salad.

4 cups water
1 teaspoon kosher salt
2 cups raw long-grain rice (see Note)
¾ pound medium shrimp
¼ pound snow peas, strings removed

SESAME OIL DRESSING
2 tablespoons champagne vinegar
½ teaspoon kosher salt
4 tablespoons safflower, sunflower, or
    canola oil
2 tablespoons Oriental sesame oil (see
    box, page 65)

1 tablespoon safflower, sunflower, or
    canola oil
1 large bunch scallions with greens,
    chopped
½ cup fresh cilantro leaves
1 large red bell pepper, seeded and
    finely chopped or thinly sliced

Bring the water to a boil, add the salt, and cook the rice until it is tender and the water has evaporated, 15 to 20 minutes. Meanwhile, simmer the shrimp in salted water to cover for 2 minutes, then drain and peel. Blanch the snow peas in boiling salted water for 1 minute, then rinse in cold water. Whisk together the dressing ingredients.

Heat the tablespoon of oil in a wok or large skillet until very hot. Add the scallion and stir until soft, about 1 minute. Add the cooked rice and stir over high heat for 3 to 4 minutes, until the rice is lightly coated with oil and mixed with the scallion. Remove the rice, and spread it out on a baking sheet to cool slightly.

While the rice is still warm, mix it in a large bowl with the dressing, shrimp, snow peas, and cilantro. Chill until the rice is cool (at least 10 minutes) and serve cold or at room temperature. Just before serving, mix in the red bell pepper (it often bleeds and discolors a salad if left in too long).

NOTE: You can also use 6 cups of cold cooked rice.

MAKE AHEAD: up to 24 hours; refrigerate

> **MENU**
>
> ❧❧
>
> **FRIED RICE SALAD
> WITH SHRIMP, SNOW PEAS,
> AND SESAME OIL**
>
> **PAPPADUMS OR FRENCH BREAD**
>
> **MANGO SORBET**
>
> ◆
>
> **ASIAN BEER**

THAI MARINATED SHRIMP SALAD

SERVES 4 TO 6 AS A MAIN COURSE

◆

*T*his is a splendid dish combining typical Thai ingredients and textures. Asian or gourmet groceries carry fish sauce and lemon grass.

1¼ pounds medium shrimp, peeled, with tails left on
¾ teaspoon freshly ground black pepper
1 tablespoon fresh lime juice
Pinch kosher salt
1 carrot, shredded
1 head Boston or red leaf lettuce, washed, patted dry, and very thinly sliced or shredded
½ cup chopped roasted unsalted peanuts
2 limes, cut in wedges and dipped in cayenne, for garnish

THAI MARINADE
3 tablespoons fresh lime juice

3 tablespoons *nam pla, nuoc mam Thai,* or Vietnamese fish sauce
2 garlic cloves, mashed to a paste (see box, page 62)
¼ large red onion, thinly sliced
2 scallions with greens, minced
One 12-inch stalk lemon grass, minced (optional), available in Asian markets
1 tablespoon chopped fresh cilantro
½ teaspoon cayenne
1 small serrano chili, seeded and minced
1 bunch fresh mint, leaves only, chopped (about ½ cup packed)

Toss the shrimp with the black pepper, lime juice, and salt. Let sit while you prepare the remaining ingredients and mix the marinade.

Sauté the shrimp in a large dry skillet in a single layer for about 5 minutes, or until pink and curled. Toss the cooked shrimp and the carrot with the marinade

MENU

THAI MARINATED
SHRIMP SALAD

GRILLED SCALLIONS
IN BASIL OIL

FRESH SLICED MANGOES

THAI OR JAPANESE BEER

and chill in the refrigerator for 10 minutes. Just before serving, put the lettuce on a large platter, arrange the shrimp on top of the lettuce, scatter the peanuts on top, and garnish with the lime wedges.

VARIATION: Substitute beef, monkfish, squid, or scallops for the shrimp.

MAKE AHEAD: marinate shrimp and carrot in refrigerator up to 24 hours ahead; arrange on platter with other ingredients just before serving

WINTER PORK LOIN, APPLE, AND HAZELNUT SALAD

SERVES 6 TO 8 AS A MAIN COURSE

◆

*T*his marvelous salad will see you through the autumn and winter, with its hearty ingredients and seasonal flavors.

MENU

❧❧

MINTY PEA SOUP

WINTER PORK LOIN, APPLE,
AND HAZELNUT SALAD

WARM CARAMEL PEARS

◆

ALSATIAN RIESLING,
GERMAN MOSEL, VOUVRAY,
CHENIN BLANC

1½ pounds pork tenderloin (or use
    leftover roast pork loin or smoked
    pork loin, sliced)
2 teaspoons dried thyme
1 teaspoon virgin olive oil
2 red apples, skins on, cut into
    eighths, cored, and evenly chopped
1 head curly endive, white part only
    (see box, page 144), washed and
    dried
2 stalks Belgian endive, root ends
    trimmed, washed, dried, and
    chopped
1 stalk celery, finely chopped
¼ head red cabbage or 2 heads
    radicchio, finely shredded
3 tablespoons raisins, golden or dark,
    plumped in hot water if not soft,
    drained
¼ cup finely chopped toasted
    hazelnuts (see box), for garnish

PARSLEY VINAIGRETTE
½ tablespoon apple cider vinegar
½ tablespoon raspberry wine vinegar
½ teaspoon freshly ground black
    pepper
½ teaspoon kosher salt
2 tablespoons finely minced fresh
    parsley
2 teaspoons Dijon mustard

1 teaspoon honey
4 tablespoons virgin olive oil, canola
    oil, or grapeseed oil

Preheat the oven to 400°. Rub the
pork with the dried thyme, brown it in the
oil in a skillet over high heat, then roast
it for 25 minutes. Cool for 15 minutes and
slice thinly.

While the pork is cooking, whisk together the vinaigrette ingredients. In a
bowl, toss all the greens, vegetables, and
fruits with 3 tablespoons of the vinaigrette. Mound attractively on a large platter. Arrange the meat in the center of the
platter on top of the salad, and drizzle
with the remaining vinaigrette. Sprinkle
with the chopped hazelnuts and serve.

MAKE AHEAD: prepare pork and vinaigrette up to 24 hours ahead; refrigerate;
assemble salad just before serving

❧❧

HOW TO TOAST AND
SKIN HAZELNUTS

◆

*Toasting hazelnuts brings out their
flavor and makes removing their
skins easier. Place the nuts in a
metal baking pan in a preheated
375° oven for 10 minutes, or until
you smell a nutty fragrance, or toast
them on high in a microwave for 3
minutes. When the skins are a
darker brown, rub the nuts vigorously in a terrycloth towel. The fric-
tion will rub off most of the skins,
but rarely all of them. They are not
really undesirable, just a little bitter.*

❧❧

POTATO, CURLY ENDIVE, CELERY ROOT, AND SAUSAGE SALAD

SERVES 6 AS A MAIN COURSE

◆

*H*ere's a hearty main-course salad that is also great as a picnic dish, since it holds and transports well.

12 small or 6 large new potatoes,
    scrubbed, boiled, and sliced
1 pound ring sausage

MUSTARD-SHALLOT VINAIGRETTE
2 tablespoons champagne or tarragon
    wine vinegar
1 large egg yolk
½ teaspoon kosher salt
¼ teaspoon freshly ground pepper
1 teaspoon Dijon mustard
½ cup virgin olive oil
1 large shallot or 3 whole scallions,
    finely chopped
⅓ cup minced fresh parsley

1 head Boston lettuce, washed and
    dried, leaves left whole
One 12-ounce jar julienned celery root,
    rinsed, drained, and sprinkled with
    fresh lemon juice (if unavailable,
    use one 14-ounce can halved
    artichoke hearts or bottoms,
    rinsed and drained)
1 head curly endive, white part only
    (see box, page 144), washed,
    dried, and torn into 1-inch pieces
2 tablespoons minced fresh parsley, for
    garnish

Boil the potatoes until tender but still firm, 15 to 20 minutes. At the same time, cook the sausage as directed in Sausage Cooked the French Way (page 78), but

MENU

◆

POTATO, CURLY ENDIVE, CELERY ROOT, AND SAUSAGE SALAD

WHOLE-WHEAT IRISH SODA BREAD

GINGER-PLUM COBBLER

◆

VOUVRAY, DRY CHENIN BLANC, RIESLING

don't brown. Whisk together the vinaigrette ingredients.

Slice the hot potatoes and toss them with half of the vinaigrette. Slice the sausage thin. Make a bed with the lettuce on a large platter. Fill one-quarter of the platter with the sausage. Fill the second quarter of the platter with the potatoes, using a slotted spoon to drain off most of the vinaigrette. Toss the celery root with half of the remaining vinaigrette and fill the third quarter of the platter. Toss the curly endive with the remaining vinaigrette and fill the fourth quarter of the platter. Garnish with the minced parsley.

MAKE AHEAD: cook potatoes and sausage, make vinaigrette, and toss cooked potatoes and celery root with vinaigrette up to 24 hours ahead; refrigerate

COUSCOUS SALAD

SERVES 6 TO 8 AS A MAIN COURSE, 10 TO 12 AS AN ACCOMPANIMENT

◆

Couscous is a perfect backdrop for this vegetable and herb–based salad. This is really a meal in itself, but if you wish, chicken, beef, or fish complement it nicely. Bulgur can be used instead of couscous, but it takes a little longer to prepare.

1 cup water or chicken stock
1 cup couscous
⅛ teaspoon kosher salt
1 large red bell pepper, seeded and finely diced
2 serrano chilies, seeded and minced
2 small tomatoes, seeded and chopped
2 zucchini, finely chopped, shredded, or thinly sliced
5 scallions with greens, minced
2 garlic cloves, mashed to a paste (see box, page 62)
2 tablespoons chopped fresh basil (see box, page 88)
½ cup chopped fresh cilantro
⅓ cup chopped fresh mint
2 tablespoons white-wine vinegar
⅓ cup virgin olive oil
Kosher salt
Freshly ground pepper to taste
6 large lettuce leaves, washed
3 ounces goat or feta cheese

Boil the water and pour over the couscous and salt in a large bowl; stir and cover. Let stand for 5 to 8 minutes, or until all the liquid has been absorbed.

Add all the chopped vegetables and herbs, the vinegar and oil, and salt and pepper to taste to the warm couscous and toss together to mix well. Taste for seasoning. Chill for at least 10 minutes. Just before serving, arrange the lettuce leaves on a large platter, spoon the salad over them, and crumble or slice the goat cheese on top.

MAKE AHEAD: mix couscous, vegetables, and seasonings up to 24 hours ahead; refrigerate; add lettuce and cheese just before serving

MENU

◆

HUMMUS

COUSCOUS SALAD

WARM BLUEBERRY CRISP

◆

LAGER BEER

WARM ASPARAGUS AND PASTA SALAD WITH HAZELNUTS AND PROSCIUTTO

SERVES 2 TO 4 AS A MAIN COURSE

◆

*T*his unusual dish was enthusiastically received by a European audience at a cooking class I taught at three-star-chef Pierre Romeyer's cooking school in Brussels. The flavors of toasted hazelnuts, asparagus, prosciutto, and balsamic vinegar are stunning when combined in one dish.

MENU

ജ

HOMEMADE BOURSIN WITH SUN-DRIED TOMATOES

WARM ASPARAGUS AND PASTA SALAD WITH HAZELNUTS, PROSCIUTTO, AND BALSAMIC VINAIGRETTE

QUICK BLACKBERRY SORBET

◆

CHARDONNAY

---

3 quarts water
1 tablespoon kosher salt
1 tablespoon olive oil
½ pound dry medium farfalle (bow-tie or butterfly pasta)
1 tablespoon virgin olive oil
1 bunch fresh asparagus (see box, page 34), thick ends snapped off, cut on a diagonal into 2-inch pieces

BALSAMIC VINAIGRETTE
½ large red onion, thinly sliced
½ tablespoon olive oil
1 shallot, minced
2½ tablespoons balsamic vinegar
1 teaspoon kosher salt, or to taste

½ teaspoon freshly ground black pepper
Scant ⅓ cup virgin olive oil (or use ¼ cup hazelnut oil and ⅛ cup virgin olive oil)

4 thin slices prosciutto, cut into 1 × ½-inch strips
⅓ cup chopped toasted and skinned hazelnuts (see box, page 120)
1 teaspoon grated lemon zest

Bring the water to a boil, add the salt and the 1 tablespoon olive oil, and cook the pasta until *al dente,* about 10 minutes. Drain and toss with the 1 tablespoon virgin olive oil. Meanwhile, cook the asparagus in 2 inches of boiling salted water in a large sauté pan for about 5 to 7 minutes, or until barely cooked through. Drain.

In a small skillet, sauté the red onion in the ½ tablespoon olive oil until lightly browned. Combine the onion with the remaining dressing ingredients in the bottom of a shallow serving bowl. Add the drained hot pasta, asparagus, prosciutto, and hazelnuts, and toss well. Sprinkle the lemon zest evenly over the top of the salad and serve warm, or chill 30 minutes in the refrigerator and serve cold.

MAKE AHEAD: prepare up to 24 hours ahead; refrigerate

LUNCHEON OR ACCOMPANIMENT SALADS

◆

OAKLEAF LETTUCE, GREEN BEAN, WALNUT, AND ROQUEFORT SALAD

SERVES 2 AS A LUNCHEON SALAD, 4 AS AN ACCOMPANIMENT

◆

*H*ere's a beautiful, easy-to-prepare salad for any season. For a perfect meal, add medium-rare New York strip steak, thinly sliced. Oakleaf lettuce is one of my favorite varieties; the eggplant-colored leaves enhance any salad.

½ pound fresh or frozen green beans, trimmed and cut into 2-inch pieces

LEMON-WALNUT DRESSING
2½ tablespoons fresh lemon juice
½ teaspoon kosher salt
½ teaspoon freshly ground black pepper
3 tablespoons virgin olive oil
3 tablespoons walnut oil

1 bunch oakleaf lettuce (or use red leaf, Boston, or romaine lettuce), washed, dried, and torn
2 ounces Roquefort cheese, crumbled or thinly sliced
⅓ cup walnut halves, toasted (see box)

TOASTING NUTS

◆

*T*oasting nuts brings out their flavor. Spread the nuts in a small metal baking pan and toast in a preheated 375° oven for 5 to 10 minutes, or until fragrant and lightly browned. Or, microwave on high for 3 minutes.

Finely chopped fresh chives or dill, for garnish
½ teaspoon grated lemon rind, for garnish

Cook the green beans, uncovered, in boiling unsalted water until tender, 4 to 6 minutes. Drain. Whisk together the dressing ingredients. Just before serving, toss the lettuce, beans, cheese, and walnuts with the dressing. Arrange on a platter, and garnish with the chives and lemon rind.

VARIATIONS: For a main-course salad, add 4 to 6 ounces pan-sautéed New York strip steak, cut in slices and served at room temperature; or half a roasted or boiled chicken without skin, cut into thin strips; or 4 to 6 ounces leftover rare roast beef, cut in thin slices.

Mesclun Salad with Goat-Cheese Croutons

SERVES 8 TO 10 AS A LUNCHEON SALAD

◆

Mesclun, a specialty of Provence, consists of young cuttings of many different kinds of tender native lettuces and herbs. The goat-cheese (*chèvre*) croutons make this a beautiful combined salad-and-cheese course; they can also be served by themselves as a delicious hors d'oeuvre. If you see small, tender, unusual lettuces in your farmer's market in spring and early summer, use them instead of or in addition to the varieties listed below. Mesclun can also be bought mixed in some stores.

1 stalk Belgian endive, root end trimmed, washed, leaves separated

1 head radicchio, washed, dried, and torn

1 head escarole, white parts only (see box, page 144), washed, dried, and torn

1 head oakleaf or red leaf lettuce, washed, dried, and torn

1 head curly endive, white parts only (see box, page 144), washed, dried, and torn

1 head Boston lettuce, washed, dried, and torn

◆ GARLICKY DRESSING

2 tablespoons balsamic vinegar

½ teaspoon kosher salt

¼ teaspoon black pepper

1 garlic clove, mashed to a paste (see box, page 62)

½ cup virgin olive oil, or ¼ cup virgin and ¼ cup extra-virgin olive oil

GOAT-CHEESE CROUTONS

1 baguette, cut into sixteen to twenty ¼-inch slices

Virgin olive oil or butter

12 ounces goat cheese

Prepare all the greens and combine in a large bowl. Whisk together the dressing ingredients. Dry the bread slices in a 350° oven for about 8 minutes, brush them on one side with oil, and spread them with the goat cheese. Just before serving, heat the croutons in the broiler 4 inches from the flame or in a 425° oven, until the cheese warms and softens but does not brown. Toss the greens with the dressing and serve on individual plates topped with two warm croutons per serving.

ROMAINE AND CHERRY TOMATO SALAD WITH A CREAMY CAESAR DRESSING

SERVES 4 AS A LUNCHEON SALAD, 6 AS AN ACCOMPANIMENT

◆

I like the crunchy textures here. This salad is quite filling; add a grilled, sliced chicken breast and you have a whole meal.

CREAMY CAESAR DRESSING
2 large egg yolks
2 small garlic cloves
5 anchovy fillets, rinsed, drained, and patted dry
⅓ cup fresh lemon or lime juice
1 tablespoon red-wine vinegar
½ teaspoon kosher salt
½ teaspoon freshly ground black pepper
⅔ cup virgin olive oil
½ teaspoon Worcestershire sauce

1 head romaine lettuce, washed, dried, and torn into pieces (see box, page 131)

16 cherry tomatoes, halved
1½ cups ½-inch store-bought croutons
⅓ cup freshly grated Italian Parmesan or crumbled feta or goat cheese

Puree all the dressing ingredients in a blender. Toss the lettuce, tomatoes, and croutons with the dressing in a large bowl, sprinkle with the cheese, and serve immediately.

MAKE AHEAD: make dressing up to 24 hours ahead; refrigerate; toss just before serving

CHUNKY GAZPACHO SALAD

SERVES 4 AS A LUNCHEON SALAD, 8 AS AN ACCOMPANIMENT

◆

*T*he great thing about this salad is that any leftovers, pureed and thinned with V-8 juice, can become tomorrow's gazpacho soup. The crisp textures of this filling salad are a perfect foil for a quiche or frittata.

CUMIN DRESSING
4 tablespoons red-wine vinegar
½ teaspoon kosher salt
½ teaspoon freshly ground black
      pepper
1 teaspoon ground cumin, toasted (see
      box, page 214)
¼ teaspoon dried basil
¼ teaspoon dried oregano
1 small garlic clove, mashed to a paste
      (see box, page 62)
3 tablespoons extra-virgin olive oil
3 tablespoons virgin olive oil
2 tablespoons V-8 juice
2 tablespoons chopped fresh parsley
      (optional)

2 cucumbers, peeled, halved
      lengthwise, seeded (see box), and
      thinly sliced
1 green bell pepper, seeded, cut
      lengthwise into ¼ × 2-inch slivers,
      then halved crosswise
1 red bell pepper, seeded, cut
      lengthwise into ¼ × 2-inch slivers,
      then halved crosswise
½ red onion, very finely minced
2 whole scallions, very thinly sliced
4 large ripe tomatoes, or 4 cups
      canned drained Italian plum
      tomatoes

CUCUMBERS

◆

*C*ucumbers taste much better in all dishes if the watery, bitter seed section is completely removed. Cut the cucumber in half lengthwise, scoop out the seeds and watery pulp with a small spoon, and discard.

---

8 leaves romaine, washed, dried, and
      broken in pieces or very finely
      shredded or sliced
1½ cups store-bought croutons
Fresh nasturtium blossoms (see box,
      page 29), for garnish (optional)

Whisk together the dressing ingredients. Toss the vegetables, lettuce, and dressing together in a bowl and refrigerate until ready to serve. Add the croutons and nasturtiums just before serving.

MAKE AHEAD: toss the vegetables with dressing up to 24 hours ahead; refrigerate; just before serving add lettuce and croutons, and toss again

POTATO AND ROQUEFORT SALAD WITH SHALLOT DRESSING

SERVES 6 TO 8 AS A LUNCHEON SALAD, 10 AS AN ACCOMPANIMENT

◆

*T*his is the most delectable potato salad I have ever tasted. Roquefort cheese, mustard, bacon, shallots, and chives all conspire here to bring optimal flavor to the humble potato.

2 pounds small new potatoes
6 slices slab bacon

SHALLOT DRESSING
3 tablespoons tarragon-flavored white-wine vinegar
¾ teaspoon kosher salt, or to taste
½ teaspoon freshly ground black pepper
3 large shallots, finely minced
1 teaspoon Dijon mustard
9 tablespoons Provençal or other extra-virgin olive oil
2 tablespoons finely minced fresh parsley

2 heads Boston, red leaf, or oakleaf lettuce, washed and dried, left whole
½ cup Roquefort cheese, crumbled
½ to ¾ cup heavy cream, Crème Fraîche (page 210), or light cream
½ bunch watercress, washed, stems removed, and dried
2 tablespoons fresh chives, finely chopped

Boil the potatoes in salted water for about 20 minutes, or until they are tender when pierced with a fork; do not overcook. While the potatoes are cooking, cook the bacon in a large heavy skillet until lightly browned. Drain on a paper towel and crumble. Prepare the dressing: Put the vinegar, salt, pepper, shallot, and mustard in a small bowl and stir until the salt dissolves. Slowly pour in the oil by droplets while whisking continuously. Whisk in the parsley and set aside.

While still warm, peel (see Note) and slice the potatoes about ½ inch thick. Place in a bowl and toss very gently with one-third to one-half of the vinaigrette. Overlap the lettuce on a large platter. Arrange the potato slices in long, even rows on top of the lettuce and arrange the watercress leaves in between the rows. Add the Roquefort and cream to the remaining vinaigrette, mix well, and spoon it over the potatoes. Crumble the bacon over the potatoes, sprinkle with the chives, and serve at room temperature. Or, if you wish, toss all the ingredients except the lettuce and watercress, and arrange the salad over the greens.

NOTE: You can cook and serve the new potatoes unpeeled if you wish; they just look neater peeled.

MAKE AHEAD: cook the potatoes and toss in vinaigrette up to 24 hours ahead; refrigerate; assemble the remaining ingredients just before serving

ENDIVE AND AVOCADO SALAD WITH TOASTED WALNUTS AND WALNUT-OIL VINAIGRETTE

SERVES 2 AS A LUNCHEON SALAD, 4 AS AN ACCOMPANIMENT

◆

*T*his is a delicious combination of ingredients, the slightly bitter flavor of endive and walnut contrasting wonderfully with the richness of avocado.

WALNUT-OIL VINAIGRETTE
2 tablespoons fresh lemon or lime juice, or champagne vinegar
2 teaspoons Dijon mustard
½ teaspoon kosher salt
¼ teaspoon freshly ground black pepper
¼ cup walnut oil
2 tablespoons canola or grapeseed oil

¼ cup coarsely chopped, toasted walnuts (see box, page 124)
2 large stalks Belgian endive, root ends trimmed, washed, and sliced crosswise into 1-inch pieces
1 large avocado, peeled, cut in

quarters lengthwise, then cut crosswise into ½-inch slices

Whisk together the vinaigrette ingredients. Just before serving, toss the walnuts, endive, and avocado with the vinaigrette and place in a colorful shallow bowl.

VARIATION: For an elegant light meal, add ¾ pound shrimp or crayfish, peeled and simmered for 3 to 4 minutes over medium-high heat.

MAKE AHEAD: toast the walnuts and make the vinaigrette up to 24 hours ahead; refrigerate

CHEESE SALAD WITH RADISHES, SCALLIONS, AND PARSLEY VINAIGRETTE

SERVES 4 AS A LUNCHEON SALAD, 6 AS AN ACCOMPANIMENT

◆

*I*nspired by home-style salads I've tasted in Switzerland and Germany, I developed this hearty, pungent dish. Served with a filling soup and a dark bread, it makes a very good Sunday supper. The Parsley Vinaigrette is excellent with roast beef or pork.

PARSLEY VINAIGRETTE
2 tablespoons champagne vinegar
½ teaspoon kosher salt
¼ teaspoon freshly ground black
    pepper
1½ teaspoons Dijon mustard
½ teaspoon dried basil
⅓ cup finely minced fresh parsley
½ cup virgin olive oil

1 head Boston, red leaf, or oakleaf
    lettuce, washed and dried
5 ounces imported Emmentaler,
    Muenster, or Havarti cheese, cut
    into ½-inch cubes
1 bunch red radishes, finely shredded

or thinly sliced in a food processor
4 scallions with 3 inches of green,
    finely chopped

Whisk together the vinaigrette ingredients. Arrange the lettuce on a platter. Toss the cheese, radishes, and scallions with the vinaigrette in a bowl and arrange on top of the lettuce.

MAKE AHEAD: prepare the vinaigrette up to 4 hours ahead; refrigerate; assemble the salad just before serving; toss the cheese, radishes, and scallions in vinaigrette

AN EASY FRENCH CAESAR SALAD

SERVES 4 AS A LUNCHEON SALAD, 6 AS AN ACCOMPANIMENT

*T*his has almost all the elements of a true Caesar salad, but with a French twist. It tastes a little different and is delicious!

2 eggs
Two ¾-inch slices French or Italian
    bread
1 garlic clove, split in half

MUSTARD VINAIGRETTE
2 tablespoons champagne vinegar
¾ teaspoon kosher salt
¼ teaspoon freshly ground black
    pepper
2 teaspoons Dijon mustard
½ cup extra-virgin olive oil

1 head romaine, washed, dried, and
    torn into large pieces (see box,
    opposite page)
6 anchovy fillets, rinsed and drained
½ cup finely grated Gruyère,
    Emmentaler, or Comté cheese

Pierce the large end of the eggs with a pin. In a small saucepan, bring water to a boil and simmer the eggs gently, uncovered, for 6 minutes. While the eggs are cooking, dry the bread in a preheated 400° oven for 5 minutes. Rub the slices on one side with the garlic, and break into croutons.

Plunge the cooked eggs in a bowl of cold water, and leave for 10 minutes. Then crack eggs, remove shells, and cut in half lengthwise.

Whisk together the vinaigrette ingre-dients. Toss the lettuce with the vinai-grette and arrange on a platter. Add the anchovies and croutons, sprinkle on the cheese, top with the egg halves, and serve.

MAKE AHEAD: prepare croutons and vinaigrette up to 24 hours ahead; refrig-erate; cook eggs and assemble salad just before serving

THE ORIGINAL CAESAR SALAD

SERVES 2 AS A LUNCHEON SALAD, 4 AS AN ACCOMPANIMENT

◆

*L*ike chili, barbecue, and bouillabaisse, much has been written and disputed about Caesar salad. This version, by far the most subtle, it seems to me, comes from my friend, artist and food stylist JoAnn Williams, who vows it is the orig-inal Caesar salad of its creator, Caesar Cardini. Follow the recipe exactly for the best Caesar salad you've ever eaten. And use the delicious anchovy croutons on other green salads.

ROMAINE LETTUCE

◆

The long (rib) end of romaine let-tuce is unattractive and undesirable in a salad. Instead of cutting off the rib of each individual leaf, I cut about 4 inches off the stalk of the head before washing. This gives nice-looking, usable leaves of lettuce and saves time. Wash the discarded stalk and use it, shredded, in soups, such as the Broccoli Soup, or in any pu-reed vegetable soup.

Six ½-inch slices French bread
6 tablespoons extra-virgin olive oil
3 garlic cloves
6 anchovy fillets
10 to 12 large romaine leaves, washed, dried, and broken in half (see box)
1 large egg
1½ to 2 tablespoons fresh lime juice
1 teaspoon Worcestershire sauce
¼ cup freshly grated Italian Parmesan
½ teaspoon freshly ground black pepper

Preheat the oven to 400°. Dry the bread slices for 5 minutes, turning them once. Brush them on both sides with 1½ tablespoons of the olive oil and return them to oven until golden-brown, 4 to 5 minutes. Meanwhile, pound together the garlic and anchovy fillets in a mortar, adding 1 tablespoon of the olive oil to make a spread. Spread the anchovy mixture evenly on the toasted bread slices, then cut these into cubes or croutons, not larger than ½ × ½ inch.

Place the romaine in a large salad bowl. In a small saucepan, bring water to a boil and cook the egg for 2 minutes. Put

the remaining 3½ tablespoons of olive oil into a small bowl, crack the egg into it, and beat the oil and egg with a whisk until well mixed.

Sprinkle the greens with the lime juice, Worcestershire, cheese, pepper, and the egg-and-oil mixture, and toss until the dressing covers all the leaves. Add the croutons and toss again. Serve immediately.

MAKE AHEAD: make the croutons up to 2 hours ahead

CLASSIC GREEK SALAD

SERVES 2 TO 4 AS A LUNCHEON SALAD, 6 AS AN ACCOMPANIMENT

◆

*T*his ample, healthy Mediterranean salad is the perfect accompaniment to grilled lamb or chicken. Try to find fresh oregano; even a small amount enhances the vinaigrette.

OREGANO VINAIGRETTE
¼ cup red-wine vinegar
¾ teaspoon kosher salt
¼ teaspoon freshly ground black
    pepper
2 teaspoons chopped fresh oregano (if
    unavailable, use ½ teaspoon dried,
    plus extra for serving)
⅓ cup extra-virgin olive oil, or 2½
    tablespoons extra-virgin and 2½
    tablespoons virgin, plus extra for
    serving

1 medium head romaine lettuce,

washed, dried, and torn (see box,
    page 131)
1 small cucumber, peeled and thinly
    sliced
4 radishes, thinly sliced
3 scallions with 3 inches green, finely
    chopped
12 large Kalamata olives
2 tomatoes, each cut into 8 wedges
¼ pound feta cheese, rinsed, drained,
    dried, and cut into ½-inch slices
2 to 4 anchovies, rinsed and drained
    (optional)
Freshly ground black pepper

Whisk together the vinaigrette ingredients. Toss all the salad ingredients except the tomatoes, feta, and anchovies with the vinaigrette and place on a large platter. Arrange the tomatoes, feta, and anchovies on top. Sprinkle with a bit

more chopped oregano and olive oil and a grinding of black pepper, and serve.

MAKE AHEAD: make vinaigrette up to 24 hours ahead; refrigerate

MIXED GREEN SALAD WITH GOAT CHEESE AND TOASTED PINE NUTS

SERVES 6 AS A LUNCHEON SALAD, 8 TO 10 AS AN ACCOMPANIMENT

*T*his delicious combination of ingredients can be served as is or "expanded" to become a main course or a light whole meal. It allows for creative and simple use of leftovers: last night's dinner becomes part of tonight's salad. Or prepare a little extra meat, chicken, or fish the night before to have enough for this light supper.

RASPBERRY-BASIL VINAIGRETTE
¼ cup raspberry vinegar
½ teaspoon kosher salt
¼ teaspoon freshly ground black
   pepper
¼ teaspoon dried basil
¾ to 1 cup Italian virgin olive oil

1 head Boston lettuce, washed, dried,
   and torn
1 head red leaf or oakleaf lettuce,
   washed, dried, and torn
1 head curly endive, white part only
   (see box, page 144), washed,
   dried, and torn
1 head radicchio, washed, dried, and
   torn
½ cup pine nuts, toasted (see box,
   page 134)
½ cup goat or feta cheese, crumbled

EXPANSION OPTIONS
Grilled, baked, or poached chicken
   breast, in thin strips
Grilled or sautéed steak, in thin slices
Warm or cold roast duck, in slices
Warm or cold roast pork loin, in strips
½ roast cornish hen, in strips
Grilled redfish fillet, in diagonal strips
Poached or grilled scallops
Cooked green beans
Roasted red peppers

Whisk together the vinaigrette ingredients. Just before serving, toss the greens with three-quarters of the vinaigrette. Taste for seasoning and arrange on a large platter. Scatter the pine nuts, cheese, and optional ingredients (if using)

on top, drizzle with the remaining vinaigrette, and serve.

NOTE: Escarole, romaine, or watercress
can be used in place of any of the lettuces.

MAKE AHEAD: make the vinaigrette and
toast the pine nuts up to 24 hours ahead;
refrigerate; assemble the salad just before serving

TOASTING PINE NUTS

*P*ut the pine nuts in a small skillet
over medium heat. Stir or shake for
3 or 4 minutes, until the nuts turn a
golden color. Be sure they don't
burn. They can also be toasted in a
preheated 350° oven for 10 minutes,
but they need to be watched and
stirred so they brown evenly.

TOASTED GOAT CHEESE IN
GREEN VINAIGRETTE

SERVES 6 AS A LUNCHEON SALAD, 8 AS AN ACCOMPANIMENT

◆

*T*his California cuisine–inspired dish can be served as a first course, a lunch
dish, or as a salad course. The greens in the vinaigrette are blanched, which
gives them more flavor when pureed.

8 ounces goat cheese, cut in 6 even
    slices
3 tablespoons extra-virgin olive oil
1¼ cups very fine fresh bread crumbs
    (prepared in a food processor),
    mixed with 1 teaspoon dried thyme

GREEN VINAIGRETTE
2 quarts water
Pinch kosher salt
1 pound fresh spinach, washed (see
    box, page 254)
1 bunch watercress (about ¼ pound),
    washed
½ cup extra-virgin olive oil

¼ cup virgin olive oil
4 tablespoons champagne vinegar
½ teaspoon kosher salt
½ teaspoon freshly ground black
    pepper

4 fresh nasturtium or begonia flowers
    (see box, page 29), for garnish
    (optional)

Preheat the oven to 450°. Put the 2
quarts of water on to boil (for blanching
the greens). Dip the goat cheese slices in
the olive oil, then roll them in the bread

crumbs. Place them on a baking sheet and refrigerate until ready to bake.

Add the salt to the boiling water, plunge in the greens, and cook, uncovered, for 2 minutes. Drain and press dry. Place the greens and the remaining dressing ingredients in a food processor and blend until finely pureed.

Bake the goat cheese for about 5 minutes, or until lightly browned and soft but not runny. Make a pool of ⅓ cup of the green vinaigrette on each of six salad plates, then place a piece of hot goat cheese on top. Garnish with the flowers if desired, and serve immediately.

SCALLOP AND LEEK SALAD WITH RASPBERRY-CHIVE VINAIGRETTE

SERVES 6 TO 8 AS A LUNCHEON SALAD, 8 TO 10 AS AN ACCOMPANIMENT

◆

*T*his delightful salad lends itself to springtime and terrace lunches very nicely.

1 cup chicken broth
4 leeks, well washed (see box, page 136) and julienned
½ pound sea or bay scallops, cleaned of sand but not rinsed (see box, page 68)

RASPBERRY-CHIVE VINAIGRETTE
3 tablespoons raspberry wine vinegar
½ teaspoon kosher salt
¼ teaspoon freshly ground white pepper
⅛ teaspoon dried marjoram
¼ cup fresh chives, finely chopped
3 tablespoons minced fresh parsley
⅔ cup canola oil, virgin olive oil, or safflower oil

1 head oakleaf or red leaf lettuce, washed, dried, and torn
¼ pound fresh mushrooms, thinly sliced (see Note)
2 stalks celery, very thinly sliced on the diagonal
1 red bell pepper, seeded and julienned
5 fresh mint sprigs, for garnish

Bring the broth to a boil in a medium saucepan and simmer the leek for about 8 minutes. Remove the leek and drain. Add the scallops to the hot broth, cook for 2 minutes, remove, and drain.

Whisk together the vinaigrette ingredients and taste for seasoning. Arrange the lettuce on a large platter. Carefully toss all the vegetables and the scallops with the dressing and arrange over the lettuce. Garnish with mint and chill for 10 minutes before serving.

NOTE: Sprinkle the mushrooms with lemon juice if cutting in advance and holding.

VARIATION: Instead of poaching the scallops in hot chicken broth, you can sear them for 1½ minutes on each side in a very hot dry skillet.

CLEANING LEEKS

◆

Leeks harbor a lot of dirt and need to be carefully washed. Cut off the root end and the green stalk, then slice the leek in half lengthwise, leaving it connected at the root end. Soak it for a few minutes in a bowl of tepid water. Swish it around, rinse thoroughly, and drain. Or slice or chop with dirt left in, then soak and rinse thoroughly in a colander.

ACCOMPANIMENT SALADS

◆

GREEN SALAD FROM NORMANDY

SERVES 6 AS AN ACCOMPANIMENT

◆

*A*lthough it may seem extravagant to use cream in place of oil, the very delicate, clean flavor of this dressing is a refreshing change from ordinary oil-based vinaigrettes. In Normandy, *crème fraîche* dressing is especially appreciated on tender spring greens and lettuces. The dressing should be made just before serving or it will thicken too much.

2 heads Boston lettuce, washed, dried, and torn
1 head oakleaf or red leaf lettuce, washed, dried, and torn

CRÈME FRAÎCHE DRESSING
⅔ cup Crème Fraîche (page 210)
2 to 3 tablespoons fresh lemon juice,

or to taste
¼ teaspoon kosher salt
Freshly ground black pepper

Prepare the greens, whisk together the dressing ingredients, and toss just before serving.

SIMPLE MIXED GREEN SALAD WITH FRENCH VINAIGRETTE

SERVES 4 AS AN ACCOMPANIMENT

◆

*N*othing is more satisfying in the course of grand or small meals than a good simple green salad. In France, a salad of greens traditionally comes after the main course, occupying its own place on the menu. But whether you serve it as a first course, with the main course, or after, keep it simple. Use two or three different kinds of greens if available, but don't add tomatoes or vegetables, especially if it is to be eaten at the end of a meal—a plain green salad serves at this point to refresh and cleanse the palate. And do use good-quality olive oils and wine vinegars—they are really worth the cost.

2 small or 1 large head Boston, oakleaf, red leaf, or romaine lettuce, washed, dried, and torn

FRENCH VINAIGRETTE
1 tablespoon red- or white-wine vinegar, balsamic vinegar, or Spanish sherry wine vinegar (never use distilled or cider vinegar)
¼ to ½ teaspoon kosher salt
¼ teaspoon freshly ground black pepper
Pinch dried basil
1 teaspoon prepared Dijon mustard (never use dry mustard)

3 to 4 tablespoons virgin or extra-virgin olive oil
½ to 1 tablespoon of one or more of the following chopped fresh herbs: parsley, chives, oregano, thyme, or basil (optional)

Prepare the greens and chill until ready to serve. Combine the vinaigrette ingredients, in the order in which they are listed, in the bottom of your salad bowl. Toss the cold salad greens with the vinaigrette just before serving.

MAKE AHEAD: prepare vinaigrette up to 3 days ahead; refrigerate

PROVENÇAL SPINACH SALAD

SERVES 4 TO 6 AS AN ACCOMPANIMENT

◆

*T*his unusual salad, made from ordinary ingredients, is particularly colorful and flavorful. I really love the aromatic effect of the thin shreds of orange peel scattered on top of the salad just before serving. Try using the zest over other salads—the orange or lemon flavor will brighten them up. The dressing has a clean, sharp taste. Use it over cooked vegetables, such as carrots, green beans, potatoes, or beets.

LEMON-AND-OIL DRESSING
2 tablespoons fresh lemon juice
7 tablespoons extra-virgin olive oil
1 teaspoon Dijon mustard
½ teaspoon kosher salt
½ teaspoon freshly ground black
    pepper
½ garlic clove, mashed to a paste (see
    box, page 62)
¼ teaspoon dried basil
¼ teaspoon dried oregano
1 tablespoon minced fresh parsley

1 stalk celery, washed and very thinly
    sliced on the diagonal
½ *each* red and green bell pepper,
    seeded and very thinly sliced
1 bunch fresh spinach, washed, dried,
and torn (see box, page 254)
1 head romaine lettuce, washed, dried,
    and torn
⅓ cup Niçoise olives (or other
    imported French or Greek black
    olives)
Zest of ½ large navel orange, cut in
    long, thin shreds

Whisk together the dressing ingredients. Toss all the salad ingredients except the orange zest with the dressing. Place on a large platter or in a very shallow bowl, and scatter the zest over the salad.

MAKE AHEAD: prepare dressing up to 24 hours ahead; refrigerate

GREEN SALAD WITH WALNUT OIL–MUSTARD VINAIGRETTE

SERVES 6 AS AN ACCOMPANIMENT

♦

Walnut oil adds a wonderfully subtle nut flavor to salad dressings. This dressing is excellent for any winter greens.

WALNUT OIL–MUSTARD VINAIGRETTE
2 tablespoons Spanish sherry wine
    vinegar
½ teaspoon kosher salt
¼ teaspoon freshly ground black
    pepper
2 teaspoons Dijon mustard
2 shallots, minced

2 tablespoons extra-virgin olive oil
2 tablespoons virgin olive oil
4 tablespoons walnut oil (see box)

4 quarts washed, dried, and torn mixed
    greens (choose as many of the
    following as you can: red leaf
    lettuce, Boston lettuce, oakleaf
    lettuce, romaine, Belgian endive,
    curly endive, escarole [see box,
    page 144], and radicchio)
½ cup walnut halves, lightly toasted
    (see box, page 124)

Whisk together the dressing ingredients. Just before serving, toss the greens with the dressing, place on a large platter, and scatter with the toasted walnuts.

VARIATIONS: Substitute hazelnuts and hazelnut oil for the walnuts and walnut oil, and add 1 cup pithless orange sections if you wish. (Instructions for toasting hazelnuts are on page 120.) Use the

NUT-FLAVORED OILS

Walnut oil is perishable and needs to be kept refrigerated. When I buy it, I always open the container at the checkout counter to see if it is fresh. If it smells rancid, I can replace it right there. It should keep in your refrigerator for 3 to 6 months, but you should always check it before using it. Hazelnut oil, which is just as flavorful, keeps much longer than walnut oil but still needs to be refrigerated.

hazelnut dressing on green beans, or over an all–Belgian endive salad.

MAKE AHEAD: toast nuts and make vinaigrette up to 24 hours ahead; refrigerate

SIMPLE FRENCH MUSHROOM SALAD

SERVES 2 TO 4 AS AN ACCOMPANIMENT

◆

*C*hampignons *au vin blanc* always appeared as a part of the varied cold hors d'oeuvres served in simple, student restaurants when I first lived in Paris. This dish is very good by itself or added to a green dinner salad. It has no oil and keeps well for several days in the refrigerator. Coriander seeds give the mushrooms a delicate piquancy.

½ pound fresh mushrooms, stems left
    on but trimmed, quartered, or
    sliced
½ cup dry white wine
2 shallots, finely minced
½ teaspoon kosher salt
¼ teaspoon freshly ground black
    pepper
1 imported bay leaf
½ teaspoon coriander seeds, crushed
    to a powder in a mortar (see box)
½ teaspoon dried thyme
Dash cayenne or hot Hungarian
    paprika
½ tablespoon fresh lemon juice
½ cup minced fresh parsley

In a heavy-bottomed 3-quart casse-role, combine the mushrooms, wine, shallot, and dry seasonings. Cook over medium heat, covered, for about 10 minutes. Remove the mushrooms and hold.

CORIANDER

◆

Coriander seeds have a delicate, light, spicy flavor that adds a nice touch to salad dressings, marinades, vegetable dishes, tomato sauces, curries, and fish. They are generally crushed in a mortar with a pestle and used in combination with other herbs and spices such as thyme, summer savory, cumin, and cayenne.

Reduce the remaining liquid by half, then add the lemon juice, mushrooms, and parsley. Chill for at least 10 minutes before serving.

MAKE AHEAD: up to 3 days; refrigerate

ITALIAN GREEN SALAD
WITH BASIL-OIL DRESSING

SERVES 4 TO 6 AS AN ACCOMPANIMENT

◆

*T*his unusual method of dressing a salad is typically Italian. The result is intriguingly different.

12 fresh basil leaves
½ cup extra-virgin olive oil
3 to 4 heads lettuce/greens (choose
    three or four of the following: curly
    endive or escarole [see box, page
    144], radicchio, spinach, or

oakleaf, red leaf, or Boston
    lettuce), washed, dried, and torn
Kosher salt
½ to 1 tablespoon red-wine vinegar, or
    to taste
Freshly ground black pepper

Puree the basil and olive oil in a blender. Place the greens in a salad bowl. Sprinkle with salt and the basil oil, then sprinkle with the red-wine vinegar. Toss, check for seasoning, add black pepper to taste, and toss again.

LEEK SALAD
IN MUSTARD-CAPER VINAIGRETTE

SERVES 4 TO 6 AS AN ACCOMPANIMENT

◆

*T*his delicious salad can be served at room temperature or chilled. It's particularly good as an accompaniment to sausage or roast chicken. The mustard-caper vinaigrette is excellent on a salad of romaine lettuce and over cooked, sliced new potatoes.

3 cups chicken broth
½ teaspoon fresh or dried thyme
8 medium leeks, trimmed, leaving only
    1 inch green, and well washed (see
    box, page 136)

MUSTARD-CAPER VINAIGRETTE
3 tablespoons champagne or tarragon
    wine vinegar
½ teaspoon kosher salt
¼ teaspoon freshly ground black
    pepper
2 to 3 teaspoons Dijon mustard
2 teaspoons small capers, rinsed
2 tablespoons minced fresh parsley
½ cup virgin olive oil

OPTIONAL GARNISHES
Roasted red peppers thinly sliced (see
    box, page 35)

1 hard-boiled egg (see box, page 114),
    finely chopped

Heat the broth until simmering. Add the thyme and leeks and simmer, uncovered, until tender, 10 to 15 minutes. Remove the leeks and drain well. While the leeks are cooking, make the vinaigrette: Mix the vinegar, seasonings, and parsley together, then slowly whisk in the oil.

To serve, place the leeks on a serving plate, drizzle with the vinaigrette, and garnish with the pepper and egg, if desired.

MAKE AHEAD: prepare up to 24 hours ahead; refrigerate

FRESH MINTED
YOGURT-AND-CUCUMBER SALAD

SERVES 4 AS AN ACCOMPANIMENT

◆

*I*n India, this salad—a *raita,* as it is called—usually includes about one teaspoon roasted ground cumin and a dash of paprika and omits the mint. It is served more as a cooling condiment than a salad. This version works well as a light complement to a spicy roast chicken or marinated grilled lamb.

2 medium cucumbers, peeled, halved, seeded, and diced (see box, page 127)
8 ounces plain low-fat yogurt
½ teaspoon kosher salt
1 tablespoon fresh lemon or lime juice
¼ cup chopped fresh mint

Combine all of the ingredients in a bowl and refrigerate until ready to serve.

VARIATIONS: Substitute chopped fresh parsley, cilantro, chives, or dill for the mint.

Add ½ peeled, seeded, finely diced tomato and ¼ teaspoon white pepper.

Omit the mint and add 1 teaspoon *each* toasted ground cumin (see box, page 214) and paprika.

MAKE AHEAD: prepare up to 24 hours ahead; refrigerate

THAI CUCUMBER SALAD

SERVES 4 AS AN ACCOMPANIMENT

◆

*T*his salad is a perfect accompaniment for any spicy Thai or Asian entrée, especially grilled *satays* made with chicken or pork, or any plainly cooked lamb, pork, beef, or chicken.

RICE-WINE VINEGAR DRESSING
3 tablespoons champagne or rice-wine vinegar
2 teaspoons water
1 tablespoon sugar
1 serrano or jalapeño chili, seeded and cut into thin rings
Pinch kosher salt

1 large cucumber, well washed, dried, skin left on and scored with a fork, cut in half lengthwise, seeded, and sliced ½ inch thick
1 tablespoon sesame seeds, toasted (see box, page 67), for garnish
Cilantro leaves, for garnish

Combine the dressing ingredients and stir to dissolve the sugar. Toss the sliced cucumbers with the dressing and chill. Serve cold in 4-ounce ramekins or small individual condiment dishes, sprinkled with the sesame seeds and cilantro.

VARIATIONS: Add any or all of the fol-lowing: 1 teaspoon fresh ginger juice (in the dressing); 1½ tablespoons finely chopped unsalted peanuts; ½ tablespoon very finely diced seeded red bell pepper.

MAKE AHEAD: prepare up to 24 hours ahead; refrigerate

Winter Salad Greens with Cranberry-Orange Vinaigrette

SERVES 6 AS AN ACCOMPANIMENT

◆

*T*art and sweet, the dressing for this colorful, festive salad makes it an excel-lent choice for a holiday meal, to complement a roast turkey or goose, pork loin, or prime ribs.

1 stalk Belgian endive, root end trimmed, washed, leaves separated

1 head curly endive, white stalks only (see box, page 144), washed, dried, and torn

1 head escarole, white stalks only (see box, page 144), washed, dried, and torn

1 bunch watercress, washed and dried, stems trimmed

1 head radicchio, washed, dried, and torn

1 head Boston lettuce, washed, dried, and torn

CRANBERRY-ORANGE VINAIGRETTE
2 tablespoons Spanish sherry wine vinegar or other red-wine vinegar

½ teaspoon kosher salt
⅓ to ½ cup olive oil
¼ teaspoon freshly ground black pepper
Finely grated rind of 1 orange
2 shallots, minced
½ cup finely minced cranberries (mince by hand or in food processor)
2 tablespoons fresh orange juice

Prepare the greens and whisk to-gether the vinaigrette ingredients. Just before serving, toss the cold, crisp greens with the vinaigrette and arrange on a large platter.

Autumn Salad of Bitter Greens, Sweet Pears, and Goat Cheese

SERVES 6 AS AN ACCOMPANIMENT

◆

A good salad course served after the main course may eliminate the craving for a rich dessert, especially if fruit or cheese figures as part of the salad. Here, the salad, cheese, and dessert courses are combined in one beautiful, flavorful dish.

1 head *each* escarole and curly endive, white stalks only (see box), washed, dried, and torn

1 head radicchio, washed, dried, and torn

1 head oakleaf or red leaf lettuce, washed, dried, and torn

1 stalk Belgian endive, root end trimmed, washed, leaves separated

1 large or 2 small ripe Comice pears, peeled and thinly sliced (if Comice are unavailable, substitute Bosc or Anjou)

HAZELNUT-OIL VINAIGRETTE
2 tablespoons balsamic vinegar

½ teaspoon kosher salt

¼ teaspoon freshly ground black pepper

1 teaspoon Dijon mustard

3 tablespoons hazelnut oil

5 tablespoons virgin olive oil

18 thin slices French bread, 3 inches in diameter

Olive oil

12 ounces goat cheese (preferably a firm, aged goat cheese such as one made in New York State), crumbled or sliced

Preheat the oven to 375°. Prepare the greens (leaving them in large pieces) and pears and whisk together the vinaigrette ingredients. Brush the bread lightly with olive oil on one side and toast in the oven until golden-brown, 5 to 7 minutes.

Just before serving, toss the pears and greens in the vinaigrette and arrange on a large platter or in a large shallow bowl. Pass the toasted French bread and the goat cheese separately.

MAKE AHEAD: make vinaigrette up to 24 hours ahead; refrigerate; slice pears and toast bread just before serving

---

❧❧ BITTER GREENS ❧❧

◆

*D*o not use the green part of the leaves of curly endive and escarole. The flavorful, usable part of these two delicious bitter lettuces is the white stalk; the green parts are tough and overly strong-tasting. The green leaves of escarole can be cooked in a soup or braised, but the green leaves of curly endive are not really good for any culinary use.

FESTIVE WINTER FRUIT SALAD

SERVES 2 AS AN ACCOMPANIMENT

◆

*A*s a brunch fruit dish, as a salad, or as a dessert after a rich meal of pork, pheasant, duck, or venison, this jewel-like combination delights with its bright colors, tart flavors, and textures. It makes a perfect addition to a Christmas breakfast.

2 ruby red grapefruit, peeled and cut in sections, pith removed
1 pomegranate
1 tablespoon orange zest, cut with a vegetable parer and very thinly sliced

Place the grapefruit in a small, shallow salad bowl. Cut the pomegranate in half and spoon out all the seeds, reserving the juice. (Be careful—pomegranate juice really stains!) Place the pomegranate seeds and juice on top of the grapefruit sections. Garnish with the orange zest and serve cold.

MAKE AHEAD: up to 24 hours; refrigerate, well-wrapped

APPLES, GRAPES, AND WALNUTS AS SALAD OR DESSERT

SERVES 4 TO 6 AS AN ACCOMPANIMENT

◆

*H*ere is a salad that serves nicely as a dessert too. I love the crisp, crunchy textures and the refreshing clean tastes of lemon and mint.

3 large eating apples (Granny Smith, Pippin, or yellow Delicious), skins on
Juice of 1 lemon
⅓ cup heavy cream, Crème Fraîche (page 210), light cream, or plain yogurt
1½ cups seedless green or red grapes, halved

1 cup walnut halves
2 tablespoons chopped fresh mint
Sprigs of fresh mint, for garnish

Cut each apple into 8 pieces, cut out the cores, and slice crosswise into ¼-inch pieces. Toss in a bowl with the lemon juice. Add the cream, grapes, walnuts, and chopped mint and toss until well mixed. Serve garnished with mint sprigs.

MAKE AHEAD: up to 4 hours, omitting the mint; refrigerate; just before serving, add a little cream and toss with the mint

APPLE, FENNEL, AND WATERCRESS SALAD

SERVES 4 AS AN ACCOMPANIMENT

◆

*T*he bright, sharp flavors and crisp textures of this easy and delicious salad beautifully complement a hearty country pâté, crusty sourdough bread, and a light red wine for a memorable winter supper.

RASPBERRY VINAIGRETTE
2 tablespoons raspberry wine vinegar
⅓ cup virgin olive oil
½ teaspoon kosher salt
¼ teaspoon freshly ground black
   pepper

2 heads fennel, trimmed, cut in half,
   and washed
2 large eating apples (Granny Smith,
   Red Delicious, Jonathan, Pippin,
   etc.), skins on
1 large bunch watercress, washed,
   stems trimmed

Whisk together the dressing ingredients in the bottom of a salad bowl. Cut out the hard core of the fennel, then chop into ½-inch pieces and place in the salad bowl. Cut each apple into 8 wedges, cut out the cores, then cut each wedge into ¼-inch pieces and place in the bowl (see Note). Toss the apples and fennel with the dressing. Add the watercress, toss until well coated, and serve.

NOTE: If making in advance, toss the apples with a little lemon juice, cover, and refrigerate.

MAKE AHEAD: prepare the fennel and apples and make the dressing up to 2 hours ahead; refrigerate; toss with the dressing just before serving

EXOTIC FRUIT SALAD

SERVES 4 TO 6 AS AN ACCOMPANIMENT

◆

*M*ake this wonderful salad/dessert in late summer when all the fruits are in season. The skin of a ripe passion fruit looks very wrinkled and shriveled, but only then is its tart flesh ripe. The sauce is also delicious served over pound cake or strawberries.

1 large papaya, peeled and sliced
1 mango, peeled and sliced
1 small cantaloupe or honeydew
    melon, peeled, thinly sliced

PASSION FRUIT SAUCE
3 tablespoons fresh orange juice
2 tablespoons fresh lime juice
2 tablespoons confectioners' sugar

Pulp and seeds of 4 passion fruit (if
    unavailable, use 2 to 3 peeled kiwi
    fruits)

Fresh mint sprigs, for garnish

Arrange the sliced fruits attractively on a large platter. Pour the sauce over the fruits, garnish with the mint, and serve cold.

♦

VEGETABLES

♦

I often prepare a favorite vegetable dish and a substantial salad for my evening meal if I've worked late. Not only is a meal of asparagus, potatoes, broccoli, or cabbage delicious and quickly made, it is also comforting knowing that vegetarian meals help keep weight down and cholesterol low, and provide necessary fiber for good health. I can happily make a meal of the Sautéed Corn Cakes, the Wild Mushroom Ragoût, or the Red Cabbage with Goat Cheese and Chives. These recipes make the flavors of the vegetables especially vivid, boosting them into the "gourmet" category. In the last few years vegetables have really come into their own as a significant element of the meal, not just as an accompanying dab of color and texture.

Quite a few fresh vegetables can be kept on hand—all members of the onion family and the firmer, or fibrous, vegetables, including fennel, carrots, cabbage, peppers, endive, and potatoes keep a good week if stored properly (see the section on Pantry Storage in chapter 1). More than a dozen of the vegetable recipes here can be made straight from the larder.

I have experimented with a little-used technique for cooking vegetables that I think is terrific—broiling and/or grilling—and many of my recipes use it. The intense heat of the broiler or the outdoor grill, besides being wonderfully quick, brings out added flavor in vegetables and eliminates the wateriness other methods often produce. I especially like the tastes of the Grilled Fennel and the Grilled Scallions in Basil Oil.

Microwaving vegetables (except potatoes, whose texture I find unpleasantly altered) is perhaps one of the best techniques for the quick cook. The trick is not to cook them too long—after about 2½ minutes the textures change. I like to combine four or six different kinds of vegetables, cut them up into same-size pieces, put them in a bowl, add 1 or 2 tablespoons of water, and microwave them. The result is delicious. I use only a little salt and pepper to season.

Blanching vegetables (cooking them, uncovered, in simmering salted water until just barely done) is also simple and fast, and yields delicious results. Pureeing cooked vegetables, such as potatoes, parsnips, turnips, sweet potatoes, carrots, winter squashes, peas, cauliflower, broccoli, leeks, and asparagus, gives the quick cook delicious, homey vegetable dishes, especially in winter. The methods described in my recipes for French Mashed Potatoes with Garlic and Cream or Puree of Peas can be applied to many other vegetables. The following puree combinations are especially good: parsnips and carrots; turnips and potatoes; sweet potatoes and carrots; butternut squash and apples; and cauliflower and potatoes. Using a *mini-pimer* or hand blender to puree in the saucepan saves dishes and fuss (see box, page 32).

HOW TO MAKE FLAVORFUL HERB OILS OR GARLIC OIL FOR SEASONING

To make herb oil for immediate use, take several sprigs of a fresh herb, such as basil, thyme, oregano, marjoram, rosemary, dill, tarragon, sage, or fennel, crush it in your hands, place it in a glass bottle, and pour in a cup or two of extra-virgin or virgin olive oil that has been heated just a minute or two so it is very warm to the touch. The heat will extract flavor from the herb quickly enough that the oil can be used right away. To make oil for future use, pour room-temperature oil over the crushed herbs and let stand at room temperature for about a week to develop flavor. Then remove the herbs and refrigerate the oil. Make up small quantities (a cup or so) and use them up quickly for best flavor. Use the same techniques for garlic oil, with 2 or 3 cloves of garlic. Crush them and add oil.

As for seasoning vegetables, the headnote for each recipe will describe in more detail the seasoning principles at work, so that you will be able to take these examples and use them to create your own vegetable dishes. I often season with homemade herb-flavored oils instead of butter to add extra flavor and eliminate cholesterol as well. These oils take only minutes to prepare and can be made ahead and kept on hand for 3 to 4 weeks (see box, opposite page).

RECIPES

VEGETABLES À LA MICROWAVE

◆

*T*he microwave does a nice job of cooking quickly without altering the textures of 1½ cups of chopped mixed vegetables *if they are cooked in the shortest possible time*—2 to 2½ minutes on high. I mix together different vegetables each time I cook, but I always try to chop or slice them so they are the same sizes, for even cooking. This makes a perfect and satisfying low-fat meal in itself.

The vegetables listed below are the ones I think do well in the microwave. Use any combination that appeals to you.

Yellow squash, patty pan squash, or
    zucchini, sliced
Red, green, or yellow bell peppers,
    seeded and sliced
Carrots, peeled and sliced
Cauliflower, in small trimmed florets
Broccoli, in small trimmed florets
Shallot or green onion, thinly sliced
Snow peas, sugar snap peas, or
    English garden peas, left whole
Asparagus, peeled and sliced
Mushrooms, sliced

Cherry tomatoes, left whole

Prepare 1½ cups vegetables and place them in a small glass bowl or microwaveproof dish. Cover with a paper plate and microwave for 2 to 2½ minutes on high. Remove and season with kosher salt and freshly ground black pepper, or Parmesan cheese, or butter or oil if you wish. Just a little basil oil, or other herb oil (page 150) drizzled on top is delicious.

ARTICHOKE TIMBALES
WITH PARMESAN
SERVES 6 TO 8

◆

A timbale is a small 4- to 6-ounce metal mold, tall and narrow, used for baking or molding vegetable or dessert custards.

This easy dish complements beef, veal, and chicken. It's perfect with a roast or any other dish that also bakes in the oven.

1 pound canned artichoke hearts,
    rinsed, drained, and pureed in a
    food processor (see Note)
2 large eggs, beaten
½ cup heavy cream
¼ cup grated Parmesan
¼ teaspoon kosher salt
¼ teaspoon freshly ground black
    pepper
¼ teaspoon dried thyme
¼ cup finely minced fresh parsley
8 leaves Italian parsley, for garnish
1 red bell pepper, seeded and cut in
    8 thin rings, for garnish

Preheat the oven to 400°. In a large bowl, combine all of the ingredients except the garnishes and season to taste. Pour into 6 to 8 small, well-buttered metal molds or custard cups. Place the molds in a baking dish and add 1 inch of hot or boiling water to the dish to make a *bain-marie.* Bake for 20 to 25 minutes, or until a knife inserted in the center of a timbale comes out clean.

To serve, invert the molds over a baking dish to remove the excess liquid, then place them on individual plates and garnish with Italian parsley leaves and red pepper rings.

NOTE: You can also use frozen artichoke hearts that have been thawed.

MAKE AHEAD: up to 24 hours; refrigerate; reheat in a 350° oven for 10 minutes

ASPARAGUS WITH SESAME OIL AND ORANGE

SERVES 2

◆

*A*sian seasonings suit asparagus marvelously well, and the waterless stir-frying technique highlights the unique flavor of asparagus much better than blanching or steaming, which often leave a watery taste. Try this recipe with green beans instead of asparagus.

½ tablespoon vegetable oil
1 bunch fresh pencil-thin asparagus,
    top 4 inches only (see Note), cut
    into 1-inch pieces
½ tablespoon grated fresh ginger

3 tablespoons fresh orange juice
Pinch kosher salt
1 tablespoon grated orange rind
½ tablespoon Oriental sesame oil (see
    box, page 65)

Heat a wok over high heat for 3 or 4 minutes. Add the vegetable oil and heat over high heat until almost smoking. Add the asparagus and cook, stirring, for 2 minutes; then add the ginger and orange juice and cook, stirring, for 1 minute. Add the orange rind and sesame oil and stir for 1 minute. Serve immediately.

NOTE: Save the trimmed parts of the asparagus spears to make a soup or a puree.

GINGER

♦

Ginger, even when finely grated, has a distinctive fibrous texture. For a more refined use, freeze knobs of fresh ginger, grate it, and squeeze through a fine strainer to get juice without the coarse fiber. Substitute twice the amount of the strained juice for grated ginger in your dish.

BROCCOLI SAUTÉED IN OLIVE OIL

SERVES 4

♦

*I*talians have a wonderful way with vegetables, always bringing out the best flavor in simple ingredients. What makes this recipe distinctive is the flavor punch provided by the garlic and dried red-pepper flakes. Try this over pasta as well as on its own.

3 quarts water
1 tablespoon salt
1 pound broccoli, florets separated, stalks trimmed, peeled, and thinly sliced
¼ cup extra-virgin or virgin olive oil
2 garlic cloves, thinly sliced
⅛ teaspoon dried red-pepper flakes (optional)

Bring the water to a boil. Add the salt and cook the broccoli florets and stalk slices, uncovered, at a rapid boil for 5 minutes, or until tender; drain.

Heat the olive oil in a large skillet. Add the garlic and red-pepper flakes (if using), and cook for a few minutes over medium heat, but don't let the garlic brown. Add the well-drained broccoli, toss to coat with the oil and seasonings, and cook over medium-high heat for 2 to 3 minutes. Serve immediately.

VARIATION: To save 5 minutes, microwave the broccoli on high for 2 minutes.

MAKE AHEAD: cook the broccoli up to 24 hours ahead; refrigerate; bring to room temperature before finishing recipe

RED CABBAGE WITH
GOAT CHEESE AND CHIVES
SERVES 2

◆

Sherry wine vinegar sets off the rich flavor of red cabbage to perfection. With the addition of goat cheese, this dish makes a hearty accompaniment to a dinner featuring pork, venison, or quail. The recipe is a version of one of California chef Jeremiah Tower's creations.

3 strips slab bacon
½ head red cabbage, core removed,
    very thinly sliced, then cut into
    3-inch-long strips
⅓ cup Spanish sherry wine vinegar
Kosher salt to taste
½ teaspoon freshly ground black
    pepper
3 ounces goat cheese, crumbled
2 tablespoons fresh chives, cut into
    1-inch pieces

Cook the bacon in a large heavy skil-

let until lightly browned. Remove, drain on a paper towel, crumble, and reserve. Add the red cabbage to the hot bacon fat in the skillet and stir over high heat until the cabbage is wilted, about 5 minutes. Add the vinegar, salt, and pepper, and continue cooking until the vinegar has cooked down and the flavors have blended. Season to taste, adding more vinegar if needed. Just before serving, put the cabbage in a serving dish and sprinkle with bacon, goat cheese and chives. Serve hot.

BRAISED CUCUMBERS
WITH DILL
SERVES 4

◆

Cucumbers are surprisingly delicious cooked and make a perfect and unusual accompaniment to fish and chicken dishes. The important thing here is to remove the seeds, which are bitter, before cooking. Simply halve each cucumber lengthwise, scoop out the watery center with a teaspoon, and turn it upside down to drain before cooking.

1 tablespoon unsalted butter
2 large cucumbers, peeled, halved, seeded, and sliced
¼ teaspoon champagne vinegar (optional)
¼ cup chopped fresh dill
¼ teaspoon kosher salt
¼ teaspoon freshly ground white pepper

Melt the butter in a heavy-bottomed 2½-quart saucepan. Add the cucumber and cook until tender, 5 to 8 minutes. Stir in the remaining ingredients and serve hot.

MAKE AHEAD: up to 24 hours; refrigerate; reheat gently

Sautéed Corn Cakes

SERVES 6

*T*hese delicate little corn cakes make a delightful accompaniment to chicken and grilled fish, and they can also be served as a delicious appetizer. Add fresh flaked crabmeat to the batter or serve it on top for a nice addition.

2 to 2¼ cups fresh corn kernels (from 4 large ears of corn), or frozen corn, thawed and drained
1 small white or red onion, very finely minced
1 celery stalk, very finely minced
1 jalapeño chili, seeded and very finely minced (optional)
1 garlic clove, mashed to a paste (see box, page 62)
3 tablespoons finely chopped cilantro (if unavailable, use fresh parsley)
½ teaspoon kosher salt
¼ teaspoon freshly ground black pepper
⅛ to ¼ teaspoon cayenne
¼ cup all-purpose flour
3 large eggs, beaten (use 4 if they are on the smallish side)

½ cup plus 2 tablespoons grated Monterey Jack cheese
2 to 3 tablespoons virgin olive oil or vegetable oil

In a bowl, combine all of the ingredients except the oil and mix well. In two large skillets, or on a heated griddle, heat the oil. Drop the batter by heaping tablespoonfuls onto the skillet, flatten, and cook until lightly browned on both sides, about 1 to 2 minutes per side. Cover with foil and keep warm in a low oven until serving. Serve hot.

MAKE AHEAD: prepare batter up to 4 hours ahead; refrigerate; sauté just before serving

SWEET CORN SOUFFLÉ
SERVES 10 to 12

◆

*T*he flavor of fresh corn cut off the cob is extraordinarily good, and cayenne and thyme season corn perfectly. This would make a fine vegetable dish with roast chicken, grilled New York strip steak, or grilled swordfish.

3 tablespoons unsalted butter
½ cup finely chopped red onion
¼ teaspoon dried thyme
3 tablespoons all-purpose flour
¾ cup whole milk
1½ cups fresh corn kernels (from
    3 large ears of corn)
1 teaspoon fresh thyme, minced
1 teaspoon fresh chives, minced
1¼ teaspoons kosher salt
¼ teaspoon freshly ground black
    pepper
Pinch cayenne
⅓ cup freshly grated Italian Parmesan
4 large egg yolks
5 to 6 large egg whites

Preheat the oven to 400°. Melt the butter in a saucepan. Add the onion and thyme, and cook over low heat until soft, about 5 minutes. Add the flour and cook for 2 to 3 minutes over low heat. Add the milk all at once, whisk, and cook for a few minutes over medium heat, until the sauce is smooth.

Add the corn, seasonings, and cheese and cook for 3 to 4 minutes. Let cool a little before adding the eggs. Whisk in the egg yolks. Beat the whites until stiff. Add a quarter of the whites to the soufflé base; mix in gently. Then fold in the rest of the whites. Do not overmix.

Pour into 10 to 12 well-buttered 4-ounce ramekins and bake for 10 to 15 minutes, or until the tops are golden-brown (see Note). Serve immediately.

NOTE: You may also bake the mixture in a well-buttered 1½-quart soufflé dish at 375° for 25 to 30 minutes, or until the top fills out and turns a golden brown.

SAUTÉED APPLES
SERVES 4

◆

I love to serve apples with hearty meats. Their delicate acidity and tartness balance the rich flavors of roast duck, turkey, pork, and quail, and grilled sausages.

4 tablespoons (½ stick) unsalted
    butter
4 medium Pippin or Golden Delicious
    apples, peeled and cored, each cut
    into 8 equal wedges
1 to 2 teaspoons sugar (optional)

Heat the butter in a heavy 12-inch

skillet until it foams. Add the apple and
sauté quickly over high heat until lightly
browned all over but not mushy, about 10
minutes. Taste for sweetness; you may
need to sprinkle with sugar to bring out
the fruit flavor. Serve hot.

MAKE AHEAD: up to 3 hours; refrigerate; reheat gently

BRAISED CHESTNUTS
WITH SHALLOTS AND THYME

SERVES 10

♦

Chestnuts are the perfect accompaniment to winter roasts—turkey, beef,
pork, duck, venison, and goose—and a welcome addition to holiday menus. Buy-
ing vacuum-packed chestnuts that are already peeled and cooked is the time-
saving trick here.

2 tablespoons unsalted butter
4 shallots, minced
Pinch sugar
½ teaspoon kosher salt
½ teaspoon freshly ground white
    pepper
1 teaspoon fresh thyme, or ½ teaspoon
    dried thyme
1 cup chicken broth
Two 10-ounce jars cooked, peeled,
    unsweetened whole chestnuts
¼ cup minced fresh parsley, for
    garnish

In a 3-quart casserole, melt the butter and cook the shallot until soft, 2 to 3
minutes. Add the seasonings, broth, and
chestnuts. Cover the casserole and simmer for about 20 minutes. Serve hot,
garnished with parsley.

MAKE AHEAD: up to 24 hours; refrigerate; reheat gently

GRILLED ENDIVE
WITH TOMATO-ANCHOVY SAUCE

SERVES 2

◆

*H*ere is a delicious vegetable to accompany a simple pasta dish. Try the sauce on grilled radicchio or grilled trout, or spread it on toasted sliced French or Italian bread to make tomato-anchovy *crostini*.

TOMATO-ANCHOVY SAUCE
4 anchovy fillets, rinsed and patted dry
½ teaspoon capers, rinsed
1 tomato, seeded and finely chopped
1 garlic clove, mashed to a paste (see
    box, page 62)
3 tablespoons minced fresh parsley
1 to 2 tablespoons fresh lemon juice or
    red-wine vinegar
¼ teaspoon freshly ground black
    pepper
¼ cup extra-virgin olive oil
¼ cup white bread crumbs (optional)

4 stalks Belgian endive, root ends
    trimmed, cut in half lengthwise
1 tablespoon extra-virgin olive oil
Kosher salt

Preheat the broiler. Make the sauce by pounding all of the ingredients in a mortar or blending in a blender or food processor.

Place the endive, cut-side down, in a small gratin dish. Drizzle with the olive oil and sprinkle with salt. Broil 4 to 5 inches from the flame for 3 to 4 minutes. With tongs, turn the endive cut-side up, drizzle with more oil if dry, and broil for another 3 to 4 minutes, or until lightly browned.

Spread the sauce over the browned endive, sprinkle with the crumbs, and heat under the broiler for 1 more minute. Serve hot, in the gratin dish.

GRILLED EGGPLANT ROLLS WITH
TOMATOES AND BASIL

SERVES 4

◆

*T*his simple, summery combination pairs splendidly with chicken, fish, or veal. It also makes a lovely light meal by itself. Put the vegetables between two slices of grilled French bread and you have a garden sandwich!

Extra-virgin olive oil or basil oil (see box, page 150)

1 large eggplant, peeled and sliced lengthwise into eight to ten ¼-inch-thick slices

One 16-ounce box Italian tomato chunks, or one 16-ounce can chopped Italian tomatoes

Kosher salt

Freshly ground black pepper

15 to 20 leaves fresh basil, finely chopped or shredded (see box, page 88)

3 sprigs fresh basil, for garnish

Preheat the broiler. Generously brush a large baking sheet with the oil. Place the eggplant slices on the sheet, and brush them with the oil. Broil the eggplant 4 to 5 inches from the flame until lightly browned and soft on one side, about 5 minutes. Remove and hold.

Pour the tomatoes and juices into a large skillet and cook over high heat until thickened, about 10 minutes. Add salt and pepper to taste; stir in the basil. Spread the tomatoes on the unbrowned side of the eggplant slices and roll each slice up lengthwise.

Place the filled eggplant rolls on a platter and keep warm in a low oven until ready to serve, or serve at room temperature. Garnish the dish with sprigs of fresh basil.

VARIATION: Leave the eggplant flat on the baking dish. Spread with the tomatoes, and sprinkle with freshly grated Italian Parmesan. Put back under the broiler until the cheese bubbles.

SAUTÉED KALE

SERVES 2

◆

*K*ale appears more often as the ubiquitous garnish for display cases of meats and fish in grocery stores than it does as a foodstuff in the home kitchen. Yet kale, by weight, is one of our most nutritious vegetables, and it's delicious too. This is my favorite quick way to cook kale—and other greens as well. The distinctive flavor of the greens is enhanced by the rich flavor of balsamic vinegar.

¾ pound fresh kale, washed, coarsest rib at base cut out, leaves coarsely chopped

2 teaspoons balsamic vinegar
Kosher salt
Freshly ground black pepper

Put the kale, with a little water still clinging to the leaves, into a hot skillet and stir for only a minute or two, until wilted. Add the vinegar and a little salt and pepper, and serve hot.

VARIATIONS: Substitute spinach, esca-role, Swiss chard, or watercress for kale. Beet greens and mustard greens can be cooked this way as well if they are small and tender. If they are larger and coarser, they need to be blanched and drained to remove the strong flavor and then added to the skillet for final cooking.

GRILLED FENNEL

SERVES 2 TO 4

*T*his is a fabulous fifteen-minute vegetable dish—quick and simple, but so delicious! Not only does broiling bring out the delicate flavor of fennel, but fennel cooked any other way takes a good thirty minutes. Serve with fish, chicken, veal, beef, or pork.

2 large or 3 medium heads fennel (see box), root ends trimmed, stalks removed, washed
1½ tablespoons extra-virgin olive oil
¼ teaspoon kosher salt
Juice of ½ lemon
½ teaspoon freshly ground black pepper

Preheat the broiler. Cut each head of fennel into 8 equal wedges, leaving the core in. Place the fennel, cut-side down, in a 9-inch gratin dish and drizzle with the olive oil. Sprinkle with salt and broil 4 inches from the flame for 4 to 5 minutes, or until lightly browned. With tongs, turn the pieces over and brown for another 4 to 5 minutes. Sprinkle with lemon juice and black pepper and serve immediately.

FENNEL

*F*ennel, or finocchio, is a bulb-shaped Italian vegetable known for its fine anise flavor. It varies in tenderness according to its age; a really fresh bulb of fennel will cook much more quickly than an older, tougher, more fibrous one. Smaller bulbs are generally more tender. Finely sliced raw fennel is a delicious crisp addition to a salad.

GRILLED LEEKS

SERVES 2

◆

*L*eeks are one of my favorite vegetables, and I love the fine flavor that grilling or broiling brings out here. This is also a wonderful first course or salad served at room temperature. Basil and thyme oil are very flavorful with the leeks.

2 large leeks, trimmed but 2 inches green left on, halved lengthwise to within 1 inch of root end, well washed (see box, page 136)
1 tablespoon extra-virgin olive oil, plus more for serving (optional)
¼ teaspoon kosher salt
¼ teaspoon freshly ground black pepper

Preheat the broiler. Cut each leek half in half again so there are eight pieces in all. Place the leeks in a gratin dish, drizzle with the 1 tablespoon olive oil, then rub the oil in so it coats the entire leek. Sprinkle with the salt and pepper and broil 4 inches from the flame for 4 to 5 minutes, or until the leeks are lightly browned. Turn over and let brown another 4 to 5 minutes, until they are tender when pierced with a knife. Sprinkle with a little more olive oil if desired and serve immediately, or serve at room temperature as a salad or first course.

FRENCH SKILLET-COOKED LETTUCE

SERVES 2

◆

*L*ettuce makes a wonderful cooked vegetable. Its delicate flavor goes well with simple dishes such as poached trout, steamed halibut, grilled sole, or sautéed veal or chicken. It also complements mushrooms, onions, shallots, or peas. This is a perfect way to use lettuce that's a little too bruised or ragged for salad. Use any kind of lettuce except iceberg.

1 tablespoon unsalted butter
2 shallots, minced
1 large head lettuce, washed, dried, and sliced into 1-inch-wide strips
Kosher salt
Freshly ground black pepper

Melt the butter in a 12-inch sauté pan or casserole. Add the shallot and cook over low heat until soft, about 2 minutes. Add the lettuce and cook over medium-high heat, stirring, until wilted, about 2 minutes. Season to taste with salt and pepper and serve hot.

VARIATIONS: Add any of the following along with the shallot: ¼ pound cooked pearl onions; ¼ pound cooked fresh green peas; 1 slice bacon or Canadian bacon, cooked and cut in thin strips; 1 to 2 tablespoons heavy cream and ¼ teaspoon sugar; 2 tablespoons chopped fresh chervil or mint.

HUNGARIAN PAPRIKA MUSHROOMS

SERVES 4

◆

*T*his dish makes an excellent vegetarian entrée served over noodles, rice, or spätzle, or a very tasty side dish for grilled chicken or fish. The Hungarian paprika gives it an unexpected depth of flavor.

2 tablespoons unsalted butter
2 tablespoons finely minced shallot or
    scallion
¾ pound fresh large white or brown
    mushrooms, washed, trimmed but
    stems left on, sliced in quarters
½ teaspoon kosher salt
¼ teaspoon freshly ground black
    pepper
½ teaspoon dried marjoram, or
    2 teaspoons fresh marjoram
2 teaspoons hot or sweet Hungarian
    paprika (see box, page 43)
¼ teaspoon all-purpose flour (don't be
    tempted to use more)
⅓ cup sour cream or Crème Fraîche
    (page 210)

COOKING MUSHROOMS

◆

*M*ushrooms need to cook fast over high heat to seal in their juices. They are much more flavorful cooked this way than when cooked so long that all their liquid is released.

Melt the butter in a large skillet. Add the shallot and mushrooms, and cook for 5 to 6 minutes over medium-high heat, stirring occasionally. Lower the heat and add the salt, pepper, marjoram, paprika, and flour. Cook for 2 to 3 minutes to develop the flavor of the paprika. Just before serving, add the sour cream and heat through, but do not boil. Place in a serving bowl and serve hot.

MAKE AHEAD: up to 24 hours; refrigerate; reheat gently

WILD MUSHROOM RAGOÛT

SERVES 6 TO 8

◆

*T*his dish is an unparalleled accompaniment to a roast or any winter meal. Or serve it on toasts or *croustades* (see box, page 251) as a marvelous appetizer or first course. It was a great favorite when I worked at Iron Horse Vineyards in Sonoma County, California. Dried mushrooms enable you to make this recipe any time of year. Fresh cèpes, morels, and chanterelles would be exquisite, but they are not all in season at the same time.

4 tablespoons (½ stick) unsalted
    butter
1 ounce dried cèpes or porcini,
    cleaned, soaked (see box),
    drained, and chopped
1 ounce dried morels, cleaned, soaked
    (see box), drained, and chopped
1 ounce dried chanterelles, cleaned,
    soaked (see box), drained, and
    chopped
1 pound medium cultivated fresh
    mushrooms, chopped
3 large shallots, minced
1 large garlic clove, mashed to a paste
    (see box, page 62)
¼ cup Crème Fraîche (page 210), or
    2 tablespoons heavy cream mixed
    with 2 tablespoons sour cream
2 teaspoons fresh thyme, or
    1 teaspoon dried thyme
1 teaspoon kosher salt
½ teaspoon freshly ground black
    pepper
Fresh lemon juice
2 tablespoons port
2 tablespoons minced fresh parsley, for
    garnish

In a large heavy skillet over high heat, melt the butter and cook all of the mushrooms with the shallot and garlic for about 5 minutes. Add the *crème fraîche* and thyme; let the mixture cook down a

---

CLEANING DRIED MUSHROOMS

◆

*T*here is a simple trick to removing the grit and sand from dried mushrooms before they are soaked. (After soaking it is nearly impossible to do so.) Put the dried mushrooms in a large colander and toss them over the sink. Keep tossing until there is no more sandy residue to be shaken loose. (You will be surprised at how much "forest dust" there is in packages of dried mushrooms.) At this point soak the mushrooms in hot-to-boiling water to cover, about 10 to 15 minutes, until they are softened but not slimy. When soft, drain, rinse, and pat dry on paper towels. If you are using several different types of dried mushrooms, soak each type separately, as sizes differ. Smaller, thinner mushrooms will soften a little quicker than larger ones.

few minutes until thickened. Season with the salt, pepper, and a squeeze of lemon. Add the port and cook for 5 minutes. Serve hot, garnished with parsley.

VARIATION: Serve on 1-inch-thick bread *croustades* (see box, page 251), brushed

with melted butter and toasted in a 375° oven until golden-brown, for an ample first course or a luncheon dish.

MAKE AHEAD: up to 1 hour; refrigerate; reheat gently

PUREE OF PEAS
SERVES 4

◆

*P*eas seem to have a lot of childhood connotations, not always positive ones. "Eat your peas" was something my mother never had to say to me, however; I always liked them. I liked them even more when I discovered this excellent recipe in France. Shallots and lettuce add a distinctive and refined flavor. This is excellent with beef, veal, lamb, and turkey dishes.

Two 10-ounce packages frozen peas
Pinch kosher salt
Pinch sugar
½ cup water
2 large shallots, chopped
6 to 8 leaves Boston lettuce
½ teaspoon kosher salt
¼ teaspoon freshly ground white pepper
2 to 4 tablespoons heavy or light cream or plain yogurt (optional)

Place the peas, salt, sugar, water, shallot, and lettuce leaves in a saucepan and simmer, uncovered, for about 8 min-

utes. Puree the mixture in a blender or food processor or with a *mini-pimer* or hand blender (see box, page 32). Season with salt and white pepper. If the puree is too thick, thin with cream or yogurt. Place in a serving bowl and serve hot.

VARIATIONS: Substitute broccoli, asparagus, or green beans for the peas, and omit the sugar.

Add about 2 teaspoons fresh chopped mint to garnish the pea puree.

MAKE AHEAD: up to 24 hours; refrigerate; reheat gently

GRILLED PEPPERS AND ONIONS
SERVES 4

◆

*T*his combination is really wonderful with grilled or pan-sautéed meats—steaks, lamb, or pork chops.

3 bell peppers (1 red, 1 green, 1
    yellow, if possible), seeded and
    quartered
2 red onions (or Vidalia onions when in
    season), cut into eighths
2 tablespoons extra-virgin olive oil
¼ teaspoon kosher salt
¼ teaspoon freshly ground black
    pepper
2 teaspoons balsamic vinegar or fresh
    lemon juice

Preheat the broiler. Place the pepper

and onion in a shallow gratin dish, drizzle with the olive oil, and sprinkle with salt and pepper. Broil about 4 inches from the flame for about 4 minutes, or until lightly browned. Turn the vegetables over with tongs and let them brown on the other side, about 4 minutes. Stir in the vinegar and serve hot or at room temperature.

VARIATION: After adding the vinegar, toss the vegetables with chopped fresh thyme, parsley, or sage.

QUICK POTATO GRATIN IN RAMEKINS
SERVES 4

◆

*T*his makes a fine accompaniment to roast or grilled lamb, beef, or pork. Garlic, thyme, and nutmeg season potatoes to perfection. The key to this recipe is to slice the potatoes paper-thin.

1 cup whole or skim milk
1 cup half-and-half
1 garlic clove, mashed to a paste (see
    box, page 62)
¼ teaspoon dried thyme, or 4 sprigs
    fresh thyme
½ teaspoon kosher salt

¼ teaspoon freshly ground black
    pepper
Pinch nutmeg
1 tablespoon unsalted butter
2 large Idaho potatoes, peeled, sliced
    paper-thin

Preheat the broiler. Place four 4-ounce ramekins on a baking sheet and put them in the oven to preheat while preparing the potatoes.

Bring the milk and half-and-half to a boil in a 2½-quart saucepan and stir in the garlic, seasonings, and butter. Add the potatoes and simmer for 10 to 12 minutes, or until tender. Divide the mix-

ture among the ramekins and broil 6 inches from the flame for 5 to 7 minutes, or until the tops are golden-brown. Serve hot.

VARIATIONS: Add 2 tablespoons freshly grated Italian Parmesan to the hot milk.
   Use half potatoes and half turnips.

MAKE AHEAD: 1 hour; leave at room temperature until serving

LEMON-GARLIC POTATOES WITH SPINACH

SERVES 4

◆

*M*emories of wonderful lemony potato dishes I had in Greece inspired this recipe. This is a perfect dish for non–meat eaters—its full flavor makes it a one-dish meal. High heat is needed throughout the cooking to brown the potatoes.

1 tablespoon extra-virgin olive oil
1 pound small new potatoes, unpeeled, cut evenly into quarters or sixths
3 large garlic cloves, mashed to a pulp (see box, page 62)
1 cup water
Juice of ½ lemon
6 to 8 ounces fresh spinach, washed and stemmed
Kosher salt
Freshly ground black pepper

Heat the olive oil in a 9-inch nonstick skillet. Add the potatoes and cook over high heat for 5 minutes, or until lightly

browned, shaking often to redistribute the potatoes so they will brown evenly. Stir in the garlic, then add the water, cover, and cook on high heat for another 5 minutes. Test for doneness, and cook a few minutes longer if needed.

Squeeze the lemon over the potatoes, add the spinach, and stir until wilted. Season with salt and pepper to taste and serve immediately.

VARIATION: Substitute chopped Swiss chard or kale for the spinach.

FRENCH MASHED POTATOES
WITH GARLIC AND CREAM
SERVES 2

◆

*T*here are mashed potatoes and mashed potatoes. This *purée de pommes de terre à l'ail* from the south of France is a potato lover's delight and perfect comfort food. French cooks demonstrate great finesse in seasoning vegetables. Here, the hint of bay leaf (always use the imported variety, never the California bay, which is much too strong for use in cooking) gives a subtle depth of flavor to simple mashed potatoes. This is wonderful with lamb, beef, pork, or venison. The recipe can be doubled or tripled.

1 quart water
3 large garlic cloves, crushed
1 imported bay leaf
Pinch dried thyme
Pinch kosher salt
1 pound russet or other baking
    potatoes, peeled and cut into
    1-inch dice
½ tablespoon unsalted butter
2 tablespoons light or heavy cream
Kosher salt
Freshly ground black pepper

Bring the water to a boil in a large saucepan. Add the garlic, bay leaf, thyme, salt, and potatoes, and boil, uncovered, for 10 to 12 minutes, or until the potatoes are cooked through. Drain the potatoes, remove the bay leaf, return the potatoes and garlic to the pan, and toss for 1 minute over medium heat to evaporate the excess moisture. Mash the potatoes and garlic with a mixer or a potato masher, mix in the butter, cream, and salt and pepper to taste, and serve hot.

VARIATION: This is a good basic recipe for making vegetable purees. Use any of the vegetables or combinations suggested on page 152, and omit the garlic.

SUMMER POTATOES
FROM THE VAUCLUSE
SERVES 4 TO 6

◆

*T*his was a favorite dish during the many summers I lived and cooked in an old farmhouse in the Vaucluse, a beautiful region of olive orchards, gardens, and vineyards about twenty miles north of Avignon, France. The potatoes really simmer in the tomato juice with thyme, rosemary, garlic, and onion as the predominant seasonings.

4 tablespoons (½ stick) unsalted
    butter or extra-virgin olive oil
1 medium red onion, chopped
1 large garlic clove, mashed to a paste
    (see box, page 62)
1 pound fresh tomatoes, seeded and
    chopped (or 1½ cups imported
    Italian tomato chunks)
3 medium bell peppers (1 green, 1 red,
    and 1 yellow, if possible), seeded
    and chopped into 1-inch pieces
2¼ pounds red or yellow potatoes, cut
    into ¾-inch pieces
1 imported bay leaf
½ teaspoon dried thyme
Pinch dried rosemary
½ teaspoon kosher salt
¼ teaspoon freshly ground black
    pepper

Melt the butter or heat the oil in a

POTATOES

The food processor turns mashed potatoes into a gluey mess! There are better ways to mash potatoes! Use an old-fashioned hand potato masher, an old-fashioned hand ricer, an electric mixer, a hand blender, or a mini-pimer. Add hot broth, milk, or butter to lighten and flavor the potatoes.

heavy-bottomed 4-quart casserole. Add all of the vegetables and seasonings, and cook over high heat for 5 minutes, stirring. Cover and cook over medium heat for about 15 minutes, or until the potatoes are cooked through.

GRILLED SCALLIONS IN BASIL OIL
SERVES 2

◆

*T*his is a delicious way to prepare a vegetable that's normally never featured by itself. Serve these with grilled or roasted meats.

2 tablespoons extra-virgin olive oil
2 large fresh basil leaves, chopped
    (see box, page 88)

2 bunches scallions, 4 inches green
    left on
Kosher salt

Preheat the broiler. Heat the olive oil over low heat in a very small saucepan. When just barely hot, remove from the heat and add the basil.

Place the scallions in a gratin dish in one layer. Drizzle with the basil oil and broil 4 inches from the flame for 3 to 4 minutes, until the scallions have browned.

Turn them over and broil another 3 to 4 minutes. Sprinkle with salt before serving.

VARIATION: Use other flavored oils such as fennel, thyme, rosemary, or oregano oil.

MAKE AHEAD: up to 30 minutes; keep warm in oven

ZUCCHINI, SCALLION, AND THREE-PEPPER SAUTÉ

SERVES 4

◆

A lot of flavor and elegance come to life in this quick summer sauté. I use the same trio of seasonings—garlic, oil, and thyme—for sautéing many other vegetables: potatoes, tomatoes, okra, corn, onions, and fennel.

1 tablespoon extra-virgin olive oil
1 bunch scallions, with 2 inches green left on, cut into 1-inch pieces
1 large zucchini, halved, cut into ½-inch slices
½ large red bell pepper, seeded and cut into ½-inch pieces
½ large yellow bell pepper, seeded and cut into ½-inch pieces
½ large green bell pepper, seeded and cut into ½-inch pieces
2 garlic cloves, mashed to a pulp (see box, page 62)
1 tablespoon fresh thyme or marjoram (if unavailable, use ½ teaspoon dried thyme or marjoram and 1

tablespoon fresh parsley)
Kosher salt
Freshly ground black pepper

Heat the oil until very hot in a large sauté pan. Add the scallion, zucchini, and pepper and cook, uncovered, stirring occasionally, for 5 minutes. When the vegetables are cooked through but not too soft, add the garlic and thyme, and salt and pepper to taste, and cook for another 3 minutes. Serve immediately.

MAKE AHEAD: up to 24 hours; refrigerate; reheat gently

BROILED TOMATOES WITH BASIL OIL
SERVES 2

◆

*B*roiled tomatoes are a great summer standby. The flavored oil gives them a distinctive aromatic taste. Any herb-flavored oil could be used instead of basil oil: thyme, rosemary, fennel, oregano, or marjoram oils, for example. Make the oil according to the directions on page 150, and keep the rest for another use.

2 large ripe tomatoes, cut in half
    between the stem end and the root
    end
Kosher salt
Freshly ground black pepper
½ tablespoon basil oil (see box, page
    150)

Preheat the broiler. Place the tomatoes, cut-sides up, in a shallow baking dish. Sprinkle with salt and pepper and drizzle with the basil oil. Broil 4 to 5 inches from the flame for 5 to 7 minutes, or until lightly browned on top.

VARIATION: Seed the halved tomatoes, salt and pepper them, and place either a very finely minced shallot or 1 large, very finely mashed clove of garlic in the cavity. Drizzle with the oil and broil.

MAKE AHEAD: broil tomatoes 1 hour in advance; do not refrigerate; reheat, or serve at room temperature

GRILLED RADICCHIO
WITH GORGONZOLA AND WALNUTS
SERVES 2

◆

*R*adicchio, though normally used in salads, is delicious grilled. The Gorgonzola and walnuts add an intriguing dimension of taste.

¼ cup lightly toasted walnuts (see box,
    page 124), coarsely chopped
2 small heads radicchio, cut into
    quarters

1 tablespoon extra-virgin olive oil
Kosher salt
2 ounces Gorgonzola cheese, softened
Freshly ground black pepper

Toast the walnuts, then preheat the broiler. Place the radicchio, curved-side up, in a gratin dish and drizzle with the olive oil. Sprinkle with salt and broil 4 inches from the flame for 3 minutes; then turn and broil for another 3 to 4 minutes, or until soft. Spread each piece with a little Gorgonzola cheese and sprinkle with walnuts. Return to the warm oven for a few minutes to melt the cheese.

QUICK SAUTÉED ZUCCHINI

SERVES 2

◆

*S*autéing zucchini over high heat brings out its flavor without leaving it soggy.

3 medium yellow or green zucchini, peeled or unpeeled, cut into ⅓-inch slices
¼ cup all-purpose flour, mixed in a paper bag with ¼ teaspoon kosher salt, ⅛ teaspoon freshly ground black pepper, and ½ teaspoon dried basil or oregano
3 tablespoons olive oil
Kosher salt

2 tablespoons finely chopped fresh parsley

Shake the zucchini slices in the paper bag with the seasoned flour. Heat the olive oil in a large skillet and sauté the zucchini over medium-high heat for 3 minutes on each side, or until lightly browned. Remove to a serving dish, sprinkle with the salt and parsley, and serve hot.

THE 10 BEST USES FOR MICROWAVE OVENS

◆

- *Cooking vegetables (keeps them crisp)*
- *Heating water, milk, or broth*
- *Melting and clarifying butter*
- *Sautéing chopped onion*
- *Toasting nuts (see pages 120 and 124)*
- *Melting chocolate (see page 188)*
- *Plumping raisins*
- *Plumping sun-dried tomatoes (see page 95)*
- *Melting honey or jam for glazes*
- *Cooking bacon*

Note: *Use paper plates for covering food instead of plastic wrap to avoid steam burns and the plastic taste that results when the plastic touches the food.*

◆

DESSERTS

◆

Without a dessert or a piece of fruit, I never feel dinner is really over. Desserts can be the simplest no-fuss course of all—the trick is to find really ripe and flavorful fresh fruit. Presented in an attractive bowl or a footed compote dish, nothing is more beautiful or appealing than fresh ripe peaches, cherries, apricots, black grapes, figs, raspberries, blackberries, melons, or nectarines.

Going one step further with fruits, combine them with a splash of fresh citrus juices or liqueurs, sweet or fortified wines, or other flavoring ingredients. A perfect navel orange is exquisite peeled, sliced, and drizzled with a little Grand Marnier or other orange liqueur. For a real treat, put sliced peaches in big wine goblets and macerate them with Muscat de Beaumes de Venise, a wonderful sweet Provençal wine that is widely available here. Strawberries take to interesting and unusual seasonings, such as a sprinkling of balsamic vinegar or a light grinding of black or freeze-dried green peppercorns. And a little *crème de cassis* (black currant liqueur) enhances all the red and black fruits. For more suggestions, refer to my list of Fabulous 5-Minute Fruit Desserts on page 176.

I've never liked desserts that are overly sweet or gooey. Most of the desserts featured in this chapter are fruit-based and are light and fresh-tasting. Delicate crisp cookies accompany fruit desserts perfectly, and I give three of my favorites here. I do sometimes like a small piece of cake for dessert; the four cakes I include in this chapter all make a nice ending to a meal and taste wonderful with coffee. I also provide several "elegant" desserts (Cold Lime Mousse, Crème Aux Fraises), and chocolate does make a distinguished appearance in Baked Chocolate and Hazelnut Mousse.

Sorbets and ice creams are relatively effortless transformations of fresh fruits. Preparation takes just a few minutes, freezing fifteen minutes to an hour—the time it takes to cook and eat your dinner! Better still, with many frozen fruits like peaches, blackberries, strawberries, and raspberries, sorbets or ice cream can be made in only five minutes merely by pureeing the partially thawed fruit with flavorings—no special freezing is required. Eight of my favorite light and refreshing fruit sorbets and ice creams are included here.

Dessert sauces are a godsend when you are pressed for time; the chocolate and apricot sauces presented here can be heated and served over ice cream, fruit, or store-bought pound cake to make quick and attractive desserts. Cream puffs filled with coffee ice cream and topped with Hot Chocolate Sauce are just plain divine! And try the exotic Passion Fruit Sauce in chapter 6 (page 147).

OUT-OF-THE-ORDINARY INSTANT DESSERTS MADE WITH READY-MADE PRODUCTS

◆

With purchases from bakeries, delis, or your grocery store, you can put together many fine quick combinations for your dessert course. There are many excellent ice creams, sorbets, pound cakes, and sauces available. Use a round or oval ice cream dipper to make the ice cream look attractive and neat, then choose your accompaniment carefully for taste and color.

- *French vanilla ice cream drizzled with cognac or Armagnac*
- *Lemon sorbet drizzled with iced vodka and garnished with fresh mint*
- *Mango sorbet, raspberry sorbet, and vanilla ice cream served side by side in the same dish*

- *Vanilla ice cream with fresh sliced peaches and raspberries*
- *Chocolate ice cream topped with toasted hazelnuts and a drizzle of Frangelico*
- *A slice of pound cake, served with coffee ice cream drizzled with hot chocolate sauce*

FRUIT-BASED DESSERTS

SORBETS AND ICE CREAM

CAKES AND COOKIES

DESSERT SAUCES

FABULOUS 5-MINUTE FRUIT DESSERTS

◆

*B*eautifully fresh, ripe fruits, harbingers of the season's change and bounty, provide you with instant desserts. When fruit is in a state of perfect ripeness, and its fresh richness can be detected in its aroma, no sauce or additional flavoring is needed. Perfect figs, raspberries, mangoes, peaches, and blackberries can stand alone, but many fruits that are picked a little less ripe than they should be can be enhanced by the addition of other ingredients. Here are some of my favorite combinations. A sprinkling of white, brown, or confectioners' sugar can be added to any of them if they are not quite sweet enough.

Sliced nectarines in chilled sweet wine

Strawberries, raspberries, and blueberries drizzled with good port

Fresh sliced pineapple macerated in imported kirsch

Sliced strawberries splashed with drops of balsamic vinegar, with a tiny amount of freshly ground black pepper *or* sugar sprinkled on top

Sliced peaches in chilled Muscat de Beaumes de Venise

Sliced peaches in chilled red wine, sweetened with a little confectioners' sugar

Raspberries and strawberries sprinkled with *eau de vie de framboise*

Orange slices drizzled with Grand Marnier or cognac

Mixed melon balls or slices (honeydew, Crenshaw, Persian, casaba, or cantaloupe) combined with fresh mint, chilled champagne, and a sprinkling of sugar and cognac

Ripe pears, sliced and sprinkled with *eau de vie de poire* or Poire William, topped with vanilla ice cream, and drizzled with hot chocolate sauce

Perfect whole strawberries dipped in hot chocolate sauce

Sliced mangoes tossed with fresh lime juice

Sliced bananas, cubed apples, and orange segments tossed with toasted coconut flakes and fresh orange juice

Dried dates stuffed with whole almonds

Dried prunes simmered in red or white wine for 20 minutes

Bananas halved, sprinkled with rum, brown sugar, and lemon juice, and baked at 400° until soft (about 10 minutes)

Grapefruit sections and pomegranate seeds tossed together with a little orange juice

Blackberries with a little *crème de cassis*

Baked apple topped with a mixture of *crème fraîche*, Calvados, and toasted hazelnuts

Pears poached in dry or sweet Marsala, sugar, and cloves for 15 minutes

Sliced mangoes, papayas, and kiwi fruit over coconut ice cream

Cherries macerated in kirsch, served over dark chocolate ice cream

Fresh peach halves drizzled with cognac or bourbon, topped with vanilla ice cream, and sprinkled with crumbled *amaretti* or macaroons

Sliced cantaloupe with fresh lime juice and thin slivers of candied ginger

Balls of watermelon, mango, and honeydew with a splash of rum and orange juice

Fresh strawberries and raspberries mixed with *crème de cassis* and *crème fraîche*

FRUIT-BASED DESSERTS

♦

COLD CHERRIES IN BRANDY

SERVES 4 TO 6

♦

*H*ere's an especially good, simple dessert you can keep on hand for up to 6 months in your refrigerator. It is superb by itself, with *crème fraîche*, or over vanilla ice cream or pound cake.

6 ounces red-currant jelly

1 pound fresh or frozen pitted sweet cherries

¼ cup cognac, Armagnac, or brandy

1 cup Crème Fraîche (page 210), for serving (optional)

Melt the jelly in a saucepan, add the cherries, and cook for 5 minutes. Let cool, add the cognac, and chill for at least 1 hour before serving or storing. Store in the refrigerator in a tightly covered jar. Spoon the cherries into individual bowls with 1 tablespoon brandy sauce per serving. Pass the *crème fraîche* if desired.

MAKE AHEAD: prepare up to 6 months ahead; refrigerate

RED AND BLACK SUMMER FRUITS
SERVES 6

*T*here's no allusion to Stendhal here, just a very colorful and refreshing summer dessert.

1 pint small fresh strawberries
1 pint fresh raspberries
1 pint fresh blackberries or dewberries
1 pint fresh blueberries
2 to 3 tablespoons sugar
¼ cup Chambord (black raspberry liqueur) or *crème de cassis*
Sprigs of fresh mint, for garnish

Clean and stem the berries and combine them in a large glass or crystal bowl. Sprinkle with sugar and liqueur and refrigerate until serving. Garnish with mint.

MAKE AHEAD: up to 1 hour; refrigerate; garnish just before serving

MELON AU PORTO
SERVES 2

*Y*ou may encounter this refreshing summer dessert in France as a first course. The French version features the special small Charentais melon from Provence—a melon so exquisitely perfumed and flavorful that after the first taste, you crave it ever after.

2 small cantaloupes, very ripe and fragrant
1 cup good-quality port (if unavailable, use a good Cabernet or Pinot Noir)
1 cup sliced cleaned and stemmed strawberries or whole cleaned and stemmed raspberries (optional)
Sprigs of fresh mint, for garnish
Crushed ice, for serving

Cut off a "lid" 2 inches below the stem end of each melon, and with a large spoon, scoop out and discard the seeds. Remove the pulp and chop it evenly. Cut a thin slice off the bottom of each melon so it sits flat. Refrigerate the melon shells until ready to serve. In a large bowl, combine the wine and melon pieces and macerate for at least 30 minutes in the refrigerator.

To serve, put the melon pieces and liquid into the melon shells, add the berries, garnish with a sprig of fresh mint, and place each melon in a bed of crushed ice in a soup plate or bowl that is sitting on a service plate.

MAKE AHEAD: prepare melon shells and macerate fruit up to 4 hours ahead; refrigerate; assemble just before serving

FRESH SUMMER FRUITS WITH COINTREAU SAUCE

SERVES 6

♦

*T*he very fine flavor of this simple sauce complements fresh berries and summer fruits extremely well. It is also excellent over pound cake or poached fruits.

COINTREAU SAUCE
3 large egg yolks, at room temperature
¼ cup sugar
4 tablespoons Cointreau, Triple Sec, or Grand Marnier
½ cup heavy cream
2 tablespoons confectioners' sugar

FRUITS (use any one or a combination equal to about 4 cups)
1 pint fresh strawberries, cleaned and stemmed, with fresh papaya slices
1½ pints fresh raspberries, rolled on a damp paper towel
3 large peaches, peeled and sliced, with 1 pint fresh blueberries
6 nectarines, peeled and sliced
1½ pints fresh blackberries or dewberries, quickly rinsed
3 fresh mangoes, peeled and sliced

Chill a mixing bowl and beaters in the refrigerator or freezer. Just before starting the recipe, warm another mixing bowl by rinsing it in hot water. Beat the egg yolks and sugar in the warm mixing bowl for about 5 minutes, or until the yolks are quite thick and a pale yellow; then beat in 2 tablespoons of the Cointreau. Place this mixture in the refrigerator until chilled.

Whip the cream and confectioners' sugar together in the chilled bowl until stiff, then add the remaining 2 tablespoons Cointreau and mix in. Gently fold the whipped cream mixture into the egg-yolk mixture; chill for 15 minutes and serve over fruit.

MAKE AHEAD: make sauce 24 hours ahead; refrigerate

SUMMER PLUM COMPOTE

SERVES 4 TO 6

◆

*P*lums are plentiful all summer long, and they benefit from cooking, especially if a little underripe. This compote keeps very well; it's a nice dessert to have on hand in your refrigerator. If you like, add a scoop of vanilla ice cream to each serving or serve with *crème fraîche* on the side.

2½ cups dry red wine
½ cup water
1¼ pounds plums, halved and pitted
Peel of ½ orange, cut in thin strips
2 cinnamon sticks
½ teaspoon allspice berries, crushed
¼ cup sugar
¼ cup port

Heat the wine and water in a non-aluminum saucepan until simmering. Add the plums, orange peel, cinnamon, allspice, and sugar, and cook gently for 10 minutes, or until the plums are soft. Add the port and pour into a serving bowl. Serve warm, at room temperature, or chilled.

MAKE AHEAD: up to 5 days; refrigerate

WARM CARAMEL PEARS

SERVES 2

◆

*T*he comforting and homey tastes of autumn come through in this easy baked dessert.

½ tablespoon unsalted butter
2 large pears, peeled, cored, and cut in quarters
2 tablespoons sugar
1½ tablespoons heavy cream

Preheat the oven to 450°. Melt the butter in a small saucepan. Mix the pear pieces with the butter, sugar, and cream in a bowl and transfer to a glass or porcelain baking dish. Bake until the sugar and cream turn a light caramel color and the pears are cooked through, 8 to 12 minutes. Serve warm.

MAKE AHEAD: up to 24 hours; refrigerate; reheat 10 minutes in a 350° oven

GRATIN OF CHERRIES AND APRICOTS WITH AMARETTI
SERVES 4 TO 6

◆

*L*oosely based on a recipe from *Gourmet* magazine, this warm fruit gratin makes a perfect finale to a cold summer supper. If you use frozen cherries, which are a good alternative to fresh (never use canned) and dried apricots, you can enjoy this delicious summery dessert year-round.

¾ pound red or black cherries, fresh
  or frozen, pitted
6 ounces ripe fresh apricots, pitted
  and sliced, or dried apricots,
  plumped in hot water for 10 minutes, drained, and cut into
  quarters
2 tablespoons imported kirsch (see
  box) or cognac
3 large egg yolks
⅓ cup confectioners' sugar
½ teaspoon finely grated lemon rind
½ cup heavy cream
½ cup crushed *amaretti* or crisp
  gingersnaps

KIRSCH

◆

*K*irsch is a clear spirit distilled from cherries. Its distinctive, delicate flavor complements all red fruits. Domestic kirsch is available, but its flavor leaves much to be desired. Imported kirsch, or kirschwasser *as it is also called, is expensive but well worth the price for the quality of flavor. Use only imported kirsch from traditional cherry-growing areas of Europe: Alsace, Germany, Switzerland, and Austria.*

Preheat the oven to 425°. Mix the fruit with the kirsch and macerate at room temperature while preparing the rest of the recipe. With a mixer, beat the yolks, sugar, and lemon rind on high speed until slightly thickened. In a separate bowl, whip the cream until stiff, then quickly fold into the yolk mixture.

Butter a 9- or 10-inch shallow-sided gratin dish. Place the fruit with its juices in the dish, pour the cream mixture evenly over the fruit, and sprinkle with the *amaretti* or gingersnaps. Bake for 5 minutes, or until lightly browned. Or broil 5 to 6 inches from the flame for 3 to 4 minutes, until the top browns lightly (don't let it burn). Serve immediately.

MAKE AHEAD: macerate the fruit in the refrigerator up to 24 hours ahead; you can finish the dish just before serving dinner and leave it out to be served at room temperature

CRÈME AUX FRAISES
SERVES 6 TO 8

◆

*T*his is a beautiful, classic, and simple French dessert.

3 pints fresh strawberries, cleaned and
    stemmed
2 tablespoons imported kirsch (see
    box, page 181)
3 tablespoons sugar
1¼ cups heavy cream
6 to 8 sprigs of fresh mint, for garnish

Put a mixing bowl and beaters in the refrigerator to chill. Puree the strawberries in a blender or food processor, then strain out the seeds by pressing the berries through a large, fine-meshed sieve.

Discard the seeds. Add the kirsch and sugar to the seedless strawberry puree, stirring to dissolve the sugar.

Whip the cream until stiff in the chilled bowl. Carefully fold the cream into the pureed strawberries. Transfer to a glass or crystal bowl, cover with plastic wrap, and refrigerate until ready to serve. Just before serving, garnish with mint.

MAKE AHEAD: up to 4 hours; refrigerate

GINGER-PLUM COBBLER
SERVES 6

◆

*T*his cobbler and a greengage plum tart I once made while living in France rate as my two most memorable plum desserts. I usually double the quantity because this cobbler is so good, guests always want seconds.

2½ pounds red or purple plums, pitted
    and halved
3 tablespoons sugar

GINGER TOPPING
1 cup all-purpose flour
¼ teaspoon baking soda
1 tablespoon ground ginger

7 tablespoons softened unsalted
    butter, cut in pieces
⅓ cup light brown sugar mixed with
    ⅓ cup white sugar
1 tablespoon chopped crystallized
    ginger (optional)

Sour cream or Crème Fraîche (page
    210), for serving

Preheat the oven to 375°. Place the plums, cut-sides up, in a baking or gratin dish and sprinkle with the three tablespoons sugar.

Prepare the topping: Combine the flour, baking soda, and ginger in a large bowl. With a pastry blender, a food processor, or an electric mixer, work the butter into the flour mixture until mealy. Add the mixed sugars and crystallized ginger, if using, and combine well. Pat the topping evenly over the plums and bake for 30 minutes. Serve warm, with a dollop of sour cream or *crème fraîche.*

MAKE AHEAD: up to 4 hours; leave in a cool place; reheat in a 350° oven for 10 minutes

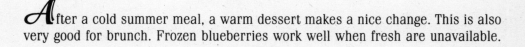

WARM BLUEBERRY CRISP

SERVES 8

♦

*A*fter a cold summer meal, a warm dessert makes a nice change. This is also very good for brunch. Frozen blueberries work well when fresh are unavailable.

4 cups fresh blueberries, quickly rinsed and dried
1 tablespoon fresh lemon juice
3 tablespoons sugar
⅔ cup all-purpose flour
⅔ cup brown sugar
1 teaspoon ground cinnamon
¼ teaspoon ground mace
½ teaspoon ground ginger
Pinch ground allspice
Pinch ground nutmeg
¼ teaspoon kosher salt
7 tablespoons unsalted butter
Plain yogurt, heavy cream, or vanilla ice cream, for serving (optional)

Preheat the oven to 375°. Butter a 9-inch square or round baking pan. Mix together the blueberries, lemon juice, and sugar and spread the mixture in the bottom of the pan.

In a bowl, combine the flour, spices, and salt and cut in the butter with a pastry blender until the mixture is crumbly. Cover the blueberries with the topping and bake for about 35 minutes, or until the topping is lightly browned and bubbling. Serve warm, with a dollop of yogurt, heavy cream, or ice cream, if desired.

VARIATION: Substitute fresh blackberries, dewberries, or raspberries for the blueberries.

RED BERRY GRATIN

SERVES 8

◆

*L*ight, delicious, and unusual, this warm summer dessert makes an excellent finale to a cold supper.

2 cups ripe strawberries, cleaned, stemmed, and cut in quarters
2 cups raspberries, cleaned and stemmed
2 tablespoons Framboise or Grand Marnier
½ cup heavy cream
3 large egg yolks, whisked
½ cup sieved confectioners' sugar
½ tablespoon finely minced orange peel
Fresh mint leaves, for garnish

Preheat the broiler. Mix the berries and liqueur and place in a 9-inch gratin dish. Whip the cream until thick; whisk in the egg yolks, confectioners' sugar, and vanilla, and spoon evenly over the berries. Broil 6 inches under the flame for 3 to 4 minutes, or until the top is lightly browned. Serve immediately, garnished with mint.

MAKE AHEAD: macerate the berries in the liqueur at room temperature up to 1 hour ahead

SOUFFLÉED DESSERT OMELET WITH GRAND MARNIER

SERVES 4 TO 6

◆

*T*his is like eating a cloud! One of my favorite desserts, this perfectly elegant and magical French concoction is also pure simplicity. In just minutes, these simple ingredients are transformed into the lightest, most delicate, and seductive sweet! Since I always have eggs, butter, sugar, and Grand Marnier on hand, I often make this when friends who have stopped by for drinks stay for dinner.

3 large egg yolks
3 tablespoons sugar
3 tablespoons Grand Marnier

3 large egg whites
1 tablespoon unsalted butter

Beat the yolks with the sugar with a whisk or a mixer until the mixture thickens slightly. Then whisk in the Grand Marnier until the sugar dissolves. In a separate bowl, beat the egg whites until stiff but not dry.

Start melting the butter over medium-high heat in a well-cured, heavy-bottomed or nonstick 9- or 10-inch skillet. Tilt the skillet so the butter coats the sides of the pan, especially the side opposite the handle, where the omelet will slide out when cooked.

In a large mixing bowl, carefully but quickly fold the whites into the yolk mixture. When the butter is just starting to brown slightly, immediately pour the egg mixture into the skillet. *Do not stir.* Cook the omelet for about 1 minute, or until the bottom is lightly browned and the eggs have puffed up a bit. Use a rubber spatula to lift up the sides to check browning.

Remove the skillet from the heat, grasp the handle, palm facing upward, and tip the skillet slightly over the middle of a large oval platter so that the omelet starts to slide out. When half of the omelet is on the platter, gently but quickly fold the second half of the omelet over it. (Your hand grasping the skillet handle will arc so that your palm faces down when you have folded the omelet over on itself.) Serve immediately.

NOTE: Do not double this recipe.

RICOTTA AND RUM DESSERT

SERVES 4 TO 6

♦

*T*his simple, satisfying, easy-to-make light dessert—a cross between cheesecake and tortoni—is perfect after an Italian meal.

1 pound part-skim ricotta cheese
½ cup heavy or light cream or plain
   yogurt
2 teaspoons white rum
½ cup granulated or confectioners'
   sugar
¼ cup chopped hazelnuts or almonds,

lightly toasted (see box, page 120)
1 ounce bitter or semisweet chocolate,
   coarsely grated
Grated rind of 1 orange
½ ounce bitter or semisweet
   chocolate, for garnish
12 *amaretti,* for serving

Place all of the ingredients except the ½ ounce chocolate and the *amaretti* in a mixing bowl and beat until well blended. Chill for at least 10 minutes. Serve cold in very small bowls, ramekins, or *pots de crème* with a little extra chocolate grated over the top just before serving. Pass the *amaretti*.

VARIATIONS: Substitute Grand Marnier or any other orange-flavored liqueur for the rum.

Substitute 1 tablespoon instant espresso for the grated orange rind.

MAKE AHEAD: up to 2 days; refrigerate

Coeur à la Crème
(Cream Cheese Heart with Fresh Berries)

SERVES 12

*T*ry this in place of cheesecake—it's the easiest party dessert imaginable, and very elegant. You need to make it at least 12 hours in advance so it can "cure," but it takes only 5 minutes to prepare. If you can find it, use mascarpone (an unsalted Italian cream cheese that is softer and richer than ordinary cream cheese); it gives a wonderful flavor.

1 pound mascarpone or cream cheese
8 ounces ricotta
4 ounces cottage cheese, drained
½ to 1 cup light sour cream or Crème Fraîche (page 210)
½ cup sugar
2 pints strawberries, blueberries, raspberries, or blackberries, or a mix of berries, cleaned and stemmed

With a mixer, beat the mascarpone until soft. Add the ricotta and cottage cheese and beat until smooth. Add the sour cream and beat until a thick, nonpouring consistency is reached. Place the mixture in a heart-shaped porcelain mold pierced with holes (see Note), lined with dampened cheesecloth, and drain over a pan in the refrigerator for 12 to 24 hours.

To serve, place a large platter over the mold and turn both over at once to unmold. Sprinkle with the sugar, and surround with the berries.

NOTE: A heart-shaped porcelain mold pierced with holes is the traditional

French equipment for this dish. If you can't find one in a gourmet cookware store, simply put the cheese mixture in cheesecloth and let it drain overnight in a regular colander placed in a large pan. Then, before serving, put the cheese mixture, still in the cheesecloth, into any 4-cup metal heart-shaped mold and press it in firmly so it takes the shape. Chill; when ready to serve, unmold onto a large platter.

MAKE AHEAD: up to 4 hours

COLD BRANDIED APRICOT MOUSSE

SERVES 8 TO 10

◆

I love the intense fruit flavor of this dessert, just a little of which goes a long way. This is an excellent dessert to keep on hand for unexpected guests. Well wrapped, it keeps a month or more in the refrigerator.

1 pound dried apricots
1 vanilla bean, sliced in half
⅓ cup brandy or cognac
3 tablespoons honey
Long thin shreds of lemon peel, for garnish
½ cup Crème Fraîche (page 210), mascarpone, sour cream, or whipped cream, for serving

In a 2½-quart saucepan, simmer the apricots with the vanilla bean in water to cover until soft, about 10 minutes. Drain the apricots, reserving ½ cup cooking liquid. Discard the vanilla bean.

In a food processor, blend the apricots with the brandy, ½ cup cooking liquid, and honey until smooth. Chill for at least 25 or 30 minutes, or quick-chill in a metal bowl in the freezer for 10 minutes.

Serve in a small glass or crystal bowl with lemon peel scattered on top and a small bowl of *crème fraîche* on the side.

MAKE AHEAD: up to 6 weeks; refrigerate, well wrapped

BAKED CHOCOLATE
AND HAZELNUT MOUSSE

MAKES 8 INDIVIDUAL MOUSSES

◆

I have to admit I'm not crazy about chocolate desserts. I prefer chocolate the way it's enjoyed in Germany and Austria—as an accompaniment to good strong coffee in late afternoon. But this wonderful, not-too-sweet or -gooey dessert can be happily consumed *anytime!* These are not cupcakes but intensely flavored individual baked mousses to be savored by eating them slowly with a small dessert spoon.

8 ounces semisweet chocolate
1 tablespoon Frangelico (hazelnut
  liqueur), white rum, or brandy
1 tablespoon heavy or light cream
3 large eggs, separated
2 tablespoons sugar
2 tablespoons all-purpose flour
⅛ teaspoon kosher salt
5 tablespoons unsalted butter,
  softened
¼ cup chopped hazelnuts
2 tablespoons confectioners' sugar, for
  topping
Candied violets, for garnish (optional)

Preheat the oven to 400°. Melt the chocolate with the Frangelico and cream over very low heat in a heavy-bottomed saucepan (see box). Remove from the heat when melted. With a mixer, beat the egg yolks for about 3 minutes, until thick and lemon-colored; then add the sugar, flour, salt, butter, and hazelnuts. Mix well. Add the melted chocolate and liqueur and mix in thoroughly.

Beat the egg whites until stiff. Stir a quarter of the whites into the batter to lighten the mixture. Then carefully fold in

MELTING CHOCOLATE

◆

*C*hocolate is tricky to melt. It seems that the more expensive the chocolate, the more difficult it is—that is, good-quality chocolate tends to melt very quickly—so use the lowest heat possible. I find it easiest to melt chocolate in a heavy-bottomed pan over the lowest heat, with a little liquid (water, cream, flavoring, or liqueur) in the bottom of the pan.

A microwave oven also works well: Break the chocolate into small pieces and place on a plate. Heat on high (1 ounce for about 45 seconds, 2 ounces for about 1 minute, 4 ounces for about 2 minutes, 8 ounces for about 3½ to 4 minutes). Never *add cold or room-temperature liquid to the hot, melting chocolate or the mixture will stiffen. Add all the recipe's liquid ingredients to the chocolate* before *melting.*

the rest of the whites. Spoon into 8 to 10 small fluted foil baking liners. (Paper cupcake liners set in well-buttered muffin tins, individual ramekins, or individual soufflé dishes could also be used.)

Bake for 20 minutes, or until mousses spring back when pressed. Remove, let cool slightly, then dust the tops with the confectioners' sugar in a small sieve. Serve warm or cool, in the foil liners, on dessert plates. Provide small dessert spoons.

MAKE AHEAD: up to 24 hours; refrigerate; or freeze up to 4 months; to thaw, leave at room temperature 4 hours, and if you wish, warm 10 minutes in a preheated 325° oven

COLD LIME MOUSSE
SERVES 12

*T*he flavor of this light, delicate mousse perfectly complements spicy food. Serve it with a mixture of fresh berries for a beautiful presentation.

6 large eggs, separated
1½ cups sugar
¾ cup fresh lime juice
1 teaspoon grated lime rind
1½ envelopes plain gelatin
⅓ cup cold water
1½ cups heavy cream
Pinch salt
Strips of lime zest, for garnish
Candied violets or fresh mint leaves,
    for garnish (optional)

With an electric mixer, beat the egg yolks, sugar, lime juice, and rind in a large bowl until the mixture thickens. In a metal cup measure, soften the gelatin in the cold water until spongy. Then place the cup measure in a small pan of simmering water so the heat dissolves the gelatin granules. Beat the dissolved gelatin into the yolk mixture. Place the bowl of yolk-gelatin mixture in a larger container filled with ice or ice water to hasten the firming of the gelatin. This should take 5 to 8 minutes.

When the yolk-gelatin mixture is syrupy and thickening, whip the cream until stiff. Fold the cream into the gelatin mixture. Whip the egg whites with salt until stiff but not dry, and fold them in.

Carefully pour the mixture into a 1½-quart porcelain soufflé dish or a crystal or glass bowl and chill in the refrigerator for 1 hour or in the freezer for 30 minutes. Serve with strips of lime zest, and candied violets or mint leaves, if desired.

MAKE AHEAD: up to 24 hours; refrigerate; or freeze for up to 24 hours

COLD LEMON RICE

SERVES 8

◆

*F*rom the lemon groves of the city of Menton in the south of France comes this very tasty, creamy, lemony rice dessert. Although you can serve it with strawberries or other fruit, or a berry sauce, I usually prefer it just plain.

2½ cups whole milk
2 cups water
1 cup long-grain or basmati rice
Rind of 1½ lemons, finely grated
⅓ cup sugar
3 large egg yolks
Juice of 1 lemon
¾ cup heavy cream
3 tablespoons sugar
Zest of ½ lemon, in thin strips, for
    garnish
4 sprigs fresh mint, for garnish

Put a mixing bowl and beaters in the refrigerator or freezer to chill. Put the milk in a 2½-quart saucepan and bring to a boil. Bring the water to a boil separately. Place the rice in a medium saucepan, add the boiling water, and cook on high for 5 minutes; drain. Add the drained rice and lemon rind to the boiling milk, cover, and simmer for 15 to 20 minutes, or until the rice is tender and the liquid has been absorbed.

Combine the ⅓ cup of sugar with the egg yolks and lemon juice. Mix this into the hot rice, and spread out on a large metal baking pan to cool quickly. Then chill in refrigerator for 20 minutes, or in the freezer for 10 minutes.

CHOPPING ORANGE OR LEMON RIND WITH SUGAR

◆

*O*range and lemon rind can be quickly chopped with sugar in a mini-chopper or a small food processor. Combining citrus peel and sugar not only makes chopping easier but yields a more intense citrus flavor because the sugar absorbs the oil.

Using a vegetable peeler, remove only the zest of the orange or lemon and none of the white, bitter pith. Chop into 2-inch lengths and place in the processor. Add 2 to 4 tablespoons of sugar and process. For a small amount, grate the peel by hand and mash it with the sugar with the back of a spoon. Use this method for cakes, cookies, and pie and tart fillings or any dessert that calls for both zest and sugar.

Be sure to rinse fruit with water and wipe dry before peeling or grating. Organic lemons and oranges are best for zest.

Whip the cream with the 3 table-spoons of sugar in the chilled bowl until stiff. Transfer the rice to a large bowl and fold the whipped cream into it. Garnish with lemon zest and mint, and serve cold.

MAKE AHEAD: chill rice mixed with sugar, egg yolks, and lemon juice up to 24 hours ahead; add whipped cream just before serving

SORBETS AND ICE CREAM

◆

QUICK BLACKBERRY SORBET
SERVES 6
◆

*T*his tart no-freeze sorbet tastes wonderful after a meal of fish or chicken.

1 pound frozen blackberries
⅓ cup *crème de cassis*
⅓ cup confectioners' sugar
1½ tablespoons fresh lemon juice

Place the frozen blackberries in a blender or food processor. Add the *crème*

de cassis, sugar, and lemon juice. Let sit for 10 minutes. Blend just enough to break up the frozen berries. Pour into a shallow metal mold and store in the freezer until ready to serve.

MAKE AHEAD: up to 4 hours

BANANA-GINGER SORBET
SERVES 2 TO 4
◆

*T*his quick dessert is a good choice to follow spicy meals. It requires frozen bananas, but since they take only half an hour to freeze, you can freeze them while you're eating dinner and prepare the sorbet at the end of the meal.

2 ripe bananas, peeled
2 tablespoons good white rum
½ tablespoon finely chopped
  crystallized ginger
¼ cup heavy cream
Sugar or honey, to taste

Wrap the bananas individually in plastic wrap and place them in the freezer for at least 30 minutes. Cut each of the frozen bananas into three or four pieces and process in a blender or food processor with the rum and ginger until well blended. Whip the cream until stiff, then fold it into the banana mixture. Sweeten to taste with sugar or honey and serve immediately, or place in a 4-cup metal mold and store in the freezer until ready to serve.

MAKE AHEAD: up to 2 hours

STRAWBERRY SORBET WITH CRÈME DE CASSIS

SERVES 6 TO 8

*C*rème de cassis (*cassis* is French for "blackcurrants") has a dense, rich, dark berry flavor. Friends of mine in Provence gather the wild black currants and make their own potent black currant "tonic," which they claim has a high concentration of vitamin B. The liqueur seems to deepen the flavor of the strawberries here and give them more color as well.

2 pints fresh strawberries, cleaned and
  stemmed
One 10-ounce package frozen
  strawberries, partially thawed
Juice of 1 lemon (about ¼ cup)
2 tablespoons *crème de cassis*
Fresh mint sprigs, for garnish

Puree the berries in a food processor or blender with the lemon juice and *crème de cassis*. Place in a shallow metal mold and freeze for about 15 minutes. Serve, garnished with mint.

MAKE AHEAD: up to 4 hours

MANGO SORBET

SERVES 4 TO 6

◆

*T*he luscious flavor of mango is brought out in this beautiful sorbet.

3 large fresh ripe mangoes, peeled and
    chopped, or enough to yield 2 cups
    fruit (if unavailable, use drained
    canned mangoes)
2 tablespoons sugar dissolved in
    1 tablespoon water
2 tablespoons fresh lime juice
2 tablespoons Grand Marnier
Fresh mint, for garnish

Puree the mango in a blender or food processor. Mix all the ingredients except the mint and freeze in an ice cream maker for 10 to 15 minutes. Serve, garnished with mint.

MAKE AHEAD: up to 5 hours; store in a metal mold in the freezer

RHUBARB-RASPBERRY SORBET

SERVES 4

◆

I like to serve this sorbet in spring and early summer, when rhubarb is in season. Its appealing tart flavor complements rich entrées. The unfrozen mixture is wonderful as a sauce over pound cake or vanilla ice cream.

1 pound fresh or frozen rhubarb, cut
    into 2-inch pieces
One 10-ounce package frozen
    sweetened raspberries
2 teaspoons fresh lemon juice
½ tablespoon minced candied ginger
2 tablespoons Chambord (black
    raspberry liqueur) or *crème de
    cassis*

Put the rhubarb in a heavy saucepan in boiling water to cover for 7 to 10 minutes; drain, and place in a food processor. Place the frozen berries on top of the rhubarb and puree. Add the lemon juice. Pour the mixture into a 4-cup decorative metal mold, stir in the ginger and Chambord, and freeze for 1 hour.

MAKE AHEAD: up to 6 hours

PINEAPPLE ICE CREAM

SERVES 8 TO 10

◆

*T*his ice cream is particularly good after spicy Asian meals.

One 20-ounce can crushed pineapple, well drained, pressed dry in a towel
1½ cups sugar
8 large egg yolks
One 10-ounce can evaporated milk
1½ cups Crème Fraîche (page 210) or heavy cream
⅓ cup light cream
3 tablespoons imported kirsch (see box, page 181)

Chill the pineapple in the freezer while making the ice cream. Beat the sugar and egg yolks in a large bowl with a mixer for about 5 minutes, until pale in color. Add the milk and cream and beat until the mixture thickens slightly. Add the kirsch. Freeze in an ice cream maker for 15 minutes. Stir in the pineapple just before removing the ice cream from the ice cream maker to serve.

MAKE AHEAD: up to 8 hours

TIPS FOR PREPARING HOMEMADE SORBET AND ICE CREAM

◆

• *All homemade sorbets and most homemade ice creams should be eaten the same day they are made; otherwise they become sticky or tacky in texture.*

• *When pureeing a frozen fruit for a sorbet in the blender or food processor, be careful not to overprocess—you'll melt it!*

• *For quickest still-freezing in the freezer, use shallow metal molds, like baking pans. Decorative metal molds with designs on the bottom are good for ice creams that need to freeze for several hours and will be turned out on a plate.*

• *Many home ice cream makers call for plain ice cubes. If yours calls for crushed ice, simply crush cubes in a food processor.*

PINEAPPLE-MINT SORBET
SERVES 6
◆

A fat-free, ultra-speedy, and refreshingly cool finale.

⅓ cup sugar (reduce to 2 tablespoons
　　if using canned pineapple)
Juice of 1 large lime
1 large pineapple, peeled, cored, and
　　cubed, or one 32-ounce can
　　pineapple chunks, drained
¼ cup finely chopped fresh mint

　　Dissolve the sugar in the lime juice.
Puree all of the ingredients in a food

processor until smooth. Place in a 4-cup
decorative metal mold or partially fill
each cup in a Teflon-coated 12-muffin tin,
and put in the freezer. It takes about 3
hours to harden in a large mold but only
1 hour in muffin tins.

MAKE AHEAD: up to 24 hours

EASY FRENCH LEMON ICE CREAM
SERVES 8
◆

*I*f you love lemon, you'll love this fabulously simple dessert. The sharp, refreshing flavor of lemon is welcome at the end of any meal in any season. This
exquisite ice cream, made with whipped cream, is typical of French homemade
ice creams and is called a *parfait*. It takes only 10 minutes to prepare and requires just a short freezing time. The whipped cream keeps the ice cream from
being icy in texture.

2 cups heavy cream
¾ to 1 cup sugar
Grated rind and juice of 2 large lemons
2 tablespoons imported kirsch (see
　　box, page 181)
Sprigs of fresh mint, for garnish

　　Whip the cream and sugar together
until thick. Fold in the rind, juice, and

kirsch. Pour into a 4-cup decorative
metal mold or spoon into a Teflon-coated
12-muffin tin for quick, easy serving.
Cover with plastic wrap and put in the
freezer. It takes about 3 hours to harden
in a large mold but only 1 hour in a muffin tin. Serve, garnished with mint.

MAKE AHEAD: up to 24 hours

CAKES AND COOKIES

◆

Provençal Orange Cake
SERVES 6

◆

A small piece of a light, well-made cake served with coffee always satisfies. This one is especially refreshing after entrées with lots of garlic! French country cakes are typically not big, high, fluffy cakes—this one is only about 1 to 1½ inches high.

8 tablespoons (1 stick) unsalted butter
½ cup sugar
2 large eggs
Grated rind and juice of 1 medium
    orange
1 cup less 1 tablespoon all-purpose
    flour
1 teaspoon baking powder

GLAZE
1 cup confectioners' sugar
⅓ cup freshly squeezed orange juice
2 tablespoons Cointreau or Grand
    Marnier

Thin slices of fresh orange, for garnish

Preheat the oven to 350°. With a mixer in a large bowl, cream the butter and sugar. Beat in the eggs, one at a time, then beat in the orange rind and juice. Combine the flour and baking powder, beat into the liquid mixture, and mix well. Butter and flour an 8- or 9-inch round or square baking pan and pour in the batter. Bake for about 35 minutes, or until the cake springs back when touched.

While the cake bakes, make the glaze. Sift the confectioners' sugar into a medium bowl. Mix in the orange juice and Cointreau, and stir until the sugar has dissolved. Place the cake in the pan on a rack, prick the surface of the cake with a small skewer, and pour the glaze mixture over the warm cake. Garnish the cake with the orange slices and serve warm, at room temperature, or cold.

MAKE AHEAD: up to 48 hours; refrigerate, covered, or freeze for up to 4 months

ESPRESSO CAKE

SERVES 6 TO 8

◆

*T*his easy cake has a wonderful texture and a fine coffee flavor. Without the icing, it makes a good "coffee cake" for breakfast or brunch.

8 tablespoons (1 stick) unsalted butter
½ cup plus onc tablespoon sugar
2 large eggs
6 tablespoons all-purpose flour
7 tablespoons cornstarch
1½ tablespoons instant espresso
    powder
1½ heaping teaspoons baking powder
2 tablespoons brewed espresso coffee

MOCHA ICING
2 ounces bittersweet chocolate
2 tablespoons brewed espresso

Preheat the oven to 350°. With a mixer, cream the butter and sugar in a large bowl. Add the eggs one at a time, beating after each addition. Sift the flour, cornstarch, instant espresso, and baking powder together. Add to the egg mixture, and blend well. Add the espresso coffee.

Butter and flour an 8-inch square or round baking pan. Pour in the batter, and bake for 30 minutes, or until cake springs back when pressed. Remove the cake from the pan and cool on a wire rack.

When the cake is cool, make the icing: Melt the chocolate in the coffee in a double boiler. Stir to mix well. Pour the warm icing over the cooled cake.

NOTE: Although espresso gives the best flavor here, you can use any double-strength dark-roast coffee instead.

MAKE AHEAD: up to 48 hours; refrigerate, covered; or freeze for 3 months, with or without icing; to thaw, leave at room temperature for 3 hours

LIGHT FRENCH COUNTRY CHERRY CAKE

SERVES 6 TO 8

◆

*T*his dessert defies description—it's not really a cake, nor is it a *clafoutis*—it's somewhere in between. But that's what I like about French country desserts—unusual textures and exceptional flavors.

One 16- to 20-ounce package frozen
cherries

3 tablespoons vanilla sugar (if
unavailable, use 3 tablespoons
sugar and 1 teaspoon vanilla
flavoring)

1 tablespoon imported kirsch (see box,
page 181)

3 large egg yolks

Juice and grated rind of 1 large lemon

3 egg whites

½ cup sugar

2½ tablespoons all-purpose flour

2½ tablespoons cornstarch

1 teaspoon baking powder

Heavy or light cream or plain yogurt
(optional)

Preheat the oven to 350°. Remove
the cherries from the freezer, place them
in a colander (they take only 5 minutes or
so to thaw), and drain. Combine the cherries with 2 tablespoons of the vanilla sugar and the kirsch. With a mixer, beat together the yolks, the remaining 1 tablespoon vanilla sugar, and the lemon rind
and juice until thickened, 2 to 3 minutes.

In a separate large bowl, beat the
whites until stiff. Begin adding the ½ cup
sugar, 1 tablespoon at a time, beating at
top speed to make a stiff meringue.

Mix together the flour, cornstarch,
and baking powder. Fold the yolk mixture
into the meringue, then sprinkle the dry
ingredients onto the mixture and carefully
fold in. Butter a 9- or 10-inch baking dish
and pour in the batter. Drop the cherries
into the batter, but do not stir. Bake for
35 minutes, or until lightly browned on
top. Serve warm, either plain or with a
dollop of cream or yogurt on top.

MAKE AHEAD: up to 4 hours; store at
room temperature

WALNUT AND ALMOND CAKE
WITH CASSIS CREAM

SERVES 10 TO 12

◆

*A*udrey Sterling, in whose wonderful kitchen I worked as a private chef at
Iron Horse Vineyards in Sonoma County, California, loved this cake, which I discovered in France years ago.

1½ cups sugar
6 large egg yolks

1 whole large egg
¼ teaspoon salt

1 cup walnuts, finely ground
1 cup almonds, finely ground
¾ cup all-purpose flour
1 teaspoon vanilla extract, or
    ¼ teaspoon almond extract
6 large egg whites
Pinch salt

CASSIS CREAM
1½ cups heavy cream
About ⅓ cup *crème de cassis*

Preheat the oven to 325°. Beat the sugar, egg yolks, whole egg, and salt in a large bowl until thick and pale. Grind the nuts separately, in a food processor or a spice grinder, to a medium or fine consistency. Combine the nuts and flour, then add to the egg mixture. Stir in the vanilla. Beat the egg whites with the pinch of salt. Stir one-quarter of the whites into the batter, then fold in the remaining whites.

Butter and flour a 10-inch springform pan and pour in the batter. Bake for about 1 hour, or until lightly browned. Cool the cake in the pan on a wire rack. Place the rack on top of the cake pan and flip to remove. Whip the cream and mix in the *cassis*. Spread the topping over the cooled cake; place on a serving dish and refrigerate until ready to serve.

VARIATION: The cake is also excellent served without the topping, and with fresh raspberries or blackberries on the side.

MAKE AHEAD: bake cake up to 24 hours ahead; wrap and refrigerate; spread with topping up to 2 hours before serving; refrigerate until serving; or freeze for up to 4 months; thaw, then spread with topping

GINGERED SHORTBREAD
SERVES 12

◆

*C*lassic shortbread takes on quite a different character with the addition of powdered ginger. This version is excellent served for a brunch or with afternoon tea. Rice flour, ground from whole-grain rice, is a traditional ingredient in Scottish shortbread, giving it a nicely granular texture.

1 cup (2 sticks) unsalted butter, cold
½ cup sugar
1¾ cups all-purpose flour, sifted
1 cup rice flour (if unavailable, mix

together ½ cup cornstarch and
    ½ cup all-purpose flour)
½ teaspoon kosher salt
1 tablespoon ground ginger

In a large bowl, cut the sugar into the butter with a pastry blender until well mixed. Combine the dry ingredients and mix them into the butter and sugar until well blended (you can use your hands, a mixer, or a food processor). Shape the dough into a ball; wrap and chill in refrigerator for 10 minutes. Preheat the oven to 350°.

Dust a carved wooden shortbread mold (see Note) heavily with flour and press the dough into it firmly to imprint the design on the bottom. Invert onto a greased baking sheet and lift off the mold. Brush off any excess flour and bake for

20 to 30 minutes. The shortbread should not brown, but it will be a very pale golden color. Leave on the baking sheet to cool. Cut, and serve at room temperature.

NOTE: If you do not have a wooden or ceramic shortbread mold, simply pat the dough into a well-buttered 8-inch pie or tart pan. Cut lightly into the dough to mark off portions. Cool in pan.

MAKE AHEAD: up to 2 days; store in a sealable plastic bag, at room temperature or in refrigerator; or freeze for up to 2 months

PANFORTE DI SIENA
SERVES 10 TO 12

◆

*N*utty, chocolaty, chewy, and full of fruit flavor and spices, *panforte*, or "strong bread," has a lot going for it. It is extremely quick and easy to prepare and keeps at least a month if well wrapped and stored in a cool place. This Italian Christmas confection remains one of my favorite holiday gifts and is a wonderful sweetmeat accompaniment for after-dinner coffee.

¾ cup whole blanched almonds
¾ cup whole unpeeled or peeled hazelnuts
4 to 5 tablespoons unsweetened cocoa powder
1½ teaspoons ground cinnamon
½ teaspoon ground allspice
½ cup all-purpose flour
½ cup candied orange peel, finely chopped

½ cup candied lemon peel, finely chopped
½ cup candied citron, finely chopped
½ cup honey
½ cup granulated sugar
¼ cup confectioners' sugar, for topping

Preheat the oven to 300°. In a bowl, mix together the first nine ingredients. In a small, heavy saucepan, bring the honey and granulated sugar to a boil and sim-mer until a little of the syrup dropped into cold water forms a soft ball, 5 to 7 minutes. Remove from the heat and quickly stir into the fruit mixture.

Turn into a well-buttered or parchment-lined 9-inch pie plate or springform pan and bake for 30 minutes.

Remove from the oven, and let cool in the pan. Sieve the confectioners' sugar over the top. Cut into thin slices and serve.

NOTE: Toast the almonds and hazelnuts, if desired (see boxes, pages 120 and 124).

MAKE AHEAD: prepare up to 1 month ahead; refrigerate

ORANGE-ALMOND TILE COOKIES
MAKES 18 TO 24 COOKIES

◆

*T*hese are the easiest and most elegant cookies I know of. In France and in fine restaurants everywhere, they typically accompany ice creams, sorbets, and fresh fruit desserts. The only trick here is to spread the batter as thin as you possibly can. They are called "tiles" because their curved shape resembles the shape of clay roof tiles.

4 tablespoons (½ stick) butter
½ cup sugar
2 large egg whites
¼ cup all-purpose flour
1 cup sliced raw almonds (skin on)
Zest of 1 orange, in 2- to 3-inch shreds

Preheat the oven to 375°. Melt the butter in a small saucepan; remove from the heat, and let cool. With a spoon, com-bine the sugar, egg whites, and flour in a bowl. Carefully mix in the cooled melted butter and then stir in the almond slices.

Butter and flour two baking sheets. Spread the batter *very thinly* into 3-, 4-, or 5-inch circles with a spatula or the

back of a spoon on the floured sheets. (This will take about 5 minutes.) Scatter the zest over the tiles and bake for 5 to 7 minutes, or until the tiles are lightly browned around the edges only.

While the tiles are baking, place four or five rolling pins or wine bottles on wire cooling racks in readiness for shaping the tiles. Remove the tiles quickly from the baking sheets with a metal spatula and curl them over the rolling pins or bottles to give the cookies a curved shape.

MAKE AHEAD: up to 24 hours; store carefully in a tightly sealed container in a dry place

CARDAMOM COOKIES

MAKES 4 TO 5 DOZEN COOKIES

◆

Cardamom's subtle flavor makes these cookies a welcome treat with ice cream, fresh fruit, and fruit desserts.

2¼ cups all-purpose flour
1 cup sugar
¼ teaspoon kosher salt
1 teaspoon ground cardamom
½ teaspoon baking powder
8 tablespoons (1 stick) unsalted butter
1 large egg
2 tablespoons brandy or rum
½ teaspoon vanilla extract
Sugar

Preheat the oven to 375°. Combine all the dry ingredients in a mixing bowl. With an electric mixer, beat in the butter, then add the liquid ingredients. Flatten the dough into a disk shape, wrap with plastic wrap, and chill in refrigerator for 10 minutes.

Place walnut-sized pieces of dough 4 inches apart on a well-buttered cookie sheet. Flatten them with the flat bottom of a glass dipped in sugar, and bake for about 7 minutes, or until pale golden. Remove to cooling racks and let cool.

MAKE AHEAD: up to 2 days; store in an airtight tin; or freeze for up to 4 months

LEMON-CORNMEAL COOKIES

MAKES 18 TO 24 MEDIUM COOKIES, 10 TO 12 LARGE COOKIES

◆

Cornmeal adds a delightful crunch to these cookies. The crispness and fresh lemon flavor make them an excellent accompaniment to fruit desserts.

½ pound (2 sticks) unsalted butter
1 scant cup sugar
2 large egg yolks
1½ teaspoons finely grated fresh
    lemon peel

1½ cups all-purpose flour
1 cup yellow cornmeal

Preheat the oven to 350°. In a large bowl, using a mixer, cream the butter and sugar. Add the egg yolks, lemon peel, flour, and cornmeal, and combine. Shape into a log, 3 inches in diameter; wrap in foil and chill in the freezer for 10 minutes.

Cut the chilled dough into thin slices. Place them carefully 1 inch apart on buttered baking sheets, and bake for 8 to 10 minutes, or until pale golden. Remove to cooling racks and let cool.

VARIATION: Dust the counter with some extra flour and roll out a sixth of the chilled dough at a time, adding flour to the countertop as needed to keep the dough from sticking. Cut out shapes with cookie cutters or freeform. Follow baking directions above.

MAKE AHEAD: up to 3 days; store in an airtight tin; or freeze for up to 4 months

DESSERT SAUCES

◆

WARM APRICOT SAUCE
MAKES ABOUT 1¼ CUPS; SERVES 6
◆

Serve this tasty sauce over ice cream, pound cake, pancakes, waffles, baked bananas, apples, or pears, French toast, or bread pudding. Or pack it in an attractive jar for a fine homemade gift. It will keep up to six months in the refrigerator.

One 10-ounce jar apricot jam
⅓ to ½ cup water
1 to 2 tablespoons imported kirsch
    (see box, page 181) or cognac

In a small saucepan, cook the jam and water until the desired pouring consistency is reached, about 5 minutes. Add the kirsch. Serve warm, or store in a glass jar in the refrigerator and reheat gently before serving.

VARIATION: If using cognac, add ½ cup toasted slivered almonds.

MAKE AHEAD: up to 6 months; refrigerate; reheat gently

HOT CHOCOLATE SAUCE

MAKES ABOUT 2½ CUPS; SERVES 10 TO 12

◆

*T*his classic sauce, delicious over ice cream, cake, or ice cream–filled cream puffs, will keep up to two months in the refrigerator.

14 ounces dark or semisweet
  chocolate, broken into pieces
3 tablespoons double-strength coffee,
  preferably espresso or dark roast
1 teaspoon vanilla extract
¼ cup confectioners' sugar
¾ cup heavy cream
1 tablespoon cognac, Armagnac,
  Cointreau, or rum

In a heavy-bottomed 2-quart sauce-pan, melt the chocolate with all of the other ingredients over very low heat (see box, page 188). Whisk until blended and serve warm, or store in a glass jar in the refrigerator and reheat gently to serve (see below).

MAKE AHEAD: up to 2 months; refrigerate; to reheat, stand the uncovered jar in a saucepan, add water to halfway up the jar, heat the water to a simmer, and simmer gently until the sauce melts (about 10 minutes)

◆

ACCOMPANIMENTS: SAUCES AND BUTTERS, CONDIMENTS, AND QUICK BREADS

◆

A sauce is a little like an edging of lace around a collar or cuff—it enhances and delights but doesn't detract from the dress itself. It can be that special touch that makes a dish really memorable.

Sauces and flavored butters provide a quick way to make a dish distinctive. They give a wide variety of flavors to simply prepared meats and vegetables. Sauté a strip steak and top it with Roquefort-Walnut Butter. Boil new potatoes and add savory Green Chili–Cumin Butter. Bake or grill a tuna steak and flavor it with the piquant Montpellier Butter. Sauté or grill a chicken breast and serve it with Romesco Sauce. The Green Sauce with Mustard and Lemon is terrific tossed with steamed zucchini or broccoli.

The simple sauces in this chapter are designed to be multipurpose—most of them can be used on meats, fish, poultry, and vegetables. Several, such as the Roquefort-Walnut Butter and the Romesco Sauce, also make excellent appetizers spread on toasted or plain French bread. And try the marvelous, oil-free Fresh Tomato and Lemon Dressing on vegetables or on bread.

In addition to the dozen quick sauces in this chapter, the salads chapter includes a large variety of vinaigrettes, marinades, and dressings, all of which can easily be adapted for other uses. For example, serve the Raspberry-Chive Vinaigrette over cold poached salmon for a marvelously flavored combination. The Spicy Peanut Sauce, served over noodles, is wonderful combined with cooled cooked chicken breast. Experimenting with these sauces will expand your sauce repertoire enormously.

Interesting condiments, homemade and store-brought, can take the place of sauces or butters in a quick meal. For example, the Red Onion, Caper, and Lemon Relish tastes wonderful with broiled salmon, and the Spicy Apricot Chutney provides a perfect complement to a grilled or roasted pork tenderloin. And most condiments have the advantage of keeping for several weeks in the refrigerator, so they can always be made well ahead of time.

Anything home-baked really personalizes a meal. The delightful quick breads in this chapter add a spark of interest when they accompany soups, main-course salads, and light or company meals. I love the Cornmeal Madeleines with Black Bean Soup Supreme; the Scallion Scones are very good with brunch dishes; and the Saffron Popovers make an elegant statement with Noisettes of Spring Lamb with Thyme and Rosemary. All the cornbreads and the biscuits freeze well.

SAUCES AND BUTTERS

CONDIMENTS

QUICK BREADS

SAUCES AND BUTTERS

♦

WATERCRESS SAUCE

MAKES ABOUT 1¼ CUPS; SERVES 4 TO 6

♦

*H*ere's a light, lemony sauce for salmon, halibut, redfish, or boiled or baked potatoes.

3 large eggs
1 bunch watercress (leaves and
　　stems), washed and dried
Juice of 2 lemons
½ teaspoon kosher salt
¼ teaspoon freshly ground black
　　pepper

Cook the eggs in the shell in boiling water for 5 minutes. Plunge them into cold water; let sit for 5 minutes, then shell. Place the cooked eggs with all the remaining ingredients in a blender or food processor and blend until very smooth. Refrigerate until ready to serve.

MAKE AHEAD: up to 2 hours; refrigerate

LIGHT BLENDER MAYONNAISE

MAKES ABOUT 1½ CUPS

♦

*A*lthough I really don't care for mayonnaise as a dressing for salad of any kind, preferring a vinaigrette or *crème fraîche* dressing, I love mayonnaise spread on bread for sandwiches. One of my favorite sandwich combinations came from a little Texas-German eatery that bakes its own bread and smokes its own turkey: a Texas smoked turkey sandwich on white bread with lemon mayonnaise. The variations will give you lots of different possibilities for interesting sandwiches and canapés. All the ingredients should be at room temperature.

1 large egg, at room temperature
2 tablespoons fresh lemon or lime
   juice
½ teaspoon kosher salt
⅛ teaspoon freshly ground white
   pepper
½ teaspoon Dijon mustard
1 cup canola oil, or other light
   vegetable oil
¼ cup finely minced fresh parsley
2 tablespoons fresh chives

Blend the egg, lemon juice, salt, pepper, and mustard in a blender or food processor. Start adding the oil, at first by drops, until the mixture thickens a bit, then in a thin stream, blending on high speed until the mayonnaise is thick and smooth. (This takes about 5 minutes.) Be careful; adding too much oil too fast to the eggs may curdle the mayonnaise. Taste for seasoning. Stir in the herbs just before using.

VARIATIONS: Substitute 1 tablespoon basil, oregano, marjoram, tarragon, or chervil for the parsley and chives.

MAKE AHEAD: prepare up to 24 hours ahead; refrigerate

FRESH TOMATO AND LEMON DRESSING

MAKES ABOUT 2½ CUPS; SERVES 4

◆

*U*se this pretty and refreshing oil-free vinaigrette as a dressing for avocados, or toss it with warm cooked vegetables such as cauliflower, broccoli, green beans, potatoes, or zucchini and serve as a salad or a vegetable side dish. It is also excellent on green salads and over steak, sautéed chicken breasts, and steamed fish.

1 garlic clove, mashed to a paste (see
   box, page 62)
3 large, fresh, ripe tomatoes, peeled
   and seeded; if unavailable, use
   3 cups canned Italian plum
   tomatoes
½ medium red pepper, seeded,
   chopped
2 tablespoons fresh lemon juice
¼ teaspoon kosher salt

Pinch cayenne
Pinch freshly ground black pepper
1 teaspoon grated lemon rind

Place all the ingredients in a food processor or blender and process until well blended. Keep refrigerated until ready to serve.

MAKE AHEAD: up to 4 hours; refrigerate

CAPER SAUCE

MAKES 5 TABLESPOONS; SERVES 2

◆

*T*his excellent sauce can be served over cooked asparagus, carrots, potatoes, broccoli, green beans, or cauliflower or over poached or steamed fish.

4 tablespoons (½ stick) unsalted
    butter

1 teaspoon tarragon, balsamic, or
    champagne vinegar
1 tablespoon drained and rinsed
    capers
1 tablespoon minced fresh parsley
⅛ teaspoon freshly ground white
    pepper

UNSALTED BUTTER

◆

*U*nsalted butter has a more delicate flavor than salted butter. Moreover, the salt added to salted butter serves not only to add flavor but also to prolong the shelf life, making it more difficult to detect when the butter has gone bad.

    In a small pan, melt the butter over very low heat. Add the remaining ingredients and heat briefly. Serve hot.

MAKE AHEAD: up to 24 hours; refrigerate; reheat gently

CRÈME FRAÎCHE

MAKES ABOUT 1 CUP

◆

*C*rème fraîche is an extremely useful item to have on hand in your refrigerator and a practical one, too, as it keeps up to three weeks. Its slightly sour, slightly nutty flavor makes it a perfect topping for many desserts. Use it in place of whipped cream or sour cream. Use it in sauces too. Just one tablespoon of *crème fraîche* gives great flavor and texture to a simple pan sauce.

1 cup heavy cream, preferably *not*
    ultrapasteurized
1½ tablespoons buttermilk

    Combine the cream and buttermilk in a glass jar with a lid and vigorously shake for about 1 minute. Remove the lid, cover the jar top with a paper towel, and put in a very warm place (75° to 85°) for 24 to 36 hours, or until the cream has thickened. Cover and refrigerate.

NOTE: *Crème fraîche* does not whip.

MAKE AHEAD: prepare up to 3 weeks ahead; refrigerate

ROMESCO SAUCE

MAKES ABOUT 1½ CUPS; SERVES 6 TO 8

◆

*T*his unusual sauce from Spanish Catalonia uses almonds to moderate the heat of chilies, creating a fabulous, rich flavor that perfectly complements grilled shellfish or baked or poached fin fish. Romesco is also delicious spread on toasted bread or used as a dip for raw or grilled vegetables. Try it spread under the skin of a chicken breast for roasting, or put a spoonful in a hot fish soup.

2 large dried ancho chilies
1 tablespoon red-wine vinegar
1 small jalapeño chili, seeded and
    chopped
3 large tomatoes
Three 1-inch slices French bread
½ tablespoon olive oil
1 sprig fresh parsley
4 to 5 large garlic cloves
½ cup whole blanched almonds
½ teaspoon kosher salt
¼ teaspoon cayenne
2 to 3 teaspoons Spanish sherry wine
    vinegar
3 to 4 tablespoons extra-virgin olive oil

Simmer the chilies with the vinegar in water to cover for 5 minutes, then split and remove the seeds. At the same time,

roast the tomatoes whole in a dry skillet until the skins are lightly browned in places; halve and remove the seeds. Fry the bread in the oil in a heavy skillet until golden, 3 to 4 minutes. Place all of the ingredients in a blender or food processor and process until well blended and thick. Taste for seasoning. Serve at room temperature.

NOTE: I make this sauce quite thick; if you wish to thin it, add more vinegar and oil.

VARIATION: Substitute hazelnuts, toasted and skinned (see box, page 120), for the almonds.

MAKE AHEAD: up to 1 week; refrigerate; bring to room temperature to serve

GREEN SAUCE WITH MUSTARD AND LEMON

MAKES ABOUT 1 CUP; SERVES 4

◆

*I*f you are tired of plain-tasting vegetables and fish, try this zippy, healthy sauce to perk up the flavor. This recipe is an adaptation of Nika Hazelton's *Sauce au Persil* from her wonderful *Swiss Cookbook*. Serve over potatoes, rice, carrots, cauliflower, green beans, or asparagus or poached, steamed, grilled, or baked fish or chicken.

1 tablespoon unsalted butter
1 tablespoon Dijon mustard
1 tablespoon fresh lemon juice
½ teaspoon freshly grated lemon rind
4 tablespoons light sour cream
1 tablespoon capers, or more to taste
½ cup stemmed fresh parsley
2 tablespoons fresh chives or green
    scallion tops
2 scallions, chopped
2 garlic cloves, mashed to a pulp (see
    box, page 62)
¼ teaspoon dried thyme
⅛ teaspoon kosher salt
⅛ teaspoon freshly ground black
    pepper

In a small saucepan, melt the butter; add the mustard and lemon juice and rind and mix well. Place the butter mixture and all of the remaining ingredients in a blender or food processor and process until well blended, about 1 minute. Check the seasoning. Serve warm.

VARIATION: Add 2 small cornichons for a slightly piquant flavor.

MAKE AHEAD: up to 4 hours; refrigerate; reheat gently

CRAB BUTTER

MAKES ABOUT 1 CUP; SERVES 6 TO 8

◆

I discovered this intriguing butter during crab season in Jackson, Mississippi, where every restaurant featured fish dishes with interesting crab toppings. Serve over any poached, grilled, baked, or broiled fish fillets.

2 to 3 ounces fresh crab meat, picked
   over
8 tablespoons (1 stick) unsalted butter
⅛ to ¼ teaspoon cayenne
⅛ teaspoon kosher salt

Pound the crab meat in a mortar with a pestle, or puree in a food proces- sor, until creamy. Add the butter and seasonings and process. Form into a ½-inch-wide log, wrap in plastic wrap, and store in the refrigerator until serving. To serve, place 1 to 3 teaspoons on top of the steaming dish to melt.

MAKE AHEAD: up to 4 hours; refrigerate

MONTPELLIER BUTTER

MAKES ABOUT ¾ CUP; SERVES 6 TO 8

◆

*M*ontpellier, a fascinating old university town on the edge of Provence, gives its name to this piquant herb butter. It's absolutely wonderful served on fish, poached eggs, or potatoes.

2 cups water
3 tablespoons minced fresh parsley
2 tablespoons minced fresh chives
1 tablespoon minced fresh tarragon or
   basil (if unavailable, use ½ tablespoon dried tarragon or basil)
8 leaves fresh spinach, washed and
   dried
1 medium garlic clove, mashed to a
   paste (see box, page 62)
1 large shallot, minced
4 anchovy fillets, rinsed and patted dry
2 cornichons, minced
1 tablespoon capers, rinsed and patted
   dry
½ teaspoon grated lemon rind
¼ teaspoon kosher salt
¼ teaspoon freshly ground black
   pepper

5 tablespoons unsalted butter
3 tablespoons extra-virgin olive oil
Fresh lemon juice (optional)

Bring the water to a boil. Drop in the fresh herbs and blanch for 1 minute; remove, drain, press dry, and put in a food processor. Add all of the remaining ingredients except the butter, oil, and lemon juice, and process until well chopped. Add the butter and process until well blended. Gradually add the olive oil until blended into a thick green sauce. Taste for seasoning, adding a little lemon juice or pepper if needed. Serve at room temperature.

MAKE AHEAD: up to 24 hours; refrigerate; bring to room temperature before serving

GREEN CHILI–CUMIN BUTTER

MAKES ABOUT ½ CUP; SERVES 4 TO 6

◆

Serve this zesty butter over corn on the cob, yellow squash, zucchini, new potatoes, cauliflower, broiled tomatoes, or grilled fish, chicken, pork, or beef.

4 tablespoons (½ stick) unsalted
    butter
1 teaspoon ground cumin
One 2-ounce can roasted, peeled green
    chilies, rinsed and patted dry
2 scallions with 3 inches of green,
    chopped
¼ teaspoon kosher salt
⅛ teaspoon freshly ground black
    pepper
4 sprigs fresh cilantro, parsley, thyme,
    or oregano

Melt the butter in a medium skillet. Add the cumin, and cook over medium-high heat for 1 minute; add the chilies and scallion. Cook, stirring, for 2 to 3 minutes, or until the scallion is soft. While hot, puree in a blender or food processor with the salt, pepper, and fresh herbs. Serve warm or cold.

TOASTING GROUND CUMIN

◆

As with cumin seeds, the full flavor of ground cumin is brought out by being heated slightly. Place the ground cumin in a small dry skillet and toast over medium-low heat for just a minute or two, until fragrant. Or cook in melted butter or oil over medium-high heat for 1 minute. Any dish that calls for cumin will benefit by toasting the cumin by either method.

MAKE AHEAD: up to 4 days; refrigerate; or freeze for up to 3 months

ROQUEFORT-WALNUT BUTTER

MAKES ABOUT ¾ CUP; SERVES 4

◆

The flavor of this delicious butter enhances grilled chicken breasts and steaks, fettuccine, cauliflower, carrots, green beans, and toast. Keep it on hand in your refrigerator or freezer.

5 tablespoons unsalted butter,
    softened
¼ cup crumbled Roquefort cheese
3 tablespoons chopped walnuts,
    toasted (see box, page 124)
¼ teaspoon freshly ground black
    pepper
Pinch kosher salt

Place all of the ingredients in the food processor and process just until the butter is blended. To serve, place 1 to 3 teaspoons on top of the steaming dish to melt.

MAKE AHEAD: up to 4 days; refrigerate; or freeze for up to 3 months

CONDIMENTS

◆

RED ONION, CAPER, AND LEMON RELISH

MAKES 1 CUP

◆

*T*his simple condiment will add zip to grilled salmon, sautéed chicken, roast beef sandwiches, or smoked-salmon canapés. It keeps in the refrigerator for two to three weeks.

1 red onion, very finely sliced or
    chopped
2 tablespoons capers, drained
2 teaspoons fresh lemon juice
½ teaspoon freshly grated lemon rind
¼ teaspoon freshly ground black
    pepper
Pinch kosher salt
1½ tablespoons extra-virgin olive oil
1 teaspoon fresh thyme leaves
1 teaspoon fresh marjoram

1 tablespoon minced fresh parsley
2 tablespoons pine nuts

Place all of the ingredients in a small bowl and mix well. Store in the refrigerator in a covered jar. This relish is good right after it is made, but the flavors develop if it stands an hour or more.

MAKE AHEAD: prepare up to 2 weeks ahead; refrigerate

MINT-VINEGAR SAUCE

MAKES 1½ CUPS

◆

*H*ere's a classic that seems completely contemporary: a tart English herbal sauce for lamb. A little of this condiment goes a long way. It's also excellent with other meats or wild game, such as venison, boar, duck, or goose.

1 cup good-quality white-wine or
    champagne vinegar
¼ cup sugar
½ cup packed chopped fresh mint
    leaves
Pinch kosher salt

Combine all of the ingredients and let stand for at least 30 minutes before serving. Serve either chilled or at room temperature.

MAKE AHEAD: up to 8 hours; refrigerate

ROASTED TOMATO SALSA

MAKES 1½ CUPS

◆

*S*erve this delicious simple salsa over fried or scrambled eggs, roasted meats, cooked dried beans, fresh green beans or other vegetables, in soups, with Mexican food, over sliced fresh avocado, over thinly sliced zucchini as a salad, or, last but not least, with barbecued foods or burgers.

2 large ripe tomatoes
1 small white onion, finely chopped
2 serrano chilies, seeded and minced
½ teaspoon kosher salt
1 tablespoon cold water
2 tablespoons fresh lime juice
1½ tablespoons chopped fresh cilantro

Preheat a small dry skillet for 2 to 3 minutes. Add the whole tomatoes and turn until they are lightly browned in places and you smell a tomato aroma, about 5 minutes. Remove the tomatoes, let cool, skin, and finely chop. In a bowl, mix all of the ingredients together. Taste carefully for seasoning, and store in the refrigerator until served.

MAKE AHEAD: up to 8 hours; refrigerate

SPICY APRICOT CHUTNEY

MAKES ABOUT 1 QUART

◆

*A*s a fabulous accompaniment to curries, pork, sausage, venison, or game birds, this delicious, easy-to-make chutney cannot be beat. It keeps in the refrigerator for up to six months. It also makes a great gift.

2 cups dried apricots, quartered or
    chopped
2 tablespoons candied ginger, finely
    chopped
1 cup golden raisins
½ lemon, peel left on, thinly sliced,
    slices quartered
1 cup yellow onion, thinly sliced, slices
    halved
1½ cups dark brown sugar
½ cup white-wine vinegar
2 garlic cloves, crushed
1½ teaspoons dry mustard
1 teaspoon dried red-pepper flakes
½ cup tomato juice

½ teaspoon salt
½ teaspoon ground cinnamon
½ teaspoon ground cloves
½ teaspoon ground allspice

Place all of the ingredients in a large, heavy, nonaluminum saucepan and simmer, uncovered, over low heat until thick, about 30 minutes. Place in sterilized jars, cover when cool, and store in the refrigerator for up to 6 months.

MAKE AHEAD: prepare up to 6 months ahead; refrigerate

HOMEMADE FRENCH MUSTARD

MAKES ABOUT 1 CUP

◆

*M*ake this easy homemade mustard for a special house gift or for your own kitchen pantry. It has a wonderful flavor. It's lighter in texture than regular mustard, so it can easily be used as a sauce. Just spread a teaspoon or so on top of any simply prepared (grilled, broiled, baked, steamed, pan-sautéed) meat, chicken, or fish dish and it will melt in, giving subtle flavor. The dry mustard needs to marinate overnight to mellow its harshness; once marinated it's a ten-minute dish.

¼ cup dry mustard
½ teaspoon kosher salt
1 tablespoon plus 1 teaspoon sugar
2 tablespoons champagne vinegar
⅓ cup plus 2 tablespoons dry white
    wine
3 large egg yolks

Combine the dry mustard, salt, sugar, vinegar, and wine in a small, non-aluminum saucepan and whisk together until smooth. Let stand at room temperature overnight.

Beat the egg yolks vigorously with a fork or whisk until slightly thickened. Add the yolks to the mustard mixture in the saucepan. Cook over low heat, whisking continuously, until the mustard thickens, 5 to 7 minutes. Do not let it boil. It will not be as thick as regular mustard when it finishes cooking, but it will thicken a little more when it is cool. Let the mustard cook, then put it in a sterilized jar or crock and store in the refrigerator up to 1 month.

NOTE: This recipe can be doubled or tripled.

♦ VARIATIONS: To make flavored mustards, stir in flavor additions while the mustard is still hot:

CAPER MUSTARD: ½ tablespoon rinsed and dried small (nonpareil) capers.

TOMATO MUSTARD: ½ to 1 tablespoon imported tomato paste concentrate from a tube, or if unavailable, regular tomato paste.

TARRAGON MUSTARD: 2 teaspoons finely chopped fresh tarragon.

HONEY MUSTARD: ½ to 1 tablespoon honey.

THYME MUSTARD: ½ tablespoon chopped fresh thyme.

CHUTNEY MUSTARD: ¼ cup finely chopped mango chutney or other chutney.

CREOLE MUSTARD: ½ teaspoon cayenne, ½ teaspoon hot Hungarian paprika, and ¼ teaspoon each dried basil, marjoram, and oregano.

MAKE AHEAD: prepare up to 1 month ahead; refrigerate

QUICK BREADS

◆

SOUR CREAM–CHILI CORNBREAD

MAKES 9 LARGE PIECES

◆

*T*his easy-to-prepare savory cornbread is always a hit at large family buffets.

6 tablespoons unsalted butter
One 16-ounce can cream-style corn
½ cup light sour cream
2 large eggs
1 cup yellow cornmeal
1 teaspoon kosher salt
1 tablespoon baking powder
4 ounces grated cheddar or Monterey Jack cheese
One 4-ounce can chopped green chilies, drained, or 2 fresh jalapeños, seeded and minced

Preheat the oven to 375°. Melt the butter in a small saucepan. Beat the melted butter, corn, sour cream, and eggs together in a large bowl. Combine the dry ingredients in a separate bowl and mix. Stir the dry ingredients into the liquid and mix well. Stir in the cheese and chilies.

Pour the batter into a buttered 9-inch square baking pan and bake for 40 minutes, or until cornbread springs back when pressed. Or bake in well-buttered and floured madeleine molds for 12 minutes, as in the recipe for Cornmeal Madeleines (page 221). Serve warm.

MAKE AHEAD: up to 8 hours; reheat in a 325° oven for 10 minutes; or freeze for up to 4 months

CORNBREAD WITH GOAT CHEESE AND SUN-DRIED TOMATOES

MAKES 9 LARGE PIECES

◆

*C*ornbread ranks among my favorite quick breads. It is homey and infinitely appealing. This version is really gourmet fare; it's wonderful for picnics too.

4 tablespoons (½ stick) unsalted
   butter
1½ cups yellow cornmeal
½ cup all-purpose flour
2 teaspoons sugar
1¼ teaspoons kosher salt
1 tablespoon baking powder
2 large eggs
1 cup whole milk
⅓ cup sour cream
4 ounces goat cheese, finely crumbled
2 ounces dry-packed sun-dried
   tomatoes, plumped in hot water
   (see box, page 95), drained, and
   chopped

Preheat the oven to 425°. Melt the butter in a small saucepan. Place the dry ingredients in a bowl and mix well. Beat together the eggs, milk, and sour cream and stir into the dry ingredients. Add the melted butter last and stir well. Scatter the goat cheese and sun-dried tomatoes evenly over the uncooked cornbread and let them sink in.

Pour the batter into a well-buttered 9-inch square baking pan and bake for 20 minutes, or until lightly browned. Or, bake in well-buttered madeleine molds for 12 minutes as in the recipe for Cornmeal Madeleines (page 221). Serve warm.

MAKE AHEAD: up to 8 hours; reheat in a 325° oven for 10 minutes; or freeze for up to 4 months

Cornmeal Spoonbread with Poblano Chilies

SERVES 4

◆

Spoonbread is usually cooked as a soufflé in a deeper dish than is called for here, but that doubles the baking time. This method gives it a slightly firmer texture, and it is just as delicious.

1¼ cups water
1 tablespoon unsalted butter
1 cup yellow cornmeal
½ cup plus 2 tablespoons all-purpose
   flour
½ teaspoon kosher salt
1 tablespoon sugar

1 large poblano chili, roasted (see box,
   page 35), peeled, seeded, and
   finely chopped
2 large egg yolks
1 cup buttermilk
1 teaspoon baking soda
2 large egg whites, beaten

Preheat the oven to 375°. In a medium saucepan, bring the water to a boil; add the butter. In a bowl, mix the cornmeal, flour, salt, and sugar. Pour these into the boiling water, stir until well mixed, and remove from heat. Stir in the chopped roasted poblanos and egg yolks and mix well. Add the buttermilk, baking soda, and beaten egg whites.

Pour the mixture into a buttered shallow 10- to 12-inch long gratin dish and bake for about 20 minutes, or until the top is browned but the center remains a little soft. Serve warm.

MAKE AHEAD: roast chilies up to 24 hours ahead; freeze spoonbread for up to 4 months

CORNMEAL MADELEINES
MAKES 30

◆

*B*y baking cornbread in madeleine mold pans, you end up with a delicious, moist, corn-studded cornbread in a neat small serving that doesn't disintegrate into a thousand crumbs. Cornmeal Madeleines can also be used as a base for a sauce—try topping them with creamed oysters for a great lunch or brunch.

5 tablespoons unsalted butter
1½ cups yellow cornmeal
½ cup all-purpose flour
2 teaspoons sugar
1¼ teaspoons kosher salt
1 tablespoon baking powder
2 large eggs
1 cup whole milk
⅓ cup sour cream
1 cup corn kernels, scraped from approximately 3 ears fresh corn, or 1 cup frozen corn, thawed
½ teaspoon freshly ground black pepper
2 tablespoons minced fresh chives

Preheat the oven to 425°. Melt the butter in a small saucepan. Place all of the dry ingredients except the pepper and chives in a bowl and mix well. In a small mixing bowl, beat the eggs, milk, and sour cream together and then stir into the dry ingredients. Add the melted butter, corn, pepper, and chives and mix well. Spoon the batter into well-buttered and floured madeleine molds and bake for 12 minutes, or until lightly browned on top. Remove immediately to a cooling rack. Serve warm.

VARIATION: Add 2 seeded and very finely minced jalapeños to the batter.

MAKE AHEAD: up to 24 hours; reheat 10 minutes in a 325° low oven; or freeze for up to 4 months

SAFFRON POPOVERS

MAKES 6 LARGE POPOVERS

◆

*S*affron's intriguing flavor graces this unusual quick bread. Serve these instead of the ubiquitous French bread with soups and salads.

¾ cup whole milk
½ teaspoon saffron threads (see box, page 98)
4 large eggs
1 cup all-purpose flour, sifted
½ teaspoon kosher salt
Pinch cayenne
Freshly ground black pepper
2 tablespoons unsalted butter, for greasing ramekins

Preheat the oven to 450°. Scald the milk in a small saucepan; remove from heat, add the saffron, and let steep for 5 minutes. Combine the eggs, saffron-milk mixture, flour, salt, cayenne, and black pepper in a large bowl and mix with an electric mixer.

Fill 6 well-buttered 4- or 5-ounce ramekins, custard cups, or soufflé dishes three-quarters full (about ½ cup batter in each). Place the ramekins on a thin baking sheet (if using a heavy sheet, increase the oven temperature 25°) and bake for about 20 to 25 minutes, or until the popovers puff high and are crusty and brown on the outside. If the popovers brown too quickly, turn the oven temperature down to 400° after 10 minutes and add 5 minutes to the baking time. Serve hot, in the ramekins.

SCALLION SCONES

MAKES 8 TO 10

◆

*T*hese are delightful for brunch, breakfast, or tea. Handle the dough as little as possible to avoid toughening it.

2 cups all-purpose flour
½ teaspoon kosher salt
1 tablespoon baking powder
¾ cup buttermilk

½ teaspoon baking soda
7 scallions (both white and green parts), finely chopped
Milk, for glaze

Preheat the oven to 350°. Place the flour, salt, and baking powder in a mixing bowl. Add the buttermilk, baking soda, and scallions into the bowl. Stir the dough gently until barely mixed.

Gather into a ball and place on the counter. Dust with a little extra flour and knead only a few times, then pat or roll out into a 10-inch circle 1 inch thick. Transfer the dough to a buttered baking sheet, cut into 8 to 10 wedges, brush each with milk, and bake for 10 to 12 minutes, or until very lightly browned. Serve warm.

MAKE AHEAD: up to 4 hours; reheat in a 325° oven for 10 minutes

CHIVE AND PARSLEY BISCUITS

MAKES 8 TO 10 MEDIUM BISCUITS

◆

*T*hese biscuits are a particularly delicious accompaniment to salads and soups.

2 cups all-purpose flour
1 scant teaspoon kosher salt
1 tablespoon baking powder
¼ cup finely chopped fresh parsley
¼ cup chopped fresh chives
1 cup light cream

Preheat the oven to 425°. Combine the flour, salt, baking powder, and herbs in a bowl. Pour in the cream, stirring only until the ingredients are lightly blended and hold together (overmixing makes biscuits tough).

Place the dough on a lightly floured surface, and knead a few times until smooth. Quickly pat or roll to a ½-inch thickness. Cut eight to ten 3-inch rounds and place them on a buttered baking sheet. Bake for about 15 minutes, or until the biscuits are lightly browned. Remove and serve hot.

NOTE: This recipe can easily be doubled or tripled.

VARIATIONS: Use only chives or parsley (½ cup).

Mix ¼ cup fresh chopped parsley or chives with ¼ cup fresh thyme, marjoram, chervil, fennel, or sage.

MAKE AHEAD: freeze for up to 4 months

CHAPTER

❧ 10 ❧

◆

WEEKEND
COOKING

◆

Weekend cooking has a completely different feel for me than weekday food preparation, where time always seems at a premium and leisure is something deferred. Meals on the weekend are really "events," anticipated and enjoyed with relish. Guests are invited to share meals and good times in the kitchen. The atmosphere is one of relaxed enjoyment, and the food in this chapter is designed to match that mood. Most of these dishes are just as quick and easy to prepare as the dishes in the rest of the book, but a few require a somewhat longer cooking time, in the oven or on top of the stove. For instance, the Roast Tuscan Pork Loin with Garlic and Herbs and the Perfect Roast Tarragon Chicken take only minutes to prepare but must roast for 1½ hours.

Roasts and braised dishes are wonderful for entertaining; not only can they cook away quietly while you and your guests enjoy apéritifs, they also add rich aromas to your kitchen. And because they are homey and unfussy foods, they connote warmth, ease, and old-fashioned hospitality. That's the spirit this cook-book reflects, I hope—a sense of *enjoyment* in preparing foods, of the pleasure of beautiful ingredients combined in simple but elegant ways to help you enjoy meals more while leading a busy, active life.

The kitchen, the hearth and heart of any home, is a tremendous draw. Even if I start serving hors d'oeuvres and wine outdoors or in the living room, every-one eventually gravitates toward the kitchen, to be right in the middle of all the preparations. If being in the kitchen with guests doesn't work for you, seek out the many recipes in this chapter and throughout the book that can be made ahead and reheated, or served cold or at room temperature.

I especially enjoy creating wonderful menus for entertaining, so at the end of this section I've listed twenty-three of my favorite menus, all using recipes from the book. These menus will give you exciting new ideas for entertaining and holiday meals throughout the year. For example, the Thanksgiving or Christmas Feast, which includes Roasted Acorn Squash Soup with Mace and Cinnamon, Squab Roasted with Five-Onion and Five-Herb Stuffing, Wild Mushroom Ragoût, Braised Chestnuts with Shallots and Thyme, Winter Salad Greens with Cranberry-Orange Vinaigrette, Dried Fruits in Chardonnay with Fresh Ginger, and Gingered Shortbread, has all the elements of a traditional meal, but this menu is jazzier, healthier, and takes much less time to prepare than the up-at-the-crack-of-dawn, twenty-pound-turkey ordeal. It can be completed in about two hours or less, from start to finish, including the dessert.

The menus I have put together in this chapter also may take a little more time to prepare than those in the rest of the book, as they are designed for lei-surely weekend cooking and entertaining.

APPETIZERS

Soups

Entrées

Side Dishes

Desserts

Brunch Dishes

APPETIZERS

◆

GOAT CHEESE
WITH HERBS IN OLIVE OIL

MAKES 6 SMALL CHEESES; EACH CHEESE SERVES 2 TO 3

◆

*M*any a wonderful impromptu meal, hors d'oeuvre, or picnic has come from marinated goat cheeses stored in my refrigerator. These make wonderful gifts, too.

½ teaspoon fennel seeds
1½ teaspoon coriander seeds
½ teaspoon black peppercorns
½ teaspoon white peppercorns
½ teaspoon dried thyme, or 3 sprigs
    fresh thyme
½ teaspoon dried rosemary, or 1 sprig
    fresh rosemary
1 teaspoon summer savory, or 3 sprigs
    fresh summer savory
2 imported bay leaves
About 2½ cups extra-virgin olive oil
6 small goat cheeses, 3 ounces each

Place all the seeds, peppercorns, herbs, and olive oil in a 1½-quart wide-mouthed glass jar. Arrange the cheeses in the jar with care, so that each is covered with seasonings. Seal tightly and refrigerate for about a week before serving. When the cheeses are gone, use the remaining oil for salads.

BAY LEAVES

◆

*L*ook for imported or Turkish bay leaf (Lauris nobilis). Do not confuse this true bay with the harsher California bay, with its long, sharply pointed, darker leaves. California bay, which is very strong, can be used in tiny amounts in hearty Mexican dishes or stews but will ruin the fine flavor of most other dishes, especially stocks and sauces.

VARIATION: Use 5 sprigs fresh basil and ½ cup sun-dried tomatoes in place of all the other seasonings or in addition to them. Remove basil after 1 week.

MAKE AHEAD: prepare up to 2 months ahead; refrigerate

SALMON CEVICHE WITH CHILIES

SERVES 6 AS AN APPETIZER OR FIRST COURSE, 4 AS A SALAD

◆

*C*eviche, a marinated scallop or redfish appetizer from Mexico, tastes marvelous with salmon, lime, and chilies. This makes a very colorful and delicious first course.

MARINADE
⅓ to ½ cup fresh lime juice
2 to 3 serrano chilies, seeded and minced
½ red bell pepper, seeded and finely chopped
2 to 3 tablespoons virgin olive oil
4 scallions, minced
2 shallots, minced
½ teaspoon kosher salt, or to taste
¼ teaspoon freshly ground black pepper
⅛ teaspoon cayenne

1 pound fresh salmon fillet, skinned and cut into ½-inch cubes
6 large radicchio or Boston lettuce leaves

Lime wedges dipped in cayenne, for garnish

Combine the marinade ingredients in a glass bowl. Place the salmon in the marinade and refrigerate for about 1 hour. Arrange the radicchio on a platter, spoon the ceviche on top, and serve with lime wedges dipped in cayenne.

VARIATIONS: Use ½ pound salmon and ½ pound red snapper, or use 1 pound bay scallops.

MAKE AHEAD: prepare up to 24 hours ahead; refrigerate

HOMEMADE BOURSIN WITH SUN-DRIED TOMATOES

MAKES ABOUT 1¼ CUPS; SERVES 6

◆

*T*his delightful hors d'oeuvre, welcome in any season, has the added advantage of being very quick to make. Serve with imported crackers, or fresh or toasted French bread or dark breads. Sliced cherry tomatoes make a nice complement.

½ pound small-curd creamed cottage
  cheese, drained
3 tablespoons sour cream
2 tablespoons heavy cream or Crème
  Fraîche (page 210)
¼ pound cream cheese
1 garlic clove, mashed to a paste (see
  box, page 62)
¼ to ½ teaspoon kosher salt
½ teaspoon freshly ground black
  pepper
½ teaspoon dried basil, or 3 leaves
  fresh basil, minced
⅛ teaspoon dried tarragon, or
  1 teaspoon fresh tarragon, minced
⅛ teaspoon dried thyme, or 1 teaspoon
  fresh thyme, chopped
2 tablespoons finely minced fresh
  parsley
½ cup dry-pack sun-dried tomatoes,
  plumped 10 minutes in hot water,
  patted dry, and finely chopped

GARNISH
8 to 10 fresh basil leaves

2 teaspoons extra-virgin olive oil
Freshly ground black pepper

Beat the cottage cheese in a mixer or food processor until fairly smooth. Mix in the sour cream, heavy cream, cream cheese, garlic, salt, and pepper, and beat or process until a creamy texture is obtained, 1 to 2 minutes. Stir in the herbs and the sun-dried tomatoes. Let cure at least an hour in the refrigerator to allow the flavors to develop.

To serve, form into several small rounds, 3 inches across and 2 inches high, and arrange on top of basil leaves on a plate. Just before serving, drizzle with olive oil and coarsely grind some black pepper over the top.

VARIATION: Beat 3 ounces of goat cheese into the cottage cheese.

MAKE AHEAD: up to 3 days; refrigerate

WALNUT FOUGASSE
(PROVENÇAL HEARTH BREAD)
MAKES 6 SMALL *FOUGASSE*; SERVES 12

◆

Fougasse, small hand-shaped flat breads, variously flavored, can be spotted in every Provençal market, usually stacked four or five deep, hanging on a nail on the side of a stall where cheeses or sausages are sold. These savory breads make a wonderful accompaniment to marinated goat cheese, olives, and tomato and cucumber salads.

2 envelopes dry yeast
4 ounces warm water
2 cups whole milk
8½ cups (2 pounds, 12 ounces) flour
1 tablespoon kosher salt
1¼ cups (2 sticks plus 2 tablespoons)
    unsalted butter, cut into pieces
1 cup chopped walnuts

Dissolve the yeast in the warm water in a large mixing bowl. Add all the milk, and half the flour and salt. With the regular mixing attachment of an electric or hand mixer, mix until the dough has a smooth, batterlike consistency. Add the remaining flour and salt and mix in with a dough hook or stir with a wooden spoon until all the flour is mixed in. Then add all of the butter and continue to mix. The dough will gradually absorb all the butter. If making by hand, knead in the butter. It will look messy at first, but the dough will gradually absorb all of the butter. Mix until the dough is smooth.

Let rise, covered, until doubled, about an hour. Punch down. Preheat the oven to 425°. With your hands, quickly mix in the walnuts, divide the dough into six equal parts, flatten to ¾ inch thick, and shape into six ovals on buttered baking sheets. Cut four 4-inch slashes in each oval, about an inch apart. Bake for 30 minutes, or until lightly browned. Serve warm or at room temperature.

VARIATIONS: Substitute 6 slices of bacon, cooked and crumbled, or ¾ cup chopped olives, or ½ cup sun-dried tomatoes, for the walnuts.

MAKE AHEAD: up to 8 hours; store, wrapped in a tea towel, at room temperature; or freeze for up to 3 months

SOUPS

COLD SENEGALESE SOUP
SERVES 4 TO 6 AS A FIRST COURSE

*H*ere's a remarkable and mysterious soup. Few people can identify the main ingredients—just apples and onions. It is a wonderfully flavorful and inexpensive alternative to its cousin, the richer, more costly vichyssoise, the classic cold creamy leek soup. The subtle touch of hotness in the background was inspired by the spicy cuisine of Senegal, once a French colony. This soup is best pureed in a blender rather than a food processor because it purees the mixture to a finer texture.

3 tablespoons unsalted butter
2 large Granny Smith apples, peeled and chopped
1 large yellow onion (or 2 small)
1½ teaspoons curry powder
4 cups chicken stock
2 to 3 drops Tabasco sauce, or ⅛ teaspoon cayenne
½ teaspoon kosher salt, or to taste
⅛ teaspoon freshly ground black pepper, or to taste
¾ cup light cream
¾ cup plain low-fat yogurt
3 tablespoons finely minced fresh parsley or chives, for garnish
12 very thin cucumber slices, for garnish

In a 2½-quart saucepan, melt the butter. Cook the apple and onion over low heat until soft, 6 to 7 minutes. Add the curry powder and cook for another minute, stirring. Add the chicken stock and simmer, covered, for about 10 minutes. Remove pan from heat and add the Tabasco, salt, and pepper and let cool slightly. Puree in a blender and chill for at least 30 minutes, or quick-chill in a metal bowl for 10 minutes in the freezer.

Just before serving, stir in the cream and yogurt. Taste and adjust the seasonings, garnish with herbs and cucumber slices, and serve very cold.

MAKE AHEAD: prepare up to 24 hours ahead; refrigerate

COLD CHERRY AND RED WINE SOUP

SERVES 4 AS A FIRST COURSE OR DESSERT

◆

Cold fruit soups are especially popular in Scandinavia but are found all over Europe. I've enjoyed this cherry soup in France, Germany, Switzerland, and Hungary. Although it was served as a first course, I like to serve it as a dessert. It is always much appreciated.

1½ pounds pitted cherries, fresh or frozen
2½ cups cold water

1 teaspoon whole cloves
1 cinnamon stick
½ cup sugar

1 tablespoon arrowroot or cornstarch
2 tablespoons red wine
1 cup chilled light red wine, such as a
    Beaujolais or Pinot Noir
½ cup heavy cream or sour cream
Fresh mint sprigs, for garnish

In a 4-quart saucepan, combine the cherries and water. Bring to a simmer, then add the spices and sugar. Cover and cook over medium heat until the cherries are soft, about 10 minutes. Remove the cherries from the liquid and chill them. Discard the cinnamon stick and cloves.

In a small bowl, whisk the arrowroot or cornstarch with the 2 tablespoons of wine until smooth. Gradually add this mixture to the hot cherry liquid, stirring over medium heat until the consistency of the soup is like heavy cream. Remove from the heat and cool, uncovered. Then refrigerate until very cold, at least 30 minutes.

Just before serving, thin the soup to the consistency of light cream with the 1 cup of wine. Stir in the cream, add the cherries, and serve, garnished with fresh mint.

MAKE AHEAD: up to 24 hours; refrigerate; add the wine, cream, and cherries just before serving

ROASTED ACORN SQUASH SOUP WITH MACE AND CINNAMON

SERVES 2 AMPLY AS A FIRST COURSE

◆

*H*ere's a winter soup that's a perfect accompaniment to a pork, goose, roast beef, or venison entrée. It has a wonderful, subtle flavor.

1 acorn, golden acorn, or butternut
    squash (1½ pounds), cut into 4
    equal wedges, large seeds removed
2 tablespoons unsalted butter
1 large yellow onion, finely chopped
1 large garlic clove, mashed to a paste
    (see box, page 62)
2¼ cups chicken broth

1 teaspoon kosher salt, or to taste
¼ teaspoon freshly ground black
    pepper
1 teaspoon sugar
1 cup heavy or light cream
¼ teaspoon ground mace
¼ teaspoon ground cinnamon

Preheat the oven to 450°. Wrap each wedge of squash tightly in foil and place the foil packages directly on the oven floor to bake. (They will cook more quickly there than on a rack and will brown slightly, giving them a good flavor.) Remove after 30 minutes or when soft.

While the squash is cooking, melt the butter in a heavy-bottomed 2-quart saucepan and cook the onion and garlic gently over medium-low heat until soft, about 10 minutes. Add the chicken broth and simmer for 10 minutes.

When the squash is done, scoop out the flesh (discarding the skin and the seeds) and add to the soup. Stir in the salt, pepper, and sugar. Simmer for 10 minutes, remove from heat, and cool slightly. Puree the soup in a food processor or blender or with a *mini-primer* (see box, page 32). Stir in the cream, lightly dust with mace and cinnamon, and serve hot.

VARIATION: To save 10 minutes on the total cooking time, cook the squash in the microwave: Cut it in half, remove the seeds, and microwave on high for 8 to 12 minutes.

MAKE AHEAD: up to 24 hours; refrigerate; reheat gently

MEXICAN POTATO, CORN, AND POBLANO SOUP

SERVES 6 TO 8 AS A MAIN COURSE

◆

*T*his vegetable soup, hearty yet subtly spicy, is from the state of Puebla in Mexico. Serve it with fresh hot corn or flour tortillas and a fresh fruit salad for an unusual light supper.

6 cups chicken broth
2 tablespoons vegetable oil
1 large red onion, minced
1 bunch whole scallions, finely chopped
2 large garlic cloves, mashed to a paste (see box, page 62)
Kernels from 3 large ears sweet corn, or 1 pound frozen corn kernels

3 small green zucchini, unpeeled, trimmed and diced
2 large tomatoes, peeled, seeded, and pureed in a food processor, or 2 cups canned Italian tomato chunks, juices drained
3 new potatoes, unpeeled, cut into 1-inch cubes
3 poblano chilies, roasted (see box,

page 35), peeled, seeded, and
chopped
1 teaspoon dried or chopped fresh
oregano
Kosher salt
Freshly ground black pepper

GARNISHES
¼ pound Monterey Jack cheese, grated
2 avocados, peeled and chopped
6 sprigs fresh coriander or parsley

MENU

**MEXICAN POTATO, CORN,
AND POBLANO SOUP**

CORNMEAL MADELEINES

**SIMPLE MIXED GREEN SALAD
WITH FRENCH VINAIGRETTE**

**COLD BRANDIED APRICOT
MOUSSE**

◆

MEXICAN BEER

Heat the chicken broth in a sauce-pan. Heat the oil in a 6-quart casserole or stockpot. Add the onion, scallion, and garlic, and cook gently until soft, about 8 minutes. Add all of the remaining vegetables and cook for several minutes. Add the hot chicken broth and seasonings and cook until the potatoes are soft, about 10 minutes. Taste for seasoning. Serve hot, garnished with grated cheese, avocado, and herbs.

VARIATION: Add ½ pound fresh flaked cooked crabmeat to the soup just before serving.

MAKE AHEAD: up to 24 hours; refrigerate; reheat gently and garnish just before serving

SOUPE AU PISTOU
(PROVENÇAL VEGETABLE SOUP
WITH PESTO)

SERVES 12 AS A MAIN COURSE

◆

*H*ere is a healthy, perfectly delicious whole meal in a pot. This fabulous chunky country soup reminiscent of a minestrone, only gutsier, with pesto (*pistou*) added at the end, is a Provençal summer specialty. The pesto is also delicious in potato soup and on pasta, and I often stir a spoonful into hot rice or sautéed tomatoes.

3 tablespoons extra-virgin olive oil
1 red onion, finely chopped
7 whole scallions, finely chopped
6 large, ripe tomatoes, chopped
2½ to 3 quarts light beef stock or
    canned beef broth
10 ounces green beans, cut into 1-inch
    pieces (if unavailable, use frozen
    beans)
4 small or 2 large zucchini, quartered
    and cut into 1-inch chunks
5 small new potatoes, peeled or
    unpeeled, cut into ½-inch chunks
3 medium carrots, scraped and cut
    into ½-inch chunks
1½ to 2 tablespoons kosher salt
½ teaspoon freshly ground black
    pepper
⅓ cup chopped fresh parsley
1 tablespoon dried thyme (do not use
    powdered)
Three 1-pound cans cannellini beans,
    rinsed and drained (see Note)
6 ounces dry capellini or vermicelli,
    broken into 3-inch pieces
1½ cups freshly grated Italian
    Parmesan

PESTO
18 fresh basil leaves, finely chopped
5 large garlic cloves
3 tablespoons extra-virgin olive oil
2 tablespoons freshly grated Italian
    Parmesan

In an 8-quart stockpot, heat the oil and sauté the onion and scallion until soft. Add the tomato and cook for 5 minutes. Add the beef stock and bring to a simmer. Add all of the chopped vegetables and seasonings and simmer for 10 to 15 minutes, or until all the vegetables are tender. Add the beans and vermicelli, and simmer for another 5 to 8 minutes.

While the soup is cooking, make the pesto. Either process all the ingredients in a food processor or mash the garlic and basil together with a mortar and pestle, slowly add the olive oil, and then the cheese. Stir the pesto into the soup, and simmer for another 2 minutes. Serve very hot, with a bowl of freshly grated Parmesan and lots of crusty French bread.

NOTE: If you prefer not to use canned cannellini, cook your own: Soak 1¼ cups dried white beans, navy beans, or Great Northern beans overnight and drain. Bring 3⅔ cups fresh water to a boil, add the beans, and simmer until done, about 1 hour. Reserve any remaining liquid to add to the soup.

MAKE AHEAD: make the pesto, grate the cheese, and prepare the soup except for adding the vermicelli and pesto up to 24 hours in advance; refrigerate; just before serving, reheat gently, check for seasoning, add the vermicelli and pesto, and simmer for 10 minutes

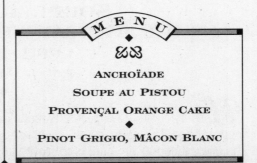

MENU
❧
ANCHOÏADE
SOUPE AU PISTOU
PROVENÇAL ORANGE CAKE
◆
PINOT GRIGIO, MÂCON BLANC

ENTRÉES

◆

SQUAB ROASTED WITH FIVE-ONION AND FIVE-HERB STUFFING

SERVES 8

◆

*S*mall roasted birds make festive entrées, especially in autumn and winter. When a large turkey just seems too much and takes too long to cook at Thanksgiving or Christmas, present these simply and quickly prepared birds.

MENU

◆

SQUAB ROASTED WITH FIVE-ONION AND FIVE-HERB STUFFING

QUICK SAUTÉED ZUCCHINI

CORNBREAD WITH GOAT CHEESE AND SUN-DRIED TOMATOES

EASY FRENCH LEMON ICE CREAM

◆

CALIFORNIA CHARDONNAY, PINOT NOIR

FIVE-ONION AND FIVE-HERB STUFFING

3 tablespoons unsalted butter
3 tablespoons virgin olive oil
8 leeks, white parts only, well washed (see box, page 136) and chopped
1 small red onion, 1 small yellow onion, and 1 small white onion, all chopped
4 shallots, minced
1 bunch whole scallions, minced

2 garlic cloves, mashed to a paste (see box, page 62)
Kosher salt to taste
Freshly ground black pepper to taste
½ tablespoon of a combination of four of the following: chopped fresh rosemary, thyme, basil, oregano, sage, and/or parsley

8 squab, quail, or Cornish hens
Kitchen string, for trussing (optional)
3 tablespoons unsalted butter, melted
Fresh sage leaves, for garnish

Preheat the oven to 425°. Heat the butter and oil in a large skillet and gently cook the leek, onion, scallion, shallot, and garlic until soft, 7 to 10 minutes. Add the salt and pepper to taste and the fresh herbs and mix well.

Stuff the squab with the onion mixture and truss if desired (see box, page 40). Place in a large roasting pan (or two small pans) and pour a little melted butter over each squab. Roast for about

35 minutes, basting often with pan juices. When the juices run clear from the thigh or breast when pierced with a knife, the birds are done. Serve one squab per person, garnished with fresh sage.

MAKE AHEAD: prepare stuffing up to 24 hours ahead; refrigerate; *do not* stuff birds until just before cooking

ROAST TUSCAN PORK LOIN WITH GARLIC AND HERBS

SERVES 6 TO 8

*T*his classic pork roast from Tuscany is wonderful hot or cold, summer or winter. It takes only 5 minutes to prepare and is then put in the oven and left alone for 1½ hours. This is truly a no-fuss main course.

5 garlic cloves, finely slivered
2 teaspoons dried rosemary
1 teaspoon dried thyme
1 teaspoon kosher salt
1 teaspoon freshly ground black
    pepper
One 4-pound boneless pork loin roast,
    at room temperature (see box,
    opposite page)
1 tablespoon extra-virgin olive oil

MENU

CANNELLINI BEAN SOUP
WITH GREENS AND PARMESAN

ROAST TUSCAN PORK LOIN
WITH GARLIC AND HERBS

GRILLED FENNEL

TARTE TATIN

GATTINARA, ORVIETO

Preheat the oven to 425°. Combine the garlic and seasonings. With a small knife, make about a dozen slits on all sides of the roast. Insert most of the garlic-herb mixture evenly into the slits, then rub the whole roast with the rest of the mixture. Drizzle with the olive oil.

Place the roast on a rack in a baking pan and roast for 30 minutes. Reduce the heat to 350°, baste, and continue roasting for another 60 minutes. Remove, let rest 10 to 15 minutes, then slice and serve.

MAKE AHEAD: roast up to 24 hours ahead; refrigerate; bring to room temperature before serving

PERFECT ROAST TARRAGON CHICKEN

SERVES 4 TO 6

◆

*T*his is my weekend staple; it's perfect for picnics, salads, and simple dinners.

3 tablespoons unsalted butter
One 3- to 4-pound roasting chicken, at
    room temperature
½ lemon
Kosher salt
Freshly ground black pepper
2 teaspoons dried tarragon, or 3 to
    4 sprigs fresh tarragon
Kitchen string, for trussing
3 strips bacon or pancetta
1 large bunch fresh watercress,
    washed and dried, for garnish

Preheat the oven to 400°. Melt the butter in a small saucepan and keep

MENU

◆

**PERFECT ROAST
TARRAGON CHICKEN**

**LEMON-GARLIC POTATOES
WITH SPINACH**

**ENDIVE AND AVOCADO SALAD
WITH TOASTED WALNUTS AND
WALNUT-OIL VINAIGRETTE**

GINGER-PLUM COBBLER

◆

**MÉDOC, BEAUJOLAIS,
PINOT NOIR**

ROASTING MEATS

◆

*L*arge cuts of poultry and meat for roasting should always be at room temperature when put into the oven. They will cook more evenly and have better flavor. Take a 3- to 5-pound roast out of the refrigerator 30 minutes to an hour before roasting, but don't leave out more than an hour.

Roasts should always sit for at least 10 and up to 20 minutes before being carved, so that the juices will have time to settle back into the tissues.

warm. Rinse the chicken in cold water, pat dry, then rub inside and out with the cut lemon. Liberally sprinkle salt and pepper both inside the cavity and on the outside of the chicken. Crush the tarragon and place in the cavity. Truss the chicken with kitchen string (see box, page 40). Spread the bacon over the breast and thighs. Place on a rack in a roasting pan.

Roast for 30 minutes. Remove the bacon and baste with the pan juices and the melted butter. Roast for another 30 minutes and baste again. Roast for a final 25 minutes but do not baste. The skin will turn golden-brown and crisp. Remove from the oven and let stand 10 to 15 minutes. Carve into eight pieces and serve on a platter, garnished with watercress.

MAKE AHEAD: up to 24 hours; refrigerate; serve cold or at room temperature

GRILLADES
AND GRITS

SERVES 8

◆

A perfect make-ahead brunch or dinner dish, this comes to us from New Orleans and the traditions and flavors of Louisiana cuisine—lots of herbs and spicy flavors. *Filé* powder is dried sassafras, and it gives a distinctive note to many Louisiana dishes.

1½ to 2 pounds boneless veal sirloin steaks, ½ inch thick

SEASONING MIXTURE
1 teaspoon kosher salt
½ teaspoon black pepper
½ teaspoon cayenne
¼ teaspoon hot Hungarian paprika
1 teaspoon dried thyme
½ teaspoon dried basil
½ teaspoon gumbo *filé* powder
2 to 3 tablespoons flour

4 tablespoons virgin olive oil
1 tablespoon unsalted butter
2 medium onions, coarsely chopped
1 cup chopped celery
2 green bell peppers, seeded and chopped
2 large garlic cloves, mashed to a paste (see box, page 62)
4 whole scallions, finely chopped
1½ teaspoons dried thyme
1 teaspoon dried basil
¼ teaspoon freshly ground black pepper
½ teaspoon kosher salt
2 cups chicken broth
2 cups chopped fresh or canned tomatoes, or 2 cups thick tomato sauce
2 tablespoons tomato paste

◆ 2 recipes Quick Grits, Southern Style (page 100; omit the cheese)
Hot vinegar-pepper sauce, bottled, as a condiment

MENU

◆

εβ

GRILLADES AND GRITS

LEEK SALAD IN MUSTARD-CAPER VINAIGRETTE

COLD LIME MOUSSE

◆

BEAUJOLAIS

Combine all of the ingredients for the seasoning mixture. Pat the meat dry with paper towels. Dust with the seasoning mixture just before cooking.

Heat 1 tablespoon of oil and the butter in a large skillet. Brown the seasoned meat on both sides, then remove. Add the remaining 3 tablespoons of oil to the skillet, and heat. Add the onion, celery, pepper, garlic, and scallion, and cook until almost soft, about 10 minutes. Add the remaining seasonings, chicken broth, tomato, and tomato paste and simmer for 5 minutes.

Place the meat in the sauce, cover, and simmer for about 40 minutes, or until the meat is tender. While the meat is cooking, prepare the grits. Serve the grillades over the hot grits and spoon the sauce on top. Pass the hot vinegar-pepper sauce.

MAKE AHEAD: make *grillades* up to 2 days ahead; refrigerate; make grits just before serving; freeze *grillades* for up to 4 months

SHEPHERD'S PIE WITH LAMB

SERVES 4 TO 6

♦

 don't know what country can truly claim creation of shepherd's pie, since it appears in so many. In France it's known as *hachis Parmentier* (after Antoine-Augustin Parmentier, a botanist who made the potato a popular vegetable in eighteenth-century France), and it usually features finely chopped or ground beef left over from a roast or stew. Whether you use leftover pork, beef, lamb, or venison, you'll find this dish a delicious and easy one to add to your repertoire of great ideas for leftovers.

MENU

SHEPHERD'S PIE WITH LAMB

GREEN SALAD WITH WALNUT OIL–MUSTARD DRESSING

COLD CHERRIES IN BRANDY, WITH GINGERED SHORTBREAD

♦

BEAUJOLAIS, PINOT NOIR, MERLOT, CAHORS, CÔTES DU RHÔNE

2½ pounds potatoes, peeled and cut into small cubes
½ cup milk

2 tablespoons freshly grated Italian Parmesan
1 tablespoon virgin olive oil or vegetable oil
3 large garlic cloves, mashed to a paste (see box, page 62)
1 large yellow onion, finely chopped
½ teaspoon dried or fresh rosemary, finely crushed (see box, page 71)
½ teaspoon dried thyme
½ teaspoon kosher salt
¼ teaspoon freshly ground black pepper
1 pound leftover roast or braised lamb, finely chopped or ground in a food processor or meat grinder
1 tablespoon unsalted butter

Preheat the oven to 425°. Boil the potatoes for 10 to 15 minutes, until tender. Drain, and mash with the milk and cheese. Meanwhile, heat the oil in a large skillet and gently sauté the garlic and onion until golden, about 8 minutes. Stir in all the seasonings, add the lamb, and cook for 2 minutes. Check seasoning.

Spread the meat-onion mixture evenly in an oiled 2½-quart gratin dish, then spread the seasoned mashed potatoes on top. Make a crisscross pattern on top with the tines of a fork, dot with the 1 tablespoon butter, and bake for 30 minutes, or until the potatoes are golden and crusty looking.

MAKE AHEAD: prepare up to 24 hours ahead; refrigerate

SIDE DISHES

◆

GOAT CHEESE AND RED ONION TIMBALES

SERVES 6

◆

*T*his is an exquisite dish inspired by Alice Waters. It's especially delicious served as a side dish with chicken or lamb. It's also very nice served with crusty sourdough bread and a green salad for lunch.

2 tablespoons extra-virgin olive oil
1 large red onion (or 2 small), finely chopped or sliced
1 garlic clove, mashed to a paste (see box, page 62)
1½ tablespoons chopped fresh thyme, summer savory, or basil
½ pound goat cheese, crumbled
5 large eggs
1 cup heavy or light cream or Crème Fraîche (page 210)
½ teaspoon kosher salt
½ teaspoon freshly ground black pepper

Preheat the oven to 350°. Brush six ½-cup ramekins, custard cups, or *timbale* molds with 1 teaspoon of the olive oil. Heat the rest of the oil in a 9-inch skillet, add the onion and garlic, and cook over medium heat for 7 to 8 minutes, or until soft. Stir in the thyme and divide the sautéed onions equally between the ramekins. Crumble the goat cheese equally over the onions.

Whisk the eggs and cream together with the salt and pepper and divide evenly among the ramekins. Place the ramekins in a baking dish and add 1 inch of hot or boiling water to the dish to make a *bain-marie*. Bake for 30 minutes, or until lightly browned on top. Serve warm or at room temperature, in the ramekins.

MAKE AHEAD: up to 24 hours; refrigerate; reheat gently on a baking sheet in a 350° oven for 10 to 15 minutes

ZUCCHINI AND TOMATO FANS
SERVES 6

The late George Garin, a great Provençal chef, is the source of this unusual and delicious hors d'oeuvre, vegetable side dish, or first course.

2 teaspoons olive oil
2 large red onions, halved and very thinly sliced
5 garlic cloves, very thinly sliced
2 to 2¼ pounds smallest, thinnest zucchini available, washed, stem ends trimmed, split in half crosswise, and each half sliced to within 1½ inches of untrimmed end to form fan shapes, making 3 or 4 long cuts in each half
6 small ripe tomatoes, halved stem end to root end and thinly sliced
1 teaspoon *each* fresh or dried thyme, savory, and oregano
1 teaspoon coriander seeds
¾ teaspoon kosher salt
½ teaspoon freshly ground black pepper
½ cup extra-virgin olive oil
⅔ cup dry white wine

Preheat the oven to 425°. Oil a very large oval or square gratin dish with the 2 teaspoons olive oil and scatter half the sliced onion and garlic on the bottom of the dish. On top of this place the fanned-out zucchini, then wedge the tomato slices, cut-sides down, in-between the zucchini cuts. Sprinkle the zucchini and tomatoes with the herbs, coriander, salt, and pepper. Scatter the remaining onion and garlic slices on top of this and drizzle with the ⅓ cup olive oil.

Pour the white wine over all, cover tightly with foil, and bake for 30 minutes. Turn off the oven and let the dish come to room temperature in the oven (about 30 minutes) if you have the time. If not, remove when done. Serve warm or at room temperature, with crusty French bread.

BRAISED RED CABBAGE WITH APPLES

SERVES 6 TO 8

◆

*T*his incredibly good combination traditionally accompanies pork or game dishes in France. It's a perfect autumn or winter offering.

4 slices bacon, cut into 1-inch pieces
2 tablespoons unsalted butter
2 yellow onions, halved and thinly
    sliced
2 pounds red cabbage, cored and
    shredded or thinly sliced
2 tart apples, peeled and chopped
1 to 2 tablespoons brown sugar
1 teaspoon kosher salt
¼ teaspoon freshly ground black
    pepper
1 imported bay leaf
1 teaspoon dried thyme
½ cup red wine
½ cup red-wine vinegar

In a heavy-bottomed 5- or 6-quart casserole, brown the bacon in the butter. Add the onion and cook over medium to medium-high heat until golden. Add the cabbage and the remaining ingredients, cover, and simmer for about 1 hour. Taste, and adjust seasonings.

VARIATION: To save a lot of time, pressure-cook the cabbage mixture at 15 pounds for 4 minutes.

MAKE AHEAD: up to 24 hours; refrigerate; reheat gently

DESSERTS

◆

BRITTANY CAKE

SERVES 8 TO 12

◆

*G*âteau Breton, this splendid simple flat cake from Brittany with a texture that's a cross between shortbread and pound cake, is a treat for breakfasts, coffees, brunches, and teas, and with fruit desserts. It is good eaten warm, but the orange flavor is more distinctive after a day or two.

½ pound (2 sticks) unsalted butter
2 large egg yolks
1 large egg
¾ cup sugar
2 cups all-purpose flour
½ teaspoon salt
½ teaspoon vanilla
⅓ cup Grand Marnier, Cointreau, or
    other orange liqueur
1 large egg, beaten

Preheat the oven to 350°. With a mixer, cream the butter in a large mixing bowl. Add the egg yolks and the whole egg, one at a time, beating well after each addition. Mix in the sugar, flour, and salt until blended. Mix in the vanilla and orange liqueur.

Turn the batter into a buttered 10- or 12-inch tart pan and spread evenly with a spatula, smoothing the surface. Brush the top with the beaten egg and, with the tines of a fork, make a deep, curved crisscross design on the top. Bake for 1 hour and 15 minutes, or until top of cake is golden. Remove and let cool in the pan. To serve, cut in thin wedges.

MAKE AHEAD: up to 10 days; store, well wrapped in foil, in the refrigerator; or freeze for up to 4 months

FRAISAGE: A TECHNIQUE FOR SMEARING PASTRY

◆

Both a basic American pie-crust dough and the French short crust pâte brisée can be made flakier by the French technique of smearing, or fraisage. As with all pastry doughs, handle the crust as little as possible. It is not necessary even to gather it up into a big smooth ball. In fact, leave the crumbly dough in the mixing bowl after you have stirred in the water.

Feel the dough with your hands to be sure the ratio of water to flour is correct—the dough should be neither too wet nor too dry. Lightly press together egg-shaped bits of dough, put them on the counter, and with a swift movement forward, smear the dough onto the counter with the heel of your hand. It should take three or four swipes. Smear the dough at least 5 inches. Don't be tempted to handle the smeared dough; just leave it on the counter. Continue quickly smearing until all the dough is used up.

Flatten the dough into a round disk shape and place it between two long pieces of wax or parchment paper. Chill the dough according to the recipe instructions, then roll it out between the two pieces of paper, which eliminates having to add extra flour to the crust. Remember, overhandling and overrolling the dough and a too-warm environment toughen a short crust.

TARTE TATIN
(CARAMELIZED UPSIDE-DOWN
APPLE TART)

SERVES 6 TO 8

◆

I love a good *tarte Tatin*; it's a fabulous dessert and very quick to make if a prepared pastry is used. It is named for the demoiselles Tatin, the two sisters who created this marvelous dessert in their inn in Normandy. It features the prize products of Normandy—apples, butter, and *crème fraîche*.

CRUST
1⅓ cups all-purpose flour
Pinch of salt
2 tablespoons sugar
6 tablespoons (¾ stick) unsalted
    butter
2 tablespoons vegetable shortening
2½ to 3 tablespoons ice water

CARAMEL
3 tablespoons water
1 cup sugar

5 large Golden Delicious apples,
    peeled, cored, and sliced into
    eighths
1 cup Crème Fraîche (page 210),
    whipped cream, or sour cream, for
    serving

Make the crust: In a bowl, combine the flour, sugar, and salt. Cut the butter and shortening into this mixture with a pastry blender or in a food processor. Stir in the water and gently combine by smearing the pastry (see box, page 245). Chill in the freezer for 10 minutes or in the refrigerator for 1 hour. Roll out into a 12-inch circle between sheets of wax pa-per and refrigerate until ready to use. Or, use a prepared pie crust.

Preheat the oven to 375°. Make the caramel: Boil the water and sugar, uncovered, in a heavy ¾-quart saucepan for about 5 minutes. Stir at the beginning to dissolve the sugar. Watch carefully; when the mixture has turned caramel-colored, pour it immediately into a buttered 10-inch glass pie plate.

Arrange the apple slices over the caramel, and loosely cover the apples with the crust. It is not necessary to trim the crust, just tuck the uneven edges of crust inside. Bake for about 1 hour, or until the crust is browned.

Remove from the oven and let sit for 1 minute, then loosen the edges with a sharp knife and carefully invert by placing a 12- to 14-inch serving plate with shallow sides over the tart and turning the tart over. Serve warm, with *crème fraîche*, whipped cream, or sour cream.

MAKE AHEAD: prepare and roll out pastry and make caramel up to 24 hours ahead; refrigerate

THE BEST AND EASIEST FRENCH CHOCOLATE CAKE

SERVES 12

◆

*T*o me, this is, bar none, the finest-tasting chocolate cake in the French dessert repertoire. Its exotic name in French, *Reine de Saba*, or the "Queen of Sheba cake," reflects nothing exotic in either ingredients or preparation. I don't know of an easier, faster, or more foolproof cake. It is equally delicious without the icing. The icing can also be used as a sauce for ice cream.

9 ounces sweet or semisweet
    chocolate
6 tablespoons water
9 tablespoons (1 stick plus
    1 tablespoon) unsalted butter
1¼ cups sugar
Scant cup ground almonds
    (3½ ounces)
¾ cup all-purpose flour, sifted
1 teaspoon baking powder
½ tablespoon cognac or rum
1½ teaspoons vanilla
4 large egg yolks, whisked
4 large egg whites

CHOCOLATE ICING
1 cup heavy cream
10 ounces chocolate (can be 5 ounces
    bitter and 5 ounces sweet or all
    semisweet)

1 cup thinly sliced raw almonds or
    hazelnuts, for decorating

Preheat the oven to 350°. Over low heat, melt the 9 ounces of chocolate in the water in a heavy-bottomed 2½-quart saucepan. Add the next eight ingredients one by one, mixing well after each addition. Be certain the mixture is not too hot when you add the yolks. Remove from the heat and pour into a large mixing bowl. Let cool to lukewarm. Beat the whites until stiff and fold into the batter.

Line the bottom of two 8- or 9-inch round cake pans or one 12-inch spring-form pan with foil or parchment paper and butter and flour the sides. Pour in the batter and bake in the middle of the oven for about 30 to 40 minutes in the two smaller pans or 40 to 50 minutes in the larger pan. Remove and let cool in the pan(s), then unmold onto a cooling rack placed on a baking sheet.

To make the icing, melt the chocolate in the cream over medium heat in a small saucepan. Stir to blend and cool until lukewarm. Then simply pour the icing over the cake while it is still on the cooling rack and decorate by pressing almond slices all around the sides.

MAKE AHEAD: bake cake, but do not ice, up to 2 days ahead; wrap well and refrigerate; make the icing up to 2 days ahead and chill; reheat gently to pour over cake; or freeze cake for up to 2 months

RUSTIC PEAR AND APPLE CLAFOUTIS

SERVES 8

◆

I have a special fondness for French country desserts—this is one I discovered while traveling through the Poitou region. A clafoutis is a dessert of fruits baked in a kind of light custard batter. It makes a wonderful homey treat for winter weekends. Orange flower water, a distinctive dessert flavoring, is the distilled essence of orange blossoms. It's widely available in shops where spirits are sold.

5 large Anjou or Bosc pears, peeled
  and sliced
3 small Golden Delicious apples,
  peeled and sliced
3 tablespoons brandy
4 large eggs
2¼ to 2½ cups whole milk, or 2 cups
  milk and the rest light cream or
  Crème Fraîche (page 210)
2 tablespoons orange flower water
1 cup all-purpose flour
½ cup plus 2 tablespoons sugar
Crème Fraîche or heavy cream, for
  serving (optional)

Toss the pear and apple slices in the brandy. In a large bowl, mix the eggs, milk, and orange flower water. In a separate bowl, mix the flour and sugar. Gradually stir the flour into the egg mixture. Add the pears, apples, and brandy to the batter and stir to combine.

Pour into a 9-x-10-inch buttered baking or gratin dish and bake for 45 to 60 minutes, or until fruits are soft and top is a pale golden color. Serve warm or chilled, plain or with *crème fraîche* or heavy cream.

MAKE AHEAD: 2 to 4 hours; refrigerate; reheat in a 350° oven for 15 minutes

DRIED FRUITS IN CHARDONNAY
WITH FRESH GINGER

SERVES 10 TO 12

◆

I made this special dessert for Alice Waters when she came to lunch at Iron Horse Vineyards during their splendid autumn harvest feasts. I was inspired by the discovery of the most beautiful and flavorful dried fruits I had ever seen,

products of a small Sonoma family farm, and an excess of bottles with small amounts of Sauvignon Blanc and Chardonnay from the daily wine tastings. (You can use any leftover white wine in this recipe, however.) Gingered Shortbread (page 199) is the perfect complement.

1 bottle Chardonnay (or other white wine, dry or fruity)
1 cup sugar
10 whole allspice berries
2 cinnamon sticks
One 5-inch knob fresh ginger, peeled and cut into ¼-inch slices
2½ pounds mixed dried fruits: cherries, peaches, apricots, apples, figs, prunes, raisins, pears
1 cup Crème Fraîche (page 210; if unavailable, use sour cream mixed with 2 tablespoons buttermilk)

In a heavy nonaluminum casserole, cook the wine, sugar, allspice, cinnamon, and ginger, uncovered, over medium-high heat until slightly syrupy, about 20 minutes. Remove the spices and ginger and discard. Add the dried fruits to the syrup (add the softer fruits, such as dried apples, last) and slowly simmer, until tender, 20 to 30 minutes.

Chill for at least 20 minutes, or quick-chill in a metal pan in the freezer for 10 minutes. Serve in small bowls with *crème fraîche.*

NOTE: I keep this on hand in a big jar in my refrigerator year-round and use it as a quick dessert, as a topping on ice cream or pound cake, on my breakfast cereal, as a pick-me-up with cookies in the afternoon, or as an accompaniment to pork or sausage entrées.

MAKE AHEAD: up to 12 months; refrigerate in a closed jar

BRUNCH DISHES

◆

PROVENÇAL HERB AND OLIVE OMELET
SERVES 2 TO 4

◆

A wonderful traditional dish from Provence, this savory omelet can be made early in the day and served at room temperature. It is also good as an hors d'oeuvre. In the cool kitchens of Provençal stone houses, this omelet may sit on the counter at room temperature all day, as an inviting snack or appetizer.

2½ tablespoons extra-virgin olive oil
1 bunch whole scallions, finely chopped
½ red onion, finely chopped
1 garlic clove, mashed to a paste (see box, page 62)
2 tablespoons mixed chopped fresh herbs: thyme, basil, oregano, marjoram, chives, parsley (use several or 1 teaspoon of each if you have all)
⅓ cup imported black olives, pitted and chopped
6 large eggs, at room temperature (see box)
½ teaspoon kosher salt
½ teaspoon freshly ground black pepper
2 tablespoons water
2 tablespoons freshly grated Italian Parmesan
Sprigs of fresh thyme, for garnish

Heat 2 tablespoons of the oil in a 9- or 10-inch nonstick skillet. Add the scallions, onion, and garlic and cook over low heat until soft, 5 to 6 minutes. Add the fresh herbs and olives and heat through.

In a bowl, mix the eggs with the salt, pepper, water, and cheese. Add the cooked vegetable mixture to the eggs and mix well. Wipe the skillet, add the remaining ½ tablespoon olive oil, heat, and pour in the egg mixture. Cook over medium-low heat until the bottom is firm and very lightly browned.

Slide the omelet out onto a large plate, invert the skillet over the plate, and turn so the omelet returns to the skillet uncooked side down. Cook over low heat until the bottom is very lightly browned.

Slide out onto a serving plate and let stand at room temperature until ready to serve. Cut into wedges and serve, garnished with sprigs of thyme.

MAKE AHEAD: up to 8 hours; store at room temperature

EGGS

◆

Eggs should be stored in the refrigerator, but they have more flavor if brought to room temperature before using. Place them in a bowl of hot water for 5 to 10 minutes to warm them up.

POACHED EGGS ON CROUSTADES WITH RED WINE SAUCE

SERVES 4

◆

*T*his Burgundian classic, *oeufs en meurette*, makes an unusual and memorable brunch dish. It is quick to prepare: The sauce and the *croustades* can be made the day before, so that the only last-minute preparations required are reheating them and poaching the eggs. The red wine sauce is exquisite with the eggs. Use a good-quality wine for the sauce and serve the same wine with the dish. The sauce is also good over sautéed, steamed, or grilled chicken and salmon.

RED WINE SAUCE
½ bottle dry red wine, preferably a
   light Pinot Noir or Beaujolais
1 cup chicken broth
1 tablespoon unsalted butter
4 slices good-quality bacon, diced or
   cut into thin strips, ¼ inch wide
4 shallots, minced
1 small garlic clove, mashed to a paste
   (see box, page 62)
2 heaping tablespoons all-purpose
   flour
½ teaspoon kosher salt
¼ teaspoon freshly ground black
   pepper
1 imported bay leaf
½ teaspoon dried thyme
2 tablespoons minced fresh parsley

CROUSTADES
Four 1- to 1¼-inch-thick slices white
   sandwich bread, trimmed of crusts
4 tablespoons (½ stick) unsalted
   butter

½ tablespoon red-wine vinegar
4 large very fresh eggs, at room
   temperature
¼ cup minced fresh parsley

Preheat the oven to 400°. Prepare the sauce: In a nonaluminum saucepan,

HOW TO MAKE BREAD CROUSTADES

◆

*T*ake an unsliced loaf of white bread and trim the crusts to make a square loaf. (Use the trimmings for bread crumbs.) Cut the bread evenly into 1- to 1¼-inch-thick slices. Spread on a baking sheet and place in a preheated 350° oven to dry out for 6 to 8 minutes. Brush the croustades on all sides with melted butter and return to the oven for 5 to 8 more minutes, until golden-brown. If you are using these as a base for serving scrambled or poached eggs, or small roasted birds, make an indentation in the middle of the soft bread before drying it out in the oven by tearing out some of the bread. Croustades can be made ahead and frozen, buttered. Thaw and warm for 10 minutes in a 350° oven and serve.

heat the wine and broth together until simmering. In a heavy-bottomed 2½-quart saucepan, melt the butter, add the bacon, and brown lightly. Remove and hold. Add the shallot and garlic and cook until soft. Add the flour to the pan and cook over low heat for 2 to 3 minutes, stirring constantly, to make a *roux*. Pour the hot liquid over the *roux* and whisk until smooth. Add the reserved bacon and seasonings and simmer gently, uncovered, about 15 minutes.

Meanwhile, make the *croustades* as directed on page 251 and heat 4 inches of water in a sauté pan to poach the eggs.

When the *croustades* and sauce are done, add the vinegar to the simmering water, crack the eggs into the water, and poach not more than 4 minutes (see box). With a spatula, skimmer, or large spoon, remove the eggs carefully to a folded towel to drain. Place the hot *croustades* on individual warmed plates, top each with an egg, pour sauce over all, sprinkle with the minced parsley, and serve immediately.

MAKE AHEAD: prepare sauce and *croustades* up to 24 hours ahead; refrigerate; reheat sauce over low heat and *croustades* for 10 minutes in a 350° oven before poaching the eggs

THE BEST WAY TO POACH EGGS

*E*ggs *for poaching should be large, very fresh, and at room temperature. To bring cold eggs to room temperature, place them in a bowl of hot water for 5 to 10 minutes. Before poaching the eggs, have everything else ready to serve (accompaniments prepared, table set, plates warm, etc.).*

In a large sauté pan, heat 4 inches of water to a simmer and add 2 teaspoons of champagne or other white-wine vinegar to the water. Crack up to six eggs directly into the simmering water, or crack them into a saucer and slip them in. Keep the water at a simmer, cover the pan, and cook the eggs gently for 4 to 5 minutes.

Remove each egg with a metal skimmer or a large spatula, place it on a terrycloth towel for a moment to absorb any water, then serve immediately.

If you wish to make the eggs ahead and hold them, slightly undercook them (remove them after 4 minutes) and place them in a shallow pan filled with cold water. They can be refrigerated for several hours or overnight if necessary. To reheat them, place them with the metal skimmer gently into simmering water. Cook for 1 minute, remove, blot on a towel, and serve immediately.

FRENCH SCRAMBLED EGGS
WITH DILL AND SMOKED SALMON

SERVES 4

◆

*H*ere's a perfect impromptu brunch or late-night supper dish. The French have wonderful techniques for just about everything, but I especially love their finesse with eggs. The texture of these eggs is very creamy, almost like a sauce, and about as far away as you can get from overcooked scrambled eggs in ungainly, ugly clumps!

Serve on toast, on toasted bread *croustades* (see box, page 251), or in hollowed-out brioches. Once you've experienced French scrambled eggs, it's hard to settle for anything less!

9 large eggs, at room temperature (see box, page 250)
¼ cup Crème Fraîche (page 210), or sour cream or heavy cream
1½ tablespoons unsalted butter
¼ teaspoon kosher salt
¼ teaspoon freshly ground white pepper
3 tablespoons chopped fresh dill (if unavailable, use 1½ teaspoons dried dill)
2 to 3 ounces smoked salmon, cut in ½-inch dice

Bring three inches of water to a boil in the bottom of a double boiler. In the top, stir the eggs, *crème fraîche*, and butter together, beating only lightly to break up the eggs. (Too much beating or mixing only toughens the eggs.) Over the simmering water, stir the eggs constantly until they are very lightly set but still very creamy. They will resemble a sauce, but they will be cooked. This takes a good 10 minutes. Stir in the salt and white pepper to taste. Add the dill and smoked salmon, combine well, and serve immediately.

SPINACH FRITTATA
WITH DILL AND PINE NUTS

SERVES 4 TO 6

◆

*T*raditional Lebanese cooking is the source of this very tasty dish. Frittatas, flat omelets with vegetables, are really best served at room temperature, which makes them very convenient for relaxed weekend meals.

3 tablespoons virgin olive oil

¼ cup pine nuts

1 bunch whole scallions, finely chopped

3 large shallots or ½ red onion, minced

½ pound spinach, stemmed, washed (see box), and coarsely chopped or cut with scissors

½ cup chopped fresh parsley

¼ cup chopped fresh dill (if fresh is unavailable, use 2 tablespoons dried dill)

3 large eggs, at room temperature (see box, page 250)

½ teaspoon kosher salt

¼ teaspoon freshly ground black pepper

½ cup low-fat plain yogurt

Heat 1 tablespoon of the oil in a large skillet. Add the pine nuts, scallion, and shallot, and cook over medium-high heat until the onion is soft, 2 to 3 minutes. Add the spinach, parsley, and dill and cook, stirring, until the spinach is wilted, 2 to 3 minutes.

Beat the eggs lightly in a mixing bowl with the salt and pepper; add the spinach mixture, and mix well. In a clean 9-inch nonstick skillet, heat the remaining 2 ta-

THE EASIEST AND BEST WAY TO WASH SPINACH

◆

Cut off the stems and plunge the leaves into a large bowl of tepid water. Swish them through the water several times to remove dirt from the crevices, then lift them out and place in a colander or strainer. Rinse thoroughly with fresh running water, spin-dry in a salad spinner, and store in sealable plastic bags in the refrigerator until ready to use. Very dirty spinach may need to be washed twice.

blespoons olive oil until hot. Pour in the egg-spinach mixture, and cook for about 1 minute over high heat, then slip out onto a large plate. Put the frittata back into the skillet on its uncooked side and cook for another minute or two. Then slip the frittata out onto a plate or platter and leave at room temperature until ready to serve. Cut into wedges and serve, topped with yogurt.

MAKE AHEAD: up to 3 hours; store at room temperature

WHOLE-WHEAT IRISH SODA BREAD

MAKES 10 TO 12 LARGE WEDGES

◆

*O*n weekends, especially, I crave homemade bread. Despite the existence of wonderful local bakeries, fresh bread made by my own hands, baked in my own oven, gives a special delight no other can. This perfect weekend bread (it keeps two days at best) is delicious for breakfast with butter and jam, goes very well with cheeses and pâtés, and accompanies a hearty soup to perfection.

2 cups whole-wheat flour
1½ cups all-purpose flour
½ cup quick-cooking oatmeal
1½ tablespoons sugar
2½ teaspoons kosher salt
1 teaspoon baking soda
1 teaspoon baking powder
3 tablespoons cold unsalted butter
1½ cups buttermilk
1 large egg
2 tablespoons quick-cooking oatmeal,
   for garnish

Preheat the oven to 350°. Combine all of the dry ingredients in a large bowl. With a large whisk or pastry cutter, cut the butter into the dry ingredients until the mixture is mealy.

Combine the buttermilk and egg in another bowl and quickly stir into the flour and butter mixture just until the dough forms a ball. Do not overmix.

Knead for 1 or 2 minutes, until smooth. Shape into one large or two small rounds. Cut a 1-inch-deep X into the top of the loaf, and sprinkle with the oatmeal. Place on a lightly buttered baking sheet and bake for 50 to 60 minutes, or until the loaf is browned and baked through: if a skewer comes out clean, the bread is done. Remove the bread to a cooling rack. Serve warm or at room temperature.

MAKE AHEAD: up to 24 hours; store well wrapped in foil or sealable plastic bag; freeze for up to 2 months

MORE MENUS FOR ENTERTAINING
◆

MEDITERRANEAN HORS D'OEUVRES PARTY

SPUR-OF-THE-MOMENT DINNER FOR FRIENDS FROM THE PANTRY AND FREEZER

EASY AND ELEGANT DINNER FOR GUESTS

LIGHT SPRING DINNER

TWO DELICIOUS SUMMER PASTA SUPPERS

INDIAN SUMMER DINNER

QUICK-AND-EASY ITALIAN SUMMER DINNER

SOPHISTICATED COLD, MAKE-AHEAD SUMMER SUPPER

LIGHT SUMMER LUNCH

HEARTY MAKE-AHEAD BRUNCH

FABULOUS FRENCH AUTUMN BRUNCH

HEARTY AUTUMN PICNIC

AUTUMN COMPANY DINNER

AUTUMN-TO-WINTER FEAST

RUSTIC WINTER LUNCH

Easy One-Dish Winter Weekend Brunch

Mediterranean Lunch or Brunch

Christmas Morning Breakfast

Thanksgiving or Christmas Feast

SOUTHWESTERN NEW YEAR'S DAY DINNER

INDEX

♦